RUGBY'S GREATEST MAVERICKS

"A refreshing and highly entertaining read that highlights some of rugby's truly great characters and serves to remind us why we fell in love with the game in the first place."
– DONAL LENIHAN, FORMER IRELAND AND LIONS PLAYER AND MANAGER

"The mix of Mavericks in this book galvanised and at times divided; they not only inspire but they demanded of the rest of us to think differently, to be creative and to reach further than we thought possible!" – JOEL STRANSKY, WORLD CUP-WINNING SPRINGBOK AND BROADCASTER

"What a great read! Thoroughly enjoyed discovering previously unknown facts about some playing contemporaries and others, all of whom brought an extra dimension to the game of rugby over the years." – ROGER M UTTLEY OBE, FORMER ENGLAND PLAYER, CAPTAIN & COACH AND LIONS PLAYER & COACH

"Luke has selected a great mix of players. They are all maverick in their own different way and show how rugby should be able to accommodate all kinds of personalities and styles."
– DAVID CAMPESE, WORLD CUP-WINNING WALLABY, COACH AND BROADCASTER

"We all love a maverick. I liked how Luke also found fresh stories that were new and surprising. A lively and fun read that's perfect for any rugby fan who loves the game's great entertainers!" – PAUL WILLIAMS, RUGBY WRITER

"A sweet and scintillating mix of stories, anecdotes and insight into some of rugby's most fascinating characters. The book's blend of legends and relative unknowns means even the most well-read rugby fan will find something new to enjoy here."
– JAMES STAFFORD, RUGBY AUTHOR AND EDITOR OF *THE EAST TERRACE*

RUGBY'S GREATEST MAVERICKS

Luke Upton

y lolfa

To Eimear, Iseult, Séamus and Úna

First impression: 2022

The publishers wish to acknowledge the support of The Books Council of Wales

Cover photograph: Martin Hunter/Getty Images
Cover design: Tanwen Haf

ISBN: 978 1 912631 39 1

Published and printed in Wales
on paper from well-maintained forests by
Y Lolfa Cyf., Talybont, Ceredigion SY24 5HE
website www.ylolfa.com
e-mail ylolfa@ylolfa.com
tel +44 1970 832 304
fax 832 782

CONTENTS

Foreword by David Campese	7
Introduction	10
Danny Cipriani	14
Ray Gravell	25
Sonny Bill Williams	38
Andy Ripley	48
Heather Moyse	62
Finn Russell	73
Waisale Serevi	84
Marnie Cunningham	94
David Campese	108
Non Evans	122
Zinzan Brooke	133
Christophe Dominici	143
Dai Bishop	154
Prince Alexander Obolensky	165

Moss Keane	176
Sergio Parisse	192
Keith Murdoch	202
Jean-Pierre Rives	212
James Small	225
David Pocock	239
Acknowledgements	250
Bibliography	253
Notes	257

FOREWORD

In my view, a maverick is not just someone who goes against the grain but is a player who genuinely wants to do something different. When I first started playing, I'd already played a lot of other sports and just wanted to have fun. With my Italian family and working-class upbringing, I wasn't from a typical Australian rugby-playing background. I didn't come into the sport with any preconceptions about what I should or shouldn't do or say. I wanted to run the ball, play an open and instinctive game and I was always confident enough to speak my mind. And this remained as true on the day I retired as when I first picked up a ball.

The mavericks that inspired me were the Ella brothers, Mark, Gary and Glen. Remarkable with the ball, they all thought the same and played with instinct. I remember playing an exhibition match with Mark – we had a scrum in our own 22 and he looked at me and simply said, "Look for me," and we traded passes all the way down the pitch to the try line. The Ellas followed on from the Seventies Wales boys like Phil Bennett, Gerald Davies, Gareth Edwards and J P R Williams: those were real mavericks and their style set the world alight. Shane Williams would be a worthy successor to them.

Back in my playing days, Serge Blanco and Jean-Baptiste Lafond were fantastic players: pure French flair. Andy Irvine lit up games for Scotland in a conservative era for them. I really liked the Irish wing Simon Geoghegan, a great player who never got the ball much – if he'd been Australian, he'd have been a sensation! I played a lot of sevens against Waisale Serevi and he had unbelievable skills, and always wanted to try things.

Today I like the small guys: the South African Cheslin Kolbe particularly, and Finn Russell for Scotland, and I enjoy watching France with Romain Ntamack and Antoine Dupont.

There aren't enough players like this and there's not nearly enough flair on the pitch. Why? Because the modern game is too dominated by coaches. Players have no idea how to think about the game themselves. If it's not working, they don't know how to change tactics. They are overcoached. We need to stop the coaches running onto the field and telling players what to do. They are the meant to be the best in the country: it should be left to them to control the game, and not their coach up in the stand with his microphone. This is part of the influence that rugby league has over union now – it's not just coaching staff, but this approach to the game and emphasis on the defence – and I think it's deeply negative.

But the worst invention in world rugby is the academy. They're run by people who were never that good at playing rugby, and they just churn out boring players who can't think for themselves, taking them out of club and school rugby, where they'd be better off. There are too many people at the top of rugby, all over the world, who don't know what they are doing.

I don't think modern rugby players are all that happy. If I was playing now, I'd still be pretty bloody good, but I wouldn't be able to just stand on the wing waiting for the ball. I'd go looking for the ball, and a lot of coaches now don't like that. I wouldn't want to play now – since turning professional, the game is too serious. Society has changed, the pressure has increased, and the sport is the worse for it. Quite simply, it's less fun.

There are a lot of great players out there, but I worry that if the crowd aren't entertained, those crowds will drift away. Here in Australia, we have four football codes vying for attention, but there are different pressures all over the world. And if kids don't get into the game, soon there won't be a game at all.

This is why I was delighted to be included and asked to write the foreword to Luke's book. It's a great mix of players he has selected. They are all maverick in their own different way and show how rugby should be able to accommodate all kinds of personalities and styles. It's the mavericks we love as kids, and it's them that get people out of their seats. We need more of these kinds of players to keep rugby exciting. Remember, it's just a game, and games are meant to be fun!

Enjoy.

David Campese
Sydney, Australia
September 2022

INTRODUCTION

NO ONE IS entirely sure why Samuel Maverick didn't brand his cattle. There are some who think the nineteenth-century Texan rancher was an early supporter of animal rights, others claim that by not copying standard practice it allowed him to collect any unbranded cattle and claim them as his own, whilst some think he was just plain lazy. Whatever, the reason, Maverick unwittingly made his surname synonymous with someone exhibiting a streak of stubborn independence – "There's an unbranded cow, it's a maverick!"

The word's origin surprised me. It's a term that everyone knows but perhaps can't always precisely define. For this book, twenty profiles of rugby players from the 1930s to the present day, the thread that runs through them all is an independence of spirit, a desire to do things their own way, a belief in their own path – which, whilst not always proved correct, is normally entertaining, typically memorable, occasionally disastrous, but always true to them.

So, with the luxury of using this broad criterion, my research has led me to players who had explosive talent on the pitch, who reinvented the game, who made their teams and nations famous, who fell out with their teammates and managers, and some who were unable to cope with the gifts they were given. Among the twenty, there are supporters of great moral causes, artists, crusaders, polymaths, pioneers and outcasts. Several are heroes, perhaps a few are villains. Some of them you will know well, others a little, a couple probably not at all. There are funny stories, hard-to-believe anecdotes (though I assure you they are true), foolish behaviour, squandered talents and terrible tragedies.

Writing this book against the backdrop of the 2021/22 season, the world of rugby is as jumbled and inconsistent as ever. There's been some real progress: the women's game is getting long overdue, if still relatively limited, resource and attention and is growing as a result. Pacific Island teams are now standing on a stronger platform than they ever have before and are about to benefit further from the change in eligibility rules. And with the next decade of World Cups confirmed, choosing the USA as hosts potentially opens up an exciting new frontier for the game.

On the other hand, despite having been professional for over a quarter of a century now, rugby union still struggles to pay its bills. Rugby Australia was probably only saved from bankruptcy by being awarded the 2027 (men's) and 2029 (women's) World Cups, International attendances are down for many nations including Wales, Japan and South Africa, in England Wasps and Worcester face financial challenges that risk their very future, there's still disagreement over what a global rugby calendar looks like – with many of the proposals appearing as greedy as they are uninspired – and underlying all these are the ticking time-bombs of long-term concussion and player-welfare issues. Anyone who has read the recent interviews with England's Steve Thompson and Wales' Ryan Jones could not have failed to be deeply moved by their struggles with early-onset dementia and to give their own or their loved one's involvement with the sport some serious thought.

Opportunities and challenges weave their way through the stories in ths book, as we look at how the problems of the past – apartheid, discrimination, the double standards of amateurism and sexism, to name just a few – impacted the lives of our mavericks.

But most of all, our twenty mavericks, from eleven nations, represent why we love rugby. These are the men and women that get us up off our seats in the ground, pub or living room – we want a good look at what they are doing. They are the ones who made us want to play the game when we were kids. They are the ones we remember when we are nostalgically looking back on the good old days. They are the ones that we want to know more about. They can be as exasperating and frustrating as they are talented and inspiring. But they are always true to themselves.

I first started thinking about this book whilst watching *The Last Dance* on Netflix. I don't know anything about basketball, and without the Covid-19 pandemic, probably like a lot of you, would never have watched a ten-hour documentary about the sport. But I absolutely loved this story of the ultra-committed icon Michael Jordan's last season with the Chicago Bulls, the mix of his teammates – the needy Scottie Pippen, the party-loving Dennis Rodman and the erudite Steve Kerr, to name just three – and how they were led by their coach, 'Zen Master' Phil Jackson, who would deploy pioneering tactics as well as Native American spirituality to get the best out of his players. Jackson was able to connect with each of his superstars in different ways, knowing precisely what was needed to make them perform – whether it was dropping them from the team, or allowing them a blowout weekend in Las Vegas. He led them to glory, when under different leadership the squad could quite have easily imploded.

This personal focus is often missing in rugby. The balance between the individual and the collective is often misjudged, and it's normally our mavericks who suffer the most.

I don't believe there is a set definition of 'maverick' that we should use – it would surely be the opposite of being a maverick if I rigidly enforced one! But there are a few definitions given by rugby players that I find powerful. Johnny Wilkinson says of Danny Cipriani that he has "the creativity, the ability to make everything look as if it's working for you. It's almost a language of its own."

Heather Moyse, a rugby great and Olympic gold medallist, brought her own experience to the matter:

> Even winning Olympic medals or playing for your country, you can be in society's eyes successful, but if you aren't doing something you love, or want to do, you're literally chasing someone else's definition of success and not your own. A real maverick knows what they want, focuses on the things that they love to do and is not swayed by other people's opinions.

Whilst Roger Uttley, talking of his friend, the late Andy Ripley, focussed less on his undoubted ability and more on his personality when he remembered, "He always made you feel better at the end of a conversation."

And at the opposite end of the spectrum, there's a description of Dai Bishop by Graham Price, who wrote, "He was his own man and went his own way, even if that way led to self-destruction."

In these chapters we'll find examples of all these aspects of being a maverick, and much more.

Quite simply, in making my selection, I wanted great players and even better stories. This is no study of statistics or medals and cups, it's a look at twenty talented, complex and free-spirited individuals, their lives and careers. The world of rugby is passionate, beautiful, inconsistent and maddening, but despite all the changes, its players remain its beating heart. They make the game what it is, and I hope I've done them and the world in which they played justice.

Happy reading!

Luke Upton,
September 2022

DANNY CIPRIANI

"As long as Danny leaves his ego at the door, like everyone else, he will be treated the same."

FACTFILE

Full name: Daniel Jerome Cipriani

Born: 2 November 1987, Roehampton, London, England

Positions: Fly half, Full back

Representative teams: Barbarians, England Saxons, England

Clubs: Wasps, Melbourne Rebels, Sale Sharks, Gloucester, Bath

Nicknames: Google, Celebriani, Cippers, Cips

"I THOUGHT JOSH Lewsey had killed Danny Cipriani..."

8 October 2008, Wasps Training Ground, West London.

In the red corner, 32-year-old Josh Lewsey MBE: former Army Officer and World Cup winner. In the blue corner, 20-year-old Danny Cipriani: three England caps, nine GCSEs and a lot of hype.

Ding Ding. Seconds Out

Lights out for Cipriani.

As fights go, it was hardly the Rumble in the Jungle.

The row was said to have blown up after Lewsey criticised teammate Cipriani for missing tackles in a training session.

It was James Haskell, another Wasps teammate, who jokingly feared for Cipriani's life, and would recall the moment in his autobiography:

> We were doing a defensive drill and Cips didn't fancy it, which wasn't a huge shock. Instead of putting his shoulder in, he was running up to the attacker and touching him with his fingertips. This didn't go down well with Josh, who gave Cips a volley of abuse. Cips told Josh where to go, and Josh told Cips never to speak to him like that again. Before Cips spoke to him like that again, I heard a bang, and when I turned around, Cips was on the floor snoring. It was like a shit version of that famous photograph of Cassius Clay towering over Sonny Liston.[1]

Another account has Cipriani telling Lewsey to "shut up, or be shut up", which saw him get sparked out.

Either way, Cipriani very much came out second best. In truth, it is the kind of event that happens every day in training, and rarely seems to cause any long-term damage to team morale. But as Cipriani – just emerging as England's next great hope – was big news at the time, the incident got out into the newspapers, who made it a big deal.

The two protagonists dealt with the fallout in the best possible way in the next Wasps fixture, a Heineken Cup match against Castres. Unfazed by the week's headlines, Cipriani kicked ten points in a 25-11 win and created a try for Lewsey, which the two men celebrated by doing some mock shadow-boxing before enveloping each other in a man hug.

Lewsey would later clarify a little of the culture that led to the flashpoint: "This isn't always a comfortable place to work in. Everyone's on each other's backs and there is a brutal honesty, but this is why we win silverware."

Whilst Shaun Edwards, then Wasps head coach, refuted the tone of many press reports that week by denying Cipriani was too big for his boots: "As long as Danny leaves his ego at the door, like everyone else, he will be treated the same. No-one at this club is questioning his commitment. He is one of the hardest-working players at the club."[2]

The moment might be just a footnote in Cipriani's story – and not even that for Lewsey, who has gone on to forge a very successful post-rugby career in financial services – but it does serve as a blinking early-warning light.

These kinds of moments would keep happening.

It's easy to dismiss Cipriani as a talented airhead, more interested in celebrity girlfriends and the trappings of success than in knuckling down, being a team player and maximising his undoubted abilities. I probably had a similar opinion of him before writing this chapter. However, whilst it might be true to a certain extent, he is a far more complex, troubled character than I had imagined. For a decade from around 2008, Cipriani would feature as much on front pages as those at the back. It can be hard to remember the precocious talent that emerged before all the baggage.

He first played club rugby at Rosslyn Park, where fellow mavericks Prince Alexander Obolensky and Andy Ripley had plied their trade, before joining the Wasps Academy and making his full debut in 2004, aged 17. Within three years he was the full back in the Wasps team that shocked Leicester in the Heineken Cup Final and he'd soon make the fly half position his own, before winning his first England cap in 2008.

Handsome, confident and talented, he was a welcome boost to an England rugby scene languishing in a long post-2003-World-Cup hangover. Many of the 2003 winners had stayed on until 2007 when an unsuccessful defence of their crown, particularly with Jonny Wilkinson's powers on the wane, proved fresh blood was needed. Cipriani, with a Heineken Cup-winner's medal already safely tucked away, seemed to perfectly fit the bill.

When viewed now, some of the coverage of his arrival on the International stage has a level of hyperbole more often found around the English national soccer team at a major tournament than in connection with a novice rugby player (perhaps with the exception of Marcus Smith). 'Messiah' is one word that comes up a lot in reports from the time. The usually measured *Observer Sport Monthly* told its readers he was the "second coming of English rugby".

There's also already a strong tabloid mythology in how he is written about. One story says he was so arrogant in his teenage years, he would do warms-up separately from his team (which he refutes: "I never, ever used to do my own warm-ups. I was always part of the team warm-up."). Another on how he chose to convert a try with a drop kick from the touchline to win a junior cup final ("The match did take place, we did win, and I did kick a touchline conversion, but I placed it and kicked it the normal way"). That in 2008, his mum was already living in a £1m house ("If anyone is prepared to pay that amount for the house, I will happily put them in touch with my mum."). And, to choose just one headline from that time relating to women, that he dated one of the Cheeky Girls, a short-lived Romanian pop duo oddly popular in the UK press – sample lyric, for those of you who don't remember: 'Come and smile, don't be shy. / Touch my bum, this is life.' ("I had one picture taken with her, that was it. I never, ever went out with her. In the media, things are made up all the time and you have to deal with that. In a way, it is upsetting. You read things written about you and you think you've got to change how you behave, but you're not like how you're being portrayed. You just have to be yourself.").[3]

The press reports about his mum are particularly interesting when looking at the Cipriani story. Although he attended independent schools and shares a surname with one of London's most exclusive restaurants, he was hardly born with a silver spoon in his mouth. Cipriani was still young when his parents split, and his father Jay, originally from Trinidad, would go back to the Caribbean when Danny was just nine, leaving his mother Anne to raise him solo. Determined to stand on her own two feet as a single parent, she passed The Knowledge, the formidable exam required to drive a black cab in London, and in doing so became one of the first female cab drivers in the city. Anne worked all hours when Cipriani was a kid to get him into the best possible schools and put him into positions to get scholarships.

After his England debut, he spoke proudly of her:

> It was hugely important that she was at the match and I owe such a lot to my mum. She is amazing and I hope that other mothers take note and realise it can work as a single parent... My mum's been amazing because she's worked so hard to provide for me. I just want to make her happy and help her work not so many hours.[4]

His natural ability, harnessed at the Wimbledon College, the Oratory School and Whitgift, saw him play rugby, football and cricket to a high standard. Offers to join the academy at Reading FC or Surrey County Cricket Club were on the table but it was rugby he chose, signing on the dotted line for Wasps, then still based in West London.

He made his England debut off the bench in a defeat to Wales in the 2008 Six Nations and would make his first start against Ireland a few weeks later.

Cipriani had been selected to start against Scotland earlier in the tournament, but two days before that match he was axed from the squad for "inappropriate behaviour" after being photographed leaving a nightclub at 12.30 a.m. He would claim that he was only there briefly, dropping off some tickets, and hadn't drunk anything, but it would delay his debut and see him warned about his future conduct.

When he did eventually start for England, he delivered a fantastic performance, claiming an 18-point haul in a 33-10 win over Ireland at Twickenham. The response was huge: "Danny Cipriani announced a new era," said ESPN, "Sweet Cipriani polishes the keys to No. 10," wrote *The Guardian*, and even the *Irish Examiner* weren't immune, describing it as an "outstanding performance".

Cipriani, in his post-match interview, gave another flash of his unpolished approach to life as a professional sportsman, in honestly (if clumsily) saying that it was the forwards, not him, who deserved the plaudits. He stated live on BBC1, "It's the fucking one to eight who deserve the Man of the Match."

This debut would not, however, be the start of a glittering International career. The Ireland game would be his third cap, and he'd only pick up another 13 in the following ten years.

16 caps and 64 points is no return at all for a man with such unbridled and exuberant natural talent – arguably the most talented player of his generation. He would never play in a World Cup or don the red shirt of the Lions.

The years that followed would be a rollercoaster of flashes of form and flair versus tabloid headlines and bust-ups with teammates and coaches.

In 2010 he left Wasps to join the Melbourne Rebels. Injuries and mixed form had blighted the end of his spell at the London club, so he decided on a fresh start Down Under. In doing so, he became the first English International to play Super Rugby for an Australian team. Rebels coach Rod Macqueen stated that Cipriani was "coming for all the right reasons. He is on the right path to the culture we are after."

The night following their first game of his debut season, a 43-0 home drubbing against the Waratahs, some of the team thought a night out was what was needed. In the early hours of the morning at a Melbourne night club, Cipriani helped himself to a bottle of vodka from behind the bar, without paying. A fine, a warning and a public apology would swiftly follow. In the next match, Cipriani slotted a conversion and six penalties – including the match-winner, with just 9 seconds left on the clock – in a 25-24 victory over the Brumbies.

Can you begin to see a pattern emerging?

After a mixed two years in Australia, scoring 122 points but also receiving a suspension for breaking a team curfew, he traded Melbourne for Sale in 2012, stating a desire to get back into the England national side as a major driver in his return.

The following year he made headlines again when he was hit by a double decker bus in Leeds on an end-of-season night out with his Sale teammates. They were doing a pub crawl known locally as the Otley Run, and he was in fancy dress when he was struck. Luckily the bus was travelling at a low speed and he only suffered a concussion. A photo of the aftermath is remarkable: the front windscreen shattered, Cipriani in a neck brace on a stretcher surrounded by paramedics, and several of his teammates in various costumes, no doubt suddenly feeling very sober, looking on concerned. The bump at least failed to shake his sense of humour, with him tweeting a few days later, "Out of hospital now. Thank you for all the well wishes, means a lot. My ribs are a bit sore. Feel like I've been hit by a bus..."

In 2015, he was back in the England side and fighting for a place in the World Cup squad. After notching 33 points, including two tries, in a rout of the Barbarians at Twickenham, he decided to have a night out. Four Espresso Martinis, a Vodka Cranberry, a flute of champagne and many hours later, he crashed his Mercedes into a taxi on a Chelsea street.

Despite trying to evade the charge by hiring a drink-driving specialist – who somehow dragged the court proceedings out for four days – Cipriani was found guilty of driving with excess alcohol. He was fined £4,500, ordered to pay £3,120 in court costs and fees, and banned from driving for 18 months.

Reading the report of the trial, there's one other slightly cringeworthy detail: that Cipriani's arrest caused great excitement at the station, and a "rugby-loving custody sergeant", after congratulating him on his performance that day at Twickenham, several times engaged in conversation about the game and said "We will look after you" to the now probably hung-over star.[5]

Cipriani wouldn't make the England squad for their home World Cup in 2015.

In 2016, he would rejoin Wasps for two more seasons, before signing for Gloucester. Whilst at the Cherry and Whites, he'd play some of the best rugby of his career, scoring 128 points in 44 appearances and being voted 2019 Player of the Year by the Rugby Players' Association.

On the back of his form at Gloucester, in the summer of 2018 he would receive an England recall for a tour to South Africa. He wasn't involved in the first Test defeat, made a substitute appearance in the second Test loss but made his first International start in a decade in the third fixture.

Nine minutes from time, with England five points ahead in a tight encounter, his moment came.

Receiving the ball 40 metres out, he looked for support but there was none. The South African defence was almost upon him when he checked inside and, moments before being clattered to the ground, clipped the ball from an impossibly awkward angle into unguarded space in the corner, where the electric Johnny May flew onto it and grounded it for the decisive try.

England would win 25-10 and take some pride from an otherwise disappointing tour.

As the Sky commentator roared, "Cipriani, with not a lot of time, on the left foot squeezes it beneath the chaser and Johnny May's pace does the rest. Cipriani was asked to come in and do something different and that was a wonderful kick."[6]

Despite this golden moment, it was almost certainly the last International that Cipriani would ever play. His performance did little to move England boss Eddie Jones, who would later write in his autobiography:

> The reaction from the press was outrageous. They thought Cipriani had proved he was a genius. It was one good moment, but he had been quiet throughout the rest of the game. At the

> end of the week in Cape Town, Danny was still a distant third behind Owen Farrell and George Ford.[7]

Jones would also add brusquely, "When a player consistently does stupid things, you don't expect him to change much." And with the Australian at the helm at Twickenham, the door back to International rugby would remain firmly closed. Cipriani would write in the *Daily Mail* in 2021:

> It's all in the past now, but I don't think Eddie really wanted me in there, to be honest. Eddie was always so reluctant to pick me. Whenever my name was mentioned, he was always so negative… If Eddie had talked positively about what I was doing, it might have been different. I was picked in the Premiership Team of the Year three years in a row and I was named Player of the Year, but Eddie always brushed over any talk about me.[8]

There would be some more negative press headlines in 2018 after an assault in a Jersey nightclub – an unsavoury incident that took place on a pre-season tour with Gloucester. He was fined £2,000 plus £250 compensation to a woman police officer, having also been found guilty of resisting arrest. Cipriani would admit he was drunk and tweet that he was "truly sorry... most importantly [to] the police."

He joined Bath in 2021, got married during lockdown and in May 2022 announced his retirement from the English Premiership. At the time of writing, his next destination is yet to be confirmed, but America is looking the most likely. Cipriani is also increasingly contributing to the media, where he cuts an entertaining, self-effacing and clearly wiser figure than in his younger days.

A keen contributor to social media, his most powerful contribution came after the suicide of TV presenter Caroline Slack, his ex-girlfriend, when he posted a moving and raw 18-minute video message on Instagram. I won't describe it in detail as I don't think I can do it justice. Suffice to say that he talks of her, and his belief that she died because of "embarrassment and shame" which had been created by the toxic culture around celebrity. In response, he opens up on his own "most embarrassing and shameful moments" from across his life, and addresses his challenges with depression, racism, drinking, sex and more.

One part that really struck a chord with me was when he recalled the response after telling his fellow players. "I told my teammates my story. I had teammates that I thought didn't even like me text me over the weekend – the most beautiful things. Why does it take someone to die to make this the case?"

It's rare to see such honesty so publicly, and I'd urge you to take some time to watch it. The link is in the notes section at the end of the book.[9]

Writing about Danny Cipriani is exhausting. The highs and the lows chase around after each other and I've left a lot of tabloid stories out as I think many are deeply unfair. This chapter only scratches the surface of his life. A wonderfully talented player – in terms of ability, one of the best of his generation – with his skills, kicking, handling and eye for opening defences, he has it all. He scratched out 16 caps but should easily have had over 50.

Someone who agrees 100% with this assessment is Sir Clive Woodward. In September 2022, *Ruck* ran an article in which the legendary England coach referred to Cipriani as the greatest talent he ever saw who failed to live up to his potential:

> On talent and skill, Cipriani should have been in the team the last ten years. He was the person to come in and take over from [Jonny] Wilkinson, he was the man ready to go. He is the only English number 10 of the past 20 years who, if I'd been coach and he had been up for selection at the same time as Jonny, could have caused big selection headaches.
>
> His skill-set was so complete. He posed an attacking threat with ball in hand and has a superb kicking game and world-class distribution. I think Wilkinson would have got the nod over him

> in the end but the fact I even mention them in the same breath shows how highly I rate Cipriani.
>
> He just seemed to be a person where coaches didn't want to talk to [him], and he was the guy you'd want to be absolutely close to and almost build the team around him.

Cipriani's challenges around his mental health are now out in the open, but for much of his career they weren't. It does make you wonder what difference it might have made to his career if he had started trying to deal with them earlier. These issues for men are now being spoken about in a way that would have been unimaginable even a few years ago, and people like Danny Cipriani opening up about them in public are a big part of making this change.

I'm fascinated to see what he does when he retires – I think he'd be a great mentor to young rugby players.

But we'll finish with the simplest and most powerful message from his video: "Be kind" – something we can all make more effort with.

RAY GRAVELL

"You wait until I get back to London and tell them I'm making a film with Ray Gravell!"

FACTFILE

Full name: Raymond William Robert Gravell

Born: 12 September 1951, Kidwelly, Carmarthenshire, Wales

Died: 31 October 2007, Spain

Position: Centre

Representative teams: Carmarthenshire, West Wales, Barbarians, Wales, British & Irish Lions

Club: Llanelli RFC

Nickname: Grav

> In our earliest years we know a patch of ground in a detail we will never know anywhere again – site of discovery and putting names to things – people and places – working with difference and similitude – favourite places, places to avoid – neighbours and their habits, gestures and stories – textures, smells – also of play, imagination, experiment – finding the best location for doing things – creating worlds under our own control, fantasy landscapes.

THIS, BY THE late Professor Mike Pearson of Aberystwyth University, is the best description I can find of *y filltir sgwâr* ('the square mile'), the Welsh concept that we all have an intimate connection with our own 'home' surroundings, even if we no longer live there. It's the standout phrase in the moving *Times* obituary for Gravell penned by his Wales teammate and friend Gerald Davies, who beautifully made the point that "for all his travelling, he never left his home, so that wherever he went, he took these unmistakable Welsh roots with him."[10]

Other countries have similar concepts, of course.

But few countries have men like Ray Gravell.

Rugby player, actor, broadcaster, singer, activist, husband, father and friend – to give you an abridged list.

Gone too soon, dying of a heart attack aged just 56, he packed many lifetimes' worth of achievements and memories into a life well lived. Even today, 15 years after his passing, he is still very much in the public consciousness and in telling family and friends I was writing this chapter, I was regaled with their own personal stories about the man.

Reading, watching and listening to the details of his life, it seems less a chronology and more a series of remarkable moments lit up by the charisma and passion of the man known around Wales and across the rugby universe as 'Grav'.

But first, to quote Dylan Thomas – another larger-than-life Welshman, who lived the other side of the Towy Estuary in Laugharne – we must "begin at the beginning", at the place that would be Grav's home all his life: the Gwendraeth Valley, or more specifically Mynyddygarreg, a village in Carmarthenshire. Born just up the road in Kidwelly, he moved to the village (where his father had grown up) when he was just three and never really left. Although his rugby took him all over the world, he always lived in the village. His house, Brynhyfryd, has a wonderful vista across towards Caldey Island to the west, the Gower Peninsula to the east and the twinkling lights of Carmarthen at night.

A keen rugby player from a young age, his warm Welsh village life came to an abrupt halt with the suicide of his father when Ray was just 14. Jack Gravell had suffered a serious back injury whilst working in a nearby colliery and would spend days in bed in agony, no longer able to work or do either of his two favourite hobbies: hunting and gardening. With the pain unrelenting and stress and money worries mounting, one cold January afternoon, with a young Ray in Ammanford playing in a trial match for West Wales, Jack took his shotgun and went alone up a nearby mountain.

It would be Ray who found his body later that day.

> I rushed forward, but as I touched his clothes, I knew it was all over. That second, I remember, was one of the of the longest I'd ever experienced – the split second between discovering Dad's body and completely breaking down... For days afterwards, dozens of people came to see us, and I had to explain to them – as well as the inquest – what happened that awful night when Dad shot himself dead with his double-barred gun... Realizing that I'd lost a special and unique person in my life, I became inconsolable: he was an adviser, friend, brother and father. I cried those bitter tears for many years.[11]

The following days, weeks and months were terribly hard on young Ray, but with support from his family, his rugby coaches and teachers at Carmarthen Grammar School ('the Gram'), he was able to focus on the positives in his life – particularly his growing ability on the rugby pitch.

But that dreadful experience and its repercussions would, of course, stay with him forever. He never lost the fear of the dark his late father had been trying to get him to overcome. Despite all the trophies and caps he won, Ray Gravell often felt a sense of nagging doubt about his own abilities. Moments before taking the field for big games, he would ask his teammates who the best centre in Wales was – just needing that little confidence boost from his own side before going out and smashing into his opponents.

I spoke to Steve Fenwick, a dear friend of Gravell's and his centre partner with Wales for many years, and asked about this aspect of his personality.

> He was the nicest guy you could ever ask to meet, but he was such a worrier about everything. People used to try and wind him up, particularly the boys from Bridgend and Cardiff. Someone would say just before kick-off, "Grav, you've lost weight – everything OK?" and he'd spend the next 20 minutes asking Phil Bennett how he thought he looked.

John Dawes, Wales coach between 1974 and 1979, remembered this aspect of Gravell's attitude well:

> You might have some players who would lose a bit of confidence, but you just knew it took one good run and they would be back in it. Ray was a perfect example of that. He was such a worrier that he would go to pieces, and you would have a job to get him on the field. It was essential for him to get involved straight away and we made sure he did. Then he was off.[12]

His Wales career might have ended before it even started, however.

The night before his debut, against France in Paris in 1975, J J Williams awoke in the early hours to find Gravell, his roommate, packing his suitcase and getting ready to go home to Mynyddygarreg because he couldn't take the pressure. A bleary-eyed JJ told him to go and let him get back to sleep, but that if he did depart, he'd never play for Wales. Gravell stopped packing, hung his clothes back up and slipped back into bed. JJ would in later life be known for his sharp opinions as a TV pundit, and on this particular occasion his bluntness was put to good effect.

The following day at the Parc des Princes, after changing into his kit, Grav promptly disappeared to the toilet to be violently sick. He calmed himself by singing songs by Welsh nationalist folk singer Dafydd Iwan, before being dragged out onto the pitch by his Llanelli teammate Derek Quinnell. Wales would win and Gravell would proudly wear the red of Wales for the next seven years.

This mix of nerves and nationalism became a familiar part of pre-match proceedings for his teammates, as Wales and Llanelli colleague Tommy David recalls:

> What Ray had, apart from his strength, speed and determination, was this enormous passion – for Llanelli and for Wales. When we had our team talk before Llanelli faced the All Blacks, there was Grav with tears running down his cheeks.[13]

For all his appearances for Wales and his tour with the Lions in 1980, the most famous game that Gravell would ever play in would be the fixture against New Zealand on 31 October 1972 that prompted his tears. Like fellow maverick Moss Keane's win over the same opposition six years later, it's a day that has transcended rugby, becoming its own cultural touchpoint.

Whereas Munster had a play, Llanelli had a song.

> Oh the beer flowed at Stradey, piped down from Felinfoel,
> And the hands that held the glasses high were strong from steel and coal,
> The air was filled with singing and I heard a grown man cry,
> Not because we'd won but because the pubs ran dry.
>
> '9–3', Max Boyce[14]

In the 1970s a visit from the All Blacks was a rare and precious thing, and this tour was something particularly special. It began in Canada in October, then headed to New York, then crossed the Atlantic. They zigzagged across the UK and Ireland for three months, spending Christmas in London (beating a Combined Services XV on Boxing Day at Twickenham) before finishing up in France in February and being allowed to return home. They don't make tours like they used to!

There was some added spice to the tour as well, in that the previous year the British and Irish Lions had visited New Zealand and won the Test series – still the only time the Lions have achieved this feat to date. The 1971 tourists were coached by the mercurial and enigmatic Carwyn James, and the All Blacks would be facing him on their 1972 tour in his regular role as Llanelli coach, hopeful of exacting some revenge.

James, in his own meticulous way, had been planning for this game for the intervening year, bringing in players to the team that season specifically with this match in mind, changing how squad rotation was used and, on the day, bringing the players all together in a hotel pre-match and travelling to Stradey Park on the same coach, rather than just meeting at the ground as was the norm.

Gravell, aged just 21, was the youngest player on the teamsheet and as the bus trundled through the crowds, he was particularly nervous. The captain that day, Delme Thomas, would recall that he was asked by James to sit next to Gravell. Putting his arm around the youngster, he told him not worry and kept him distracted all the way to the ground with a non-stop stream of small talk. Shortly afterwards, Thomas would deliver a deeply intense team talk, and after some final deft insights from James, the team emerged to a raucous Stradey Park, packed full of 22,000 expectant and vocal Llanelli fans.

They weren't to be disappointed. A Roy Bergiers try after just three minutes set the home team on their way, and in a pulsating game they'd run out 9-3 winners. Gravell put in a tremendous defensive shift, and a few minutes from the end he was trampled underfoot by the soon-to-be-disgraced Kiwi Keith Murdoch, leaving him nearly unconscious. The referee that day, clearly keen not to delay the game's end, shouted at Gravell to get up, and he just about managed to get to his feet. With his vision blurred and his head swimming, he somehow saw out the last few minutes before being mobbed by a huge pitch invasion as the referee blew the most famous victory in Llanelli's history.

This was, of course, still in the amateur era. Gravell had been at work as a lineman for the Electricity Board the day before, but on such a special day he'd get a reward. "I was given an envelope with the largest sum I'd ever received from the club – a huge amount of money at the time – £10 of 'beer money'. It was the first time I'd held a £10 note – there was not much of it left by the end of the evening!"[15] This is approximately £147 in today's money, but sounds like it helped Gravell do his bit in ensuring, as the song goes, that the pubs were all drunk dry.

Gravell's coach that day, and for a large part of his Llanelli career, was Carwyn James – a true maverick as well, although I doubt he'd have used that word to describe himself. Part of his pioneering approach as club coach was to oversee the development of the youth teams, and this is where the two men first met. From these early days, James' impact on Gravell would greatly increase, with the player later describing him as "the person who had the greatest influence on me as an individual."

A deep and complex character, James knew exactly how to get the best out of Gravell on the pitch as well as fostering his wider interests off it.

There's a touching story of Gravell, who as we've already heard was partial to singing the songs of Dafydd Iwan prior to matches, sometimes being joined by the light tenor of James on the chorus. Gravell was developing a growing awareness of Welsh history and culture, something which James would help encourage.

If the 20 mavericks in this book would accept a manager, it would be a job for James, a man who wanted to entertain and always told his charges that "it's a game for the mind as well as the body." Perhaps fittingly, despite besting the All Blacks as coach of the Lions, Llanelli and in 1973 also the Barbarians, he never got the Wales job. His single-minded approach, zeal for reform and control over the team selection process intimidated the committee men of the WRU into never giving the top job to the most talented coach Wales has ever had.

James' influence, however, lived long with all the players he worked with. And perhaps with none more than Gravell, visible most strongly from 1997 in his role at the National Eisteddfod – the annual celebration of culture and the Welsh language in Wales.

For those of you that haven't experienced the National Eisteddfod, it's a festival of culture and literature, a fair, a trade show and an annual reunion. Parts of it have a strong druidic flavour, with prizes given for poetry and prose under the auspices of the Gorsedd of Bards – the national association of poets, writers, musicians, artists and others who have each made a distinguished contribution to the Welsh nation, language and culture.

During the ceremonies an important role is played by the Grand Sword Bearer, who holds a great blade aloft during key moments. This role has been held by several prominent Welsh individuals, but few can have been better-suited or prouder of the role than Ray Gravell – or Ray o'r Mynydd ('Ray from the Mountain'), as he was known in bardic circles. Clad all in white with a hood and a gold chain, lifting an ancient-looking sword – bigger even than him – Gravell proved to be a powerful force during many Eisteddfodau in the 2000s, in a role that often attracted more attention than that of the Archdruid himself.

Today the Bearer of the Grand Sword is Robin o Fôn ('Robin from Anglesey'), also known as Robin McBryde, the former Wales and Lions player and coach who took over the role after Gravell stood down. A fellow Llanelli legend and a powerful figure in his own right, as well as a friend of Gravell's, he's one of the few men who could have stepped into such big shoes.

Years before being chosen to represent centuries of Welsh culture, there came another honour: the call to join the 1980 Lions tour to South Africa. It was a difficult and controversial tour, as often proves the case – but particularly so in 1980, as the British and Irish governments thought there should be no involvement with a country still under the firm grip of apartheid. Gravell, like many on the tour, knew the realities of life in South Africa and did wrestle with the issue, before deciding that "a personal protest from Raymond Gravell wouldn't have helped their fight – because I still believe that keeping in contact and having a quiet influence can be effective."[16]

An injury-hit squad eventually succumbed 3-1 in the Test series, although they won every non-Test match. Gravell himself would feature in each of the four Tests, crossing for a try in the second match.

One of the most special features of a Lions tour is the mixing of players from the different nations as they put aside the rivalries for a common goal, for a few weeks at least.

Irish fly half Ollie Campbell recalls meeting Grav for the first time in a London hotel, prior to departure to South Africa:

> He came over to me and welcomed me, and he said that he was delighted to meet me. He said, "I hear you're quite shy," and then he added, "I am too" – before disproving this in the days, weeks, months and even years ahead.

Gravell's role in a tour match against the Orange Free State also looms large in Campbell's memory:

> Grav had made a tackle on his opposite number, De Wet Ras. This happened in the first play of the game and was so late it was almost posthumous. It went unseen and unpunished by the referee. Interviewed on the TV afterwards, Grav said in all seriousness that he had been told from a very young age to get his first tackle in early, even if it was late! That was the beginning and the end of the interview.[17]

Fellow Lions tourists Clive Woodward and Bill Beaumont would both become lifelong friends with Gravell, whose Welsh nationalism was never exclusionary – even to those most English of players!

Steve Fenwick recalled another memory from touring with him, this time with Wales in Australia:

> We were in Sydney, running out on the pitch, when a bloke in the stand shouted at Grav, "Go home, you Pommy bastard." Grav stopped in his tracks and ran right over to him. The Aussie looked terrified as he got up in his face, then he said, "Call me a Welsh bastard, but never a Pommy bastard." The fella said shakily, "Sorry mate, I didn't know the difference." Grav ran back onto the pitch, and we were all cracking up!

Returning from South Africa, Gravell would assume the captaincy at Stradey Park in the 1980/81 season. He continued to play for Wales until 1982 and would be part of the Llanelli squad that defeated another set of Southern Hemisphere visitors in 1984 – this time Australia – before injury brought down the curtain on his rugby career in 1985, after 485 matches.

The end of his playing days opened up more time for his burgeoning broadcasting career. He proved to be a popular, lively and knowledgeable voice in both Welsh and English, and expanded from just covering rugby to presenting lifestyle and music shows. He would record his own music and built a solid portfolio of acting roles.

Beginning with small Welsh-language parts, he would progress into a range of films, featuring alongside Jeremy Irons and Juliette Binoche in the Oscar-nominated *Damage* in 1992 and working with Hollywood legend Peter O'Toole in *Rebecca's Daughters*.

And of all the stories I've read about Gravell – and there are many: keeping this chapter to our wordcount has been a challenge! – it's him meeting the actor best known for his role as Lawrence of Arabia that is my favourite.

They are filming in the Brecon Beacons and, already nervous, Grav is startled to find he has sat down for make-up next to O'Toole. Marina, the make-up artist, begins the conversation:

> Marina: Peter, this is Ray.
> Peter (looking at the mirror in front of him): How are you?

Ray: Fine, thank you, Mr O'Toole!
Marina: He's played a bit of rugby you know...
Peter: You've played rugby, have you? Who did you play for?
Ray: I played 485 games for Llanelli during the 1970s and early 1980s.
Peter: That's a lot. Did you play against JPR?
Ray: Mr O'Toole, I am honoured and privileged to have played with, and against, JPR, Gareth and Gerald.
Peter (seeming suspicious): Which other teams did you play for?
Ray: I represented Wales, the Barbarians, and the British Lions as a centre three-quarter... without forgetting Carmarthenshire!
Peter: You played for Wales! Who was the finest centre you played against?
Ray: That has to be the Ulsterman, Michael Gibson. A true gent.
Peter (now standing up, having scattered make-up bottles everywhere and staring at Ray): You fucking played against Mike Gibson? You're not that man mountain, Ray Gravell?
Ray: Well, yes, I am!
Peter: Well, fucking hell! You wait until I get back to London and tell them I'm making a film with Ray Gravell![18]

For the next two weeks of filming, Peter O'Toole spent every spare minute with Gravell. A huge rugby fan, he was full of questions about the game and they must have been quite the pair on set!

Elected president of Llanelli RFC in 1998, Ray Gravell was always busy, in demand for his warmth, his knowledge and his pure Gravness! But in 2000 he was diagnosed with diabetes and in 2007 his right leg was amputated below the knee because of a related infection. It was at this point that he handed the Sword Bearer role to Robin McBryde. He kept working, and not long after his operation he led out his two young daughters, Gwenan and Manon, onto the Stradey Park pitch ahead of a match, wearing shorts and with his prosthetic leg – complete with Llanelli Scarlets badge – on display for all to see.

With his recovery from the operation going well, there's a particular cruelty to the heart attack which cut short his life, aged just 56. On holiday with his family in Spain, it happened just six months after the amputation, and 35 years to the day after he was part of the Llanelli team which inflicted that famous defeat on the All Blacks.

The news of Gravell's death shocked the world of rugby and all of Wales. There can't have been many more popular figures in contemporary Welsh culture, and his strength and commitment on the pitch was matched by his warmth and humanity off it. A complex man, part of a special time in Welsh history when the national team was enjoying a golden era and nationalism was reawakening, he brought together the best aspects of these twin developments.

His funeral was as close to a state one as can be delivered in Wales. Held at his beloved Stradey Park, around 10,000 mourners attended from all over Wales to see Gravell's flag-draped coffin carried onto the field by six Llanelli players, from past and present. Speakers included then First Minister Rhodri Morgan, who praised the "combination of his common humanity and his almost Bambi-like vulnerability."

Historian Hywel Teifi Edwards said, "We always knew he was special. A Vitamin C of a Welshman. He was a rarity, a begetter of stories about himself in his own lifetime. There was a distinct touch of the *Mabinogion* about him. Stories will be told about him with gusto in years to come by people who never met him, and I'm quite convinced that stories were fashioned with Grav in mind centuries ago." Whilst Dafydd Iwan, whose songs had meant so much to Grav, sang '*Duw, Mi Wn y Daw*' ('My God, I Know You Will Come').

The following spring at the Wales v. France game in Cardiff, Gravell's daughters led the Wales team on to the pitch carrying the Triple Crown plate and the coaching staff and players wore number 13 shirts bearing Gravell's name.

It was as a big a send-off as Gravell deserved.

Never tempted to head north to rugby league (there's no *y filltir sgwâr* in Widnes or Warrington), as a hard-running and even harder-tackling centre, he would have fitted well into today's game and its demands.

The famous rugby cartoonist Gren summed up Gravell's on-field reputation by drawing a fan waving a banner with the slogan: "Gravell eats soft centres." And his toughness certainly helped create the space and time for his golden-era colleagues like JPR, JJ and Gerald Davies to weave their magic.

But unlike so many players, his reputation grew after hanging up his boots. Gravell was far, far more than a great rugby player. There was a rare combination of innocence and excitement about him that made such an impact on those he met. And in researching this chapter, I've realised this must number at least half of the Welsh population!

Speaking to Steve Fenwick, he clearly still misses his friend:

> He was the proudest Welshman I ever met. And always true to himself. We came into the Welsh team together and said, whatever happens, we help each other out. We played as a real partnership in all our caps. Mind you, he still battered me when we played against each other for our clubs! Once, he absolutely slammed into me, knocking me out. I remember coming round, lying on the floor, and him looking down at me, grinning, "You alright, Steve?" This was classic Grav: big hits then a smile and a joke.

Ollie Campbell also had a nice line on him. "Grav was like an onion. There were so many layers to him. And every layer was good, too. It's said that to be forgotten is to die twice. Grav will never be forgotten."[19]

But let's give Carwyn James, writing in *The Guardian* a few years before his own death, the final word on the great man: "Gravell is passionately Welsh. Llywelyn, the last Real Prince of Wales, died in 1282, but spiritually Gravell belongs to his army."[20]

SONNY BILL WILLIAMS

"It wasn't a perfect journey, but the lessons have helped shape me into the man I'm proud to be off the field today."

FACTFILE

Full name: Sonny William 'Bill' Williams

Born: 3 August 1985, Auckland, New Zealand

Positions: Second row, Lock, Centre

Representative teams: New Zealand Sevens, Barbarians, New Zealand (Rugby League), New Zealand

Clubs: Toulon, Canterbury, Crusaders, Chiefs, Panasonic Wild Knights, Counties Manukau, Blues (rugby union); Canterbury-Bankstown Bulldogs, Sydney Roosters, Toronto Wolfpack (rugby league)

Nicknames: SBW, Money Bill, $BW

ON MOST DAYS a stroll through the impressive St Joseph Boys' facilities in Sallynoggin, a low-key working-class suburb in the south of Dublin, will take you past a host of football matches. These pitches belong to a club that since 1953 has been the home of many boys and girls who have gone on to pull on the green jersey of Ireland. But it was no footballer in the spotlight here in February 2022. Go past the pitches and into the large sports hall and you'll find yourself in the current home of Monkstown Boxing Club. If you'd taken a trip here at this time, right in front of you would have been two boxing rings, a dozen or so heavy bags, and – if you were lucky – Andy Lee training his latest protégé.

Lee is a serious guy. An Irish Olympic boxer and former World Champion who retired in early 2018 with a record of 35 wins from 39 professional fights. A second cousin of Tyson Fury who, in winning the WBO middleweight title, became the first member of the travelling community to win a major world title. Likeable and erudite, he is married to a classically trained violinist, and is a co-founder of a theatre and musical performance company.

The Irishman, however, only won a world title once. At the end of winter 2022, he was spending every day with someone who had won two rugby world titles with the All Blacks in 2011 and 2015, and a third in boxing in 2013.

Hammering the gloves with all the force that his 6' 3", 18st frame would allow was Sonny Bill Williams.

"I know he's a busy man. I know he's a wanted man by great fighters, so I'm very grateful that he's let me come over here and do some work with him," said Williams of Lee.

"He has as much as me – probably more than me, actually – in terms of high-performance knowledge and professionalism," Lee says of Williams. "That mindset... he's transferring a lot of things that he learned over all those years in rugby into boxing. I can see it especially in his preparation."[21]

Boxing is the third sport that Williams is seeking to master, the recently retired All Blacks centre having begun his career in, and twice returned to, rugby league. What took this superstar of the modern game to a municipal gym in Dublin was the opportunity to train with Lee ahead of a fight against another sport switcher, the controversial Australian-Rules-player-turned-boxer Barry Hall, in Sydney in March 2022.

His hard work in Sallynoggin paid off, with Williams destroying Hall in just two minutes, knocking him down first after just 45 seconds and then twice more before the fight was stopped. Now there's talk of Williams facing Jake Paul, the millionaire YouTuber turned boxer. Not one for the boxing purists perhaps, but a fight that would attract a lot of attention – not to mention a significant purse.

Whilst Williams has developed a love of boxing, his taste for the Sweet Science was originally born of a more prosaic reason – he needed the money.

But first let's rewind to the start of the story. Born in 1985 in Auckland to a Samoan father and a half-New Zealand, half-Australian mother, Sonny Bill was the second of four children. He grew up in a working-class, sporty family. His younger sister Niall represents New Zealand in sevens rugby, picking up a silver medal at the 2016 Olympics, a gold at the women's Rugby World Cup Sevens in 2018 and most recently a bronze at the 2022 Commonwealth Games. The big hits and outrageous offloads Sonny Bill Williams is known for were first born in his backyard and out on the street, playing rugby with his siblings and cousins. And a look at some of Niall's highlights on YouTube shows that she shares the same skills and thirst for physicality as her big brother.

School wasn't easy, though. Sonny Bill suffered severe burns on his legs in an accident when he was little, and as he'd recall in 2021:

> In primary school, I used to get called "Kentucky Fried Chicken legs"... I remember walking down the corridor and girls stopping and saying, "Oh my God, look at his legs." I never wore shorts to school from then.
>
> When we look at the Polynesian players, they're really big and physical and strong, and here I was: this little white skinny, lanky fella claiming to be Samoan. Well, for anyone that thought otherwise, I was going to show them – and that's where the shoulder charge came from.[22]

Money was tight throughout his childhood, and this added further fuel to his determination: "Coming from pretty much nothing, I strove so hard to get Mum a house with wallpaper on it. I pushed the boundaries, I trained my butt off because that's all I knew – because I wanted to succeed, be something, create something and give something to my family."[23]

The young Sonny Bill excelled in sprinting, the high jump and cross country and he could have had a future in athletics, but once in secondary school it was rugby league that would become his focus. Whilst playing junior rugby in Auckland, he was spotted by the Canterbury-Bankstown Bulldogs and moved to Sydney at just 16 as the youngest-ever player to sign for a National Rugby League (NRL) team. He would make his full debut two years later. After only a handful of club games, he became the youngest-ever New Zealand rugby league International player, pulling on the black jersey aged 18. As a point of comparison, the youngest-ever rugby union All Black is Jonah Lomu, who was 19.

Williams would spend four successful years with the Bulldogs, but it was his departure which would lead to his first boxing bout. By 2007 he was a rugby league superstar and signed a bumper five-year contract to keep him at the Bulldogs until 2012. Just nine months later, he walked out on the sport and left the country on his Samoan passport to join rugby union outfit Toulon in France. This acrimonious exit would be described by some as the 'greatest act of treachery in the game's history'.

Williams would recall in 2021:

> Although I was playing some great footy at the time when I took off, I was deeply, deeply unhappy off it.
>
> I wish that I had the mindset that I have now because it wouldn't have went down the way it went down. I would have been more confident to stand up and say, "This is how I'm feeling, this is what needs to change." I just felt like I needed to escape, but what I found out was that when I ran, the man in the mirror, the problems I was facing, were staring straight back at me in the mirror in France.[24]

Williams was at this point a hard-partying fixture of the gossip pages and he would later be open about his drinking and drug-taking during this period. Some salacious stories in particular coloured his reputation. One article in the press about a dalliance with a young lady resulted in him reportedly buying up copies of all the newspapers in his area to stop his girlfriend finding out.

And no, it didn't work.

The move to France might have been an attempt to shake off some bad habits, but it would prove an expensive one. To get out of the contract, he had to pay one million Australian dollars to the Bulldogs – money that, despite the big wages at Toulon, he didn't have. A fellow multi-sport athlete, Australian rugby-league-star-turned-world-champion-boxer Anthony Mundine, came to his rescue. He gave Williams a loan – understood to be in the region of $750,000 AUD – and as part of the repayment, asked him to join the undercard of one of his fights.

Sonny Bill hadn't previously been into boxing beyond watching the odd big fight on TV, but this unorthodox entry into the sport was the beginning of something quite special. Williams would tell an Irish journalist in 2022:

> So, it was through necessity, and then... Well, to begin with, I was a little bit of a fish out of water. I didn't even know how to throw a jab or a one-two, y'know? But I hang my hat on hard work and dedication. "I may not be there now but I will test the waters as much as I can." And that's where the love affair began.[25]

His first opponent was a fellow Kiwi: Gary Gurr, aka 'The Baboon'. A builder by trade, a rookie brawler by form, but a world champion in his mind. At the weigh-in, he turned the air blue with expletives before shoving Williams in the chest and telling the crowd he'd knock out his opponent in the first round, so he could "get to the bar".

Williams stopped Gurr just one minute and 22 seconds into the second round. And a week later he played for the Barbarians against the Wallabies in Sydney.

So began a boxing career that would duck and weave through his successes in both codes of rugby.

In June 2011 he fought the Tongan Alipate Liava'a, aka 'God's Finest Man', who juggled the twin careers of boxing and gospel singing, with Williams winning a unanimous points decision. The fight was billed as 'The Clash for Canterbury' and became one of the biggest fundraisers for the city's earthquake appeal. Sky donated the money from its pay-per-view sales, and Williams gave $100,000 NZD from his share of TV sales – one of the biggest individual donations by a sportsperson to a disaster appeal ever.

The following year, Williams won the New Zealand Professional Boxing Association (NZPBA) Heavyweight Championship after knocking out Clarence Tillman III.

In early 2013, the standard of the opposition would be raised a level when he took on the South African Francois Botha, who (though by this time past his peak at 44) had previously fought Mike Tyson, Lennox Lewis, Evander Holyfield and Wladimir Klitschko, among other elite pugilists. New Zealand and South Africa have delivered many heavyweight matches on the rugby pitch, and these two giants went hard at it for 10 rounds before the Kiwi secured a unanimous points decision and with it the vacant WBA International Heavyweight title.

Sonny Bill Williams was a boxing World Champion, less than 18 months after winning the rugby equivalent at the Rugby World Cup in Auckland.

He'd made his International rugby union debut in 2010 as only the second-ever player (and the first since the 1920s) to pull on the black jersey in union after first playing for the league Test team. Williams had returned to New Zealand from France earlier that year, to sign with Canterbury and the Crusaders and agree an unprecedented contract with the New Zealand

Rugby Union that allowed him to continue with his boxing when schedules permitted.

From his first appearance he became a regular in the squad, even if he wasn't always in the starting XV. He had to be satisfied with coming off the bench in the World Cup Final victory over France in 2011, just as he would four years later in the win over Australia at Twickenham, coming on at half time and providing Ma'a Nonu with a brilliant offload to set up the match's decisive try.

But it was perhaps what happened after the game that made more headlines for Williams. As the All Blacks do their lap of honour, a 14-year-old English schoolboy, Charlie Line, runs onto the pitch to try and celebrate with the players. Before he can reach them, he's brutally rugby tackled by a security guard, making an audible, slightly comic yelp as he's bundled into the turf.

On seeing this, Williams intervenes, rescuing the slightly woozy teenager and escorting him back to his mum in the stand. Then, much to everyone's bewilderment, he gives young Line his World Cup-winners medal to keep. He explained:

> I was walking around doing a lap of honour with the boys and a young fella came running out and he got smoked by the security guard, like full-on tackled him. I felt sorry for the little fella. If that was a younger brother or cousin, I would have given the security guard a hiding. But I just picked the kid up and took him back to his old lady and tried to make the night more memorable for him: better [for the medal] to be hanging around his neck than mine.

This moment was beamed around the world, and the photos are very sweet. But one senses some annoyance about the spotlight on Charlie from his family, who on the Monday after the final had to issue a statement: "Charlie is now back at school and focussing on his studies. He won't be taking part in any media interviews."[26]

Charlie kept his medal. And Williams was later furnished with a replacement by the tournament organisers. Everyone was a winner!

In between World Cup wins, Sonny Bill had spent a year back in League with the Sydney Roosters and a spell with Union side Panasonic Wild Knights in Japan. Williams can never be accused of being a man who would grow too comfortable in his surroundings.

And there was another off-field change in 2009 that would prove to be the most important of all – his conversion to Islam. Despite his behaviour shaking him enough to leave New Zealand for a fresh start in France, his lifestyle continued in Europe, as he told the BBC:

> Look, I chased girls. I drank alcohol, spent lavishly, and thought I was someone that I wasn't. I lived that life and, in my experience, what did it give me? Hollowness and emptiness in my heart.
>
> It took a few years for the process, but I found Allah, I found Islam and it really allowed me to turn the wildness in myself into positivity. With the way that I have driven as a sportsman to succeed, those two together have allowed me to reach where I am today.[27]

Williams acknowledges that Muslims today can be forced to "almost be embarrassed" about their religion, but he is immensely proud of his faith. A week after the Christchurch Mosque attacks in March 2019, which saw 51 people murdered by a white supremacist, Williams visited the city and met members of the community as an act of solidarity. Given his high profile in New Zealand, he felt it was his duty to represent those communities of which he is a part.

His switching between codes, his sometimes unconventional approach to his career, the boxing and without a doubt his faith have led to a section of the rugby public never truly embracing Williams. He responds:

> Well, I think to an extent, you always feel like an outsider. I'm a Polynesian and to top it off I'm a Muslim as well. So, you always have that kind of deep-down feeling that you are an outsider — but at the same time, that doesn't stop you from giving it a crack and being authentic and being a good person, y'know?[28]

Journalist Alan Duff, co-author of Sonny Bill Williams' autobiography *You Can't Stop the Sun from Shining*, has a particular admiration for his beliefs:

> To become a Muslim – or start the process of conversion, at least – only a few years after 9/11, when most of the Western world considered Islam and terrorism to be inextricably linked, takes more than courage. That decision not only put his stellar sporting reputation at risk, it exposed him to the odium of the prejudiced and the ignorant, and not a few otherwise rational people whose minds had been turned by those horrific attacks. Sonny will tell you he was no different: he once conflated Islam with terrorism, as I did myself. But through its teachings, Sonny discovered a deep inner healing and peace.[29]

Before his retirement in 2019, SBW found time for one more World Cup, picking up a bronze medal in Japan in his 58th and final cap for the All Blacks. His union club career concluded with two years with the Blues in Super Rugby, then he turned back to League, to play in the British system for the first Transatlantic rugby team, Toronto Wolfpack in Canada. His two-year deal was reportedly worth up to £2.6m a year, making him the highest-paid player in the history of either code.

His signing was huge for the fledgling outfit, with Williams described as the "LeBron James of rugby" when he arrived. Unfortunately, the knee injury that he'd had problems with for most of his career began to really hamper his fitness, and he managed just five appearances before Covid-19 forced a shutdown of the league. The Wolfpack's finances took a battering and, allied with the problems of pandemic-era travel, they had to leave the UK system for the newly launched North American Rugby League (NARL).

Williams duly left Canada and finished up his career with a brief second spell at Sydney Roosters before announcing his retirement on Instagram in March 2021. A picture of him with his wife and family accompanied a note telling his 1 million+ followers:

> A massive thank you to the public & fans for all the support over the last 17 years. To my many teammates, thanks for the lessons and help along the way. It wasn't a perfect journey by any means but the lessons have helped shape me into the man I'm proud to be off the field today.

Writing about Sonny Bill Williams' career can be a slightly bewildering affair, with the big New Zealander as kinetic off the field as he was on it. One of the most successful cross-code athletes in sport, he's played league, union and sevens at the highest level all over the world and lifted two rugby world cups, as well as winning two boxing belts – with that particular journey still ongoing. He has gone from the hedonistic and chaotic lifestyle that made him a favourite of the Antipodean tabloids to the deeply religious and committed husband and father to four young children seen in his more recent photos and videos on Instagram.

He's not been without his critics: as we've noted, his frequent moves and country- and code-hopping have led some to label him – I think unfairly – as Money Bill or $BW. But I doubt that Williams cares about this. He has his family, inner peace, a drawer full of medals, and is still aiming to dominate in one of his sports. And he's done everything his own way. At just 36, it's going to be fascinating to see what he chooses to aim his considerable talents towards next.

ANDY RIPLEY

"He always made you feel better at the end of a conversation."

FACTFILE

Full name: Andrew George Ripley OBE

Born: 1 December 1947, Liverpool, England

Died: 17 June 2010, Lingfield, Surrey, England

Position: No. 8

Representative teams: Middlesex, President's XV, England XV, Barbarians, England, British & Irish Lions

Club: Rosslyn Park

A FAVOURITE DISCUSSION topic for sports fans everywhere is who would win in confrontations that couldn't possibly happen. We are talking, "Who would win if Mike Tyson fought Muhammad Ali?", "Who was really the greatest footballer, Pelé or Diego Maradona?", "Would the 1970s Wales rugby team be as dominant today as they were then?", "How would Ayrton Senna do in a modern F1 car?" The questions go on and on, and so can the arguments – that's the beauty of them, as there's no way of providing a definitive answer.

But for the memorably named American figure-skating champion Dick Button, the question "Who is America's best athlete?" had been in his head since he won the James E Sullivan Memorial Trophy, awarded to the USA's best amateur athlete, in 1949. In the 1960s, retired from competing and the founder of a TV production company, he decided to try and bring his idea to life. He presented to the American Broadcasting Company (ABC) a pitch for a TV show that brought together athletes from different sports to compete directly against each other in events that were not their own, in one competition "that tested strength, speed, stamina and hand-eye coordination. And out of it came *Superstars*."[30]

The show launched in America in 1973 and a British version followed later the same year. It was filmed at Crystal Palace and was won by 400 m Olympic gold medallist David Hemery, with Welsh rugby favourite Barry 'the King' John coming runner-up as they competed across several disciplines. Shown by the BBC on New Year's Eve, it was a ratings smash and would be a TV fixture for the next 12 years.

Now, if you ask anyone who remembers the British version of *Superstars*, they'll likely recall one of a few things: a jaunty theme tune, English footballing superstar Kevin Keegan having a nasty fall off his bike, the unlikely elevation to national fame of judoka Brian Jacks, and the immense charm and tremendous strength of Andy Ripley.

The England and Lions man took part in several editions of *Superstars*, winning his 1981 British heat and qualifying for an international championship in Eilat, Israel. Watching the slightly grainy footage on YouTube, it's an entertaining if slightly eccentric programme, with a talented, eclectic field that also includes English rugby league winger Keith Fielding, Irish canoeist Declan Burns (who set a new world record for vertical pull-ups during the show's 'gym test', with 55 in 60 seconds), the South African F1 champion Jody Scheckter and German footballing great Gerd Müller.

Ripley emerged triumphant. A tremendously strong runner, he won the 800 m as well as the basketball competition and cycling (where he had to dodge a car that had somehow found its way onto the supposedly closed road where the race was taking place) and scored well in the canoeing. On a promenade surrounded by Israeli holidaymakers and schoolchildren, and towering over the marketing director of the event's sponsor (a long-defunct cruise company), he was presented with the trophy as Europe's best multi-discipline athlete.[31]

Ripley's fame now extended beyond just the world of rugby, as he recalled years later:

> *Superstars* was really just garbage TV, perhaps even the trailblazer for all these reality TV shows that pollute our screens today. My God, perhaps I am in some way responsible for *Celebrity Big Brother*... I'd never been recognised on the street for my rugby exploits, but the moment I appeared on *Superstars*, I couldn't even pop down to my local Marks & Spencer's without being mobbed. OK, that's a slight exaggeration, but you know what I mean. "Here, aren't you that bloke off *Superstars* that does the rowing and the running?" Being a natural-born attention seeker, I loved it and milked it for all it was worth.[32]

That Ripley managed to be so successful in *Superstars*, against many younger competitors, is testimony to his status as one of the last great Corinthian athletes – that is, someone who prides themselves in the playing of the game, amateurism and its associated values, rather than desperately hunting wins, trophies and rewards.

Physically imposing and with a natural aptitude for hard work and setting and achieving lofty goals, in addition to his rugby career he earned success in the City and got a Masters from Cambridge at the age of 50 – where he also came very close to being a part of the Boat Race crew. He did, at the age of 51, set an indoor rowing world record for his age group.

This, however, only tells part of his story.

Ripley was born in Liverpool in 1947, the youngest of five children, but spent most of his youth in Bristol after his parents separated. He didn't start playing rugby until his late teens. After graduating from the University of East Anglia, he moved to London to work for Price Waterhouse (as PwC were known then) and turned up for a trial at Rosslyn Park. Ripley found a natural home at the south-west London club – which also boasts two of our other mavericks, Danny Cipriani and Prince Alexander Obolensky, as former players – staying there for his entire career. He played his first game for the 4th team in autumn 1969, but by Christmas he was in the 1st team. He was representing Middlesex in the County Championship by 1971 and a year later he received a call for the England team to face Wales at Twickenham.

Wales would win that game 12-3, but Ripley loved every minute of it:

> Every rugby International will tell you that the first cap is special and it's true. I'll never forget the moment when I emerged from the changing room and sprinted onto the Twickenham pitch. It's addictive, I loved it… the noise, the smell, the adrenalin, everything… you just want it to last forever.[33]

England would lose all their games in the 1972 Five Nations, so few gave them much of a chance as they set off that summer for Johannesburg to play South Africa on African soil for the first time ever. The hosts had lost only one of their previous 14 home matches – to New Zealand, in a series they won 3-1.

England went into the Test match at Ellis Park having won five and drawn one of their warm-up matches, but even then their 18-9 win, with a team featuring four debutants, stunned the rugby world. Ripley, at 6' 5" and with long flowing locks tumbling out of his headband, was at his dynamic best in this match, and the performance kick-started his International career and brought England out of a slump.

The following season would see Ripley a member of an England team that received a standing ovation for simply running onto the pitch at Lansdowne Road at the height of the Troubles. This had never happened before, and is likely never to happen again, but as Irish great Fergus Slattery bluntly put it years later:

> If England didn't come it would have fucked up rugby union and Ireland would have been bollixed because now England, Scotland and Wales wouldn't have come to Dublin and you wouldn't have known when they were coming back. There would have been no Five Nations. It would have gone down the toilet.[34]

1973 was a particularly vicious time in the years of the Troubles, throwing England's arrival for the match into serious doubt. The previous season, security worries had seen Wales and Scotland refuse to take a trip across the Irish Sea and that year's Five Nations had not been completed.

In the first four weeks of the year, while England's position was being debated, 18 people had died in sectarian violence. A year prior to the game, in the days following Bloody Sunday – when British paratroopers shot 26 unarmed civilians during a protest march in Derry, killing 14 – the British Embassy in Merrion Square had been attacked and burnt down. It was still in ruins as arguments raged over whether England should visit Dublin.

In the end it was decided that England would fulfil the fixture. And despite the heavy security, Ripley took it all in his usual droll stride:

> We concealed our apprehension beneath humour. We played musical chairs whenever we travelled on the team bus, reasoning that the dozens of IRA snipers perched on the rooftops would find it harder to hit one of us if we were always swapping seats.[35]

Roger Uttley, a friend of Ripley's who won his first England cap that day, recalled to me that the full impact hadn't hit him at first:

> International games just didn't have the same focus as they do today. Yes, I was conscious of the Troubles, but I barely read a newspaper and only watched a few snippets of news a day. I was making my debut, so was focussed on that. It was only when we arrived, with the huge Garda protection and the amazing reception we received, that I got the scale of it. Being greeted like that by the Irish fans was fantastic and hugely welcomed.

David Duckham, one of Ripley's teammates that day, still feels emotional about that match:

> The moment when we took the field, there was this most almighty roar. Such a moment. One or two of us were in tears. It even brings tears to my eyes talking about it now. I can't believe any of us were consciously aware of any danger, but the fact was this was when we were most vulnerable. I just felt we had the comfort of 50,000 spectators and the warmth of the welcome was such I couldn't believe anything would happen.[36]

In the end the game passed without incident, and Ireland recorded an 18-9 win over the visitors. The England captain, Gloucestershire farmer John Pullin, uttered perhaps the most honest but poignant words ever spoken at a post-match dinner: "We may not be very good," he said, "but at least we turn up."

Later in 1973 Ripley would be part of an England team that defeated New Zealand 16-10 in Auckland, and the following year the Lions would come calling for their tour to South Africa. He had completed the journey from playing social rugby straight out of university to the pinnacle of the British and Irish game in just five years.

Many tipped Ripley to start the Tests but Welshman Mervyn Davies kept him out of the team, a huge hit on Jan Ellis in the first Test setting the tone for both a hugely physical series and Davies' own performances. 'Merv the Swerve' had huge admiration for Ripley, describing him as "the best and certainly the most awkward" No. 8 he'd ever played against.

Speaking to *Rugby World* in 2010, Davies recalled the battle he'd had with Ripley for that No. 8 spot:

> I knew I was under pressure and Andy made me a better player by pushing me so hard. I read recently that he was deeply disappointed at not getting into the Test side, but he never once revealed that while he was on tour. He just knuckled down and made me work even harder. He used to embarrass me in training with his sprinting prowess and he was a superb all-round athlete. He was a true athlete who played rugby. But above and beyond that he was a great man to tour with. Off the field he was a magnificent character who was always great company.[37]

Fellow Lions tourist Roger Uttley remembered the tour fondly when speaking to me:

> Andy liked to give the impression he was very cool and that he didn't take life too seriously and, in his own words, "just rocked up". In essence, though, he was a secret trainer and always prepared assiduously for the challenges he got involved in, a major factor in why he was so successful in his sporting achievements and in life in general.
>
> In South Africa, he was kept out of the team by Mervyn Davies – who, yes, probably was a better player – and he would pretend it didn't bother him, but it did. It was the biggest disappointment of his life. He wanted to be the best at everything he did. But it was an amazing tour: the competition for places was immense, and those scrummaging sessions had to be seen to be believed. But I was glad it wasn't the professional era – there was lots of fun to be had as well! Luckily the press was with us on our nights out!

Ripley might have been frustrated at his absence from the Test teamsheets, but he was in good company. The 'dirt-trackers' – those non-Test players – included top-class internationals like Mike Burton and Tommy David. Another non-starter, the late Irish hooker Ken Kennedy, did, however, return from the tour with a new fiancée – Miss South Africa 1973 – so he at least managed to make the most of his time out of the Test team.

This was no ordinary tour, though. Quite simply, the 1974 Lions rewrote the history books. They won 21 consecutive matches in South Africa and drew the final Test to become the first Lions team to beat the Springboks in a four-match series for 78 years. Over the 22 matches played on the tour, they scored 719 points, which included 107 tries. Such was the damage inflicted on the hosts that South African Rugby Board President Danie Craven, presenting Springboks blazers to six new caps after their defeat in the third Test, turned on them and said, "It hurts me to be giving you these, because you have not earned them."[38]

Whilst Ripley was part of the team winning the midweek fixtures as part of the all-conquering Lions, he was certainly not taking it all too seriously. The team manager, Alun Thomas, was a strong disciplinarian when it came to dress and behaviour. A schoolteacher by profession, the Welshman found Ripley's relaxed approach to authority, and in particular the dress code, a unique challenge.

At an ambassadorial reception early in the tour, Ripley arrived wearing shorts and a T-shirt, looking more like he was set for the beach than for hobnobbing with the great and good of South African society. Thomas was aghast, sternly telling Ripley, "There's another official function on Friday. You will wear the tour blazer, grey trousers, and tie. Don't dare turn up in anything else."

Ripley, true to form, did exactly what he was told and sported the blazer, trousers and tie – but nothing else! No shirt, socks or shoes! Thomas' reaction is perhaps best left unrecorded. And if this had happened in the era of camera phones and social media, I have no doubt that #Ripley would have been trending!

Writing in 2005, Ripley recalled going to a Lions squad reunion dinner:

> None of us would have missed the tour for the world. Whereas in '74 tour manager Alun Thomas would get annoyed because I'd never wear my blazer, now, over 30 years on, I wear it with pride. Got there eventually, Alun.[39]

His fellow Lion, the Welsh full back J P R Williams, recalled Ripley warmly:

> His long hair and sandals were often frowned upon, but he proved to be a second Francis of Assisi, showing remarkable kindness to animals.

This was shown during the tour when he came across two sick, orphaned kittens and took them under his wing, nursing them back to health. He then placed an advert in the local paper for "two Lions cubs", available to a good home.

Another story from the Lions' time in South Africa was recalled by Bobby Windsor, who remembered a trip into a township for a day. Everyone was back on the bus at the end of the day, except for Ripley. When he eventually arrived back at the hotel, he was, according to the Welsh hooker, "wearing nothing but a leopard skin. He'd given away every bit of his Lions kit – tracksuit, shirt, shorts, socks, trainers – the lot. What a fantastic bloke."

Ripley's talents extended far beyond just the rugby field and the *Superstars* programme. I've already mentioned his rowing success, and he was a champion athlete, competing in the 400 m at a national level, and also a triathlete and a qualified canoe instructor. He spoke fluent French and was known to sometimes commentate in the language. And as for his day job, he was an accountant, working successfully in the City of London for several large firms, including Midland Bank, Citibank and the United Bank of Kuwait.

Being a player in the amateur era meant he had to juggle professional commitments with the demands of top-class rugby, and even though he was no longer in the England squad when he was featuring in *Superstars*, the Rugby Football Union kept a close eye on him. For coming third in the World edition in 1981, he pocketed $15,600.

Except he didn't.

Soon after the programme was broadcast, he got a call from the RFU Secretary, who told him how much he'd enjoyed watching Andy on TV. Ripley knew exactly why he was receiving the phone call and duly offered a donation of precisely $15,600 to the RFU benevolent fund. "Oh Andy, how generous," came the reply.

If he had won that that edition of *Superstars*, he would have won $35,000 and under the rules of the time, that would have turned him professional. And given him a lifetime ban from rugby union.

Another story from Ripley's juggling of commercial commitments was about the time he somehow found himself with two boot sponsors to please – so wore a different brand on each foot.

He played his last game for England in 1976, although he would carry on playing for Rosslyn Park until 1988, finally calling it a day with his beloved club aged 41.

When writing about the life of Andy Ripley after the peak of his playing career, it's really a tale of two books.

In 1985, he published *Ripley's Rugby Rubbish: The Essential Ego and Massage Book*, a book so eccentric it's almost impossible to describe. It's a collection of pictures (largely from his career) with funny captions, vaguely autobiographical recollections that are in no particular order, musings on the difference between club sides and International teams, a history of rugby and politics (featuring a picture of Edward Heath with the caption 'Hello boys' – somewhat risqué considering the rumours that swirled around the former Prime Minister) and much more. As I can't really properly describe it, I'd urge you to try to track down a copy instead.

But my favourite bit is perhaps his flow chart 'How to become an England rugby forward', which includes the questions 'Have you been to public school?', 'Can you count up to eight?' and 'Do you belong to Wasps/Harlequins and know the selectors?' and answers as varied as 'Apply to join Cardiff RFC', 'Unless you are as big as a gorilla and can do 100 metres in 10 seconds – take up windsurfing' and 'Apply directly to be a committee member'.[40]

He appeared on the popular BBC chat show *Wogan* to promote the book, but described it as a "load of old twaddle" and again, to avoid the wrath of the RFU, gave away all the profits to the National Society for the Prevention of Cruelty to Children (NSPCC). As he remarked in the brief foreword to what he called a "load of junk", he gave the money away "because, not only do I want to be the President of the Rugby Football Union in 1994, but also because I am a truly wonderful person and books like this don't make much money."[41]

The second book, 2007's *Ripley's World: The Rugby Icon's Ultimate Victory Over Cancer* (with a revised edition in 2008 entitled *Ripley's World: The Enthralling Story of the British Lion's Most Crucial Battle*), also reflected his unique approach to life, but from a very different perspective. Yes, it does cover some parts of his life and playing career, but the vast majority is written in diary form, detailing his diagnosis and treatment for prostate cancer between 2005 and 2007. It's honest, open, informative, funny, sad and his character shines through.

Unlike so many rugby books, it really is his voice on the pages. He brushes over many of his rugby glories, instead focussing on his life at the time – the immense love for his wife and children, his vast set of mates and his resolute commitment to physical activity (mainly rowing, waking at 5.30 a.m. to get out on the Thames in the dawn light), even whilst undergoing tough medical treatment. An analytical man, as befitting his accountancy training, he learns a lot about his illness and the treatment, and explains things clearly to the reader. He also doesn't shirk the details of the effects of cancer, the entry on the realities of going to the toilet in the night in particular being a wonderful slice of black humour.

Alongside some big laughs, there are some powerful sections. One that I returned to twice to reread was an entry about a trip to Greece with his two daughters before they went back to university, when he considers his approach to his disease.

> Perhaps my way of 'being positive' is what I would call embracing life, loving life, making the most of whatever is left, enjoying friends and family and the minutiae of stuff, like the clean white-linen tablecloth in front of me. Is this desperate? Well, yes, but so what? I am desperate, but I love and embrace life in all its colours and shapes and sizes. If this is being positive, then in spite of wherever I stand with regard to the medical position, I know I will be positive forever.[42]

The same entry goes on to say how he is weakest at his happiest. He cries as he sits there on a beach in the Greek sunshine, next to his beloved daughters, before taking them for a "beach-boy iced coffee with an extra scoop of vanilla ice cream."

All the royalties from this book go to the Prostate Cancer Society and the 2007 version ends on a positive note, with him seemingly have beaten cancer.

Sadly, cancer, no respecter of fitness, reputation or any amount of *joie de vivre*, returned a year later, and Andy Ripley died in 2010. He was just 62 and left behind a wife, son and two daughters. In his later years, he became a campaigner tirelessly raising both funds for and awareness of the disease, of which there are now over 52,000 new cases in Britain and 1.4 million worldwide every year.

Ripley received an OBE for his efforts in 2010, receiving special dispensation from Buckingham Palace to receive it before the formal announcement of the Queen's Birthday Honours as his illness was so advanced. The pictures of him being presented with it by the then Prince of Wales – blind, pale, painfully skinny and sitting in a wheelchair – were a brutal reminder of the cruel ravages of the disease when compared to the strong, vibrant and handsome Ripley we all knew. But proud to the end, even in this, he increased awareness of prostate cancer and the need for men to get checked regularly.

The news of Ripley's untimely passing was met with sadness from all corners of the rugby world, with warm memories and funny stories flooding in.

When speaking to Roger Uttley, it's clear the affection he still has for old friend Ripley, and how he still misses him:

> He was best my best friend, and I remember saying at the memorial, I think he made everyone feel the same way. He was a great friend to everyone he met. He was a bloke's bloke, but ladies liked him as well because he was a charming individual who cared and was interested in other people. He always made you feel better at the end of a conversation.

Fellow maverick Jean-Pierre Rives, a contemporary of Ripley's in the French back row, once said, "Rugby needs people like Andy. You can still meet people like him in the game, and that proves to me that rugby still has spirit."

To go back to our earlier point about Ripley having a Corinthian spirit, the way he lived and approached the game wouldn't have worked today. Whilst I am sure he would have enjoyed being able to focus a little more on the physical aspects of the game, I suspect life as a professional rugby player would have bored him senseless. An endless routine of training, gym, coffee shops, video analysis, sponsor commitments and the intense social-media spotlight would not have matched his unique personality or approach to the game.

I asked Roger Uttley if he and Ripley would have preferred to play in the professional era:

> I remember speaking to Andy about this, and we both thought we'd be good enough but were glad we weren't. For us it was recreation. We were as professional as we could be, and we all made personal or professional sacrifices. But going back to your job on Monday morning brought you back to reality. I like the combination. The boys today are so conditioned for rugby and often not a lot else. Plus, some of the collisions – wow! I am lucky. I do ache. But nothing to what the boys today will have after they retire.

When the English game turned professional in 1995, Ripley's club Rosslyn Park remained amateur. In an interview, he made clear what he thought had been lost with the new moneyed game: "Friendship and loyalty have been smashed. Rugby has lost its heroes. I want to have heroic figures out there. If they're chasing a few quid like me, I don't like it. It devalues them. It means they are marionettes, puppets, manipulated by people with money." He went on to admit he was a "nostalgic, sentimental old buffer".[43]

This is classic Ripley: a serious point made in an erudite way, but with a dose of humour or self-deprecation. As *The Scotsman* said of him, "few played rugby like Ripley, and fewer still could live a life as full and unorthodox."

Everyone who met Ripley liked him. Whilst he was gone far too soon, as well as being a father, husband, friend and rugby player, he was a one-off, a true eccentric, a character, and he fitted more into one short lifetime than most people would in two or three.

HEATHER MOYSE

"I told him that if they thought I was too much of a risk, I would understand and would find my own way. For me, rugby was not negotiable."

FACTFILE

Full name: Heather Moyse

Born: 23 July 1978, Summerside, Prince Edward Island, Canada

Position: Full back

Representative teams: Canada sevens, Canada

Clubs: University of Waterloo, University of Toronto, Ontario, Prince Edward Island, Blackrock College RFC (Ireland), Caribs and Trinidad Northern (Trinidad)

Nickname: Moyzie

As a child, Heather Moyse was a big fan of *Choose Your Own Adventure* books. Many of you will remember them but if not, they were children's stories where the reader takes the role of the main character, and every few pages, faces two or three options. You pick one, and it takes you to a specific page and you continue your journey from there. For example, the tale might take you to a castle and there you have three doors in front of you: one might lead to treasure, one plunge you into a dungeon and another take you face to face with a dragon. It gives the reader the choice to influence the story and how it ends. Moyse would later realise that devouring these stories was teaching her a valuable lesson in choice and consequences. But unlike the route through a 1980s children's book, there would be no limit on what Moyse – not just a rugby great, but a modern Canadian sporting icon – could achieve.

A four-time Olympian in the bobsleigh, Moyse won a gold medal at the 2010 Winter Games in Vancouver, and another in 2014 in Sochi. Then there's the International cycling and an Antarctic expedition, before we even mention her remarkable rugby career.

Her story begins on Prince Edward Island, the smallest of the ten Canadian provinces, nestled off the east coast in the Atlantic Ocean and home to just over 150,000 people. A charming place full of beaches, farms, and small towns, it was made famous as the setting of another successful children's book, *Anne of Green Gables*. It was in high school that Moyse first picked up a rugby ball and she played for three years. But in her first few years at the University of Waterloo in Ontario, it was track and field and soccer that she focussed on.

Then one day, she was asked by the boyfriend of a friend to fill in with a local rugby team desperately short of numbers ahead of a tournament. Initially reluctant as she hadn't played in two years, as soon as she got on the pitch, it all changed.

> The first time I got my hands on the ball and ran almost the full length of the field to score a try, I knew I wouldn't be going back to soccer. Not because I scored, but because of the thrill of running with the ball in my hand and the sense of community within the sport. I hadn't realized how much I had missed playing rugby. That night, before the rugby tournament was even over, I called my soccer coach and explained how I was feeling. I loved the girls on my team, had so much respect for my coach, and sincerely enjoyed my time with them, but I loved rugby.[44]

Within two years of reigniting her love of rugby, in 2000 she was called into the Canadian U23 team for a series of games against the United States. But Moyse had a problem: the women's rugby teams in the area where she was working that summer didn't start training until the autumn. So she took the logical approach, and found a men's team and asked if she could train with them. They said yes, and she spent the summer training with the Halifax Tar Heels. What began as a challenge became an opportunity:

> I had about twenty big brothers looking out for me, who were excited as I was about my opportunity to represent Canada later that year. It was extremely physical, and training with those guys really pushed me. It was the best thing I could have done.[45]

The following year, having graduated as an Occupational Therapist, she'd live and work in Dublin and play for Blackrock College RFC – a former club of Irish legend Brian O'Driscoll, with whom Moyse would connect later on – before moving to Trinidad and Tobago. The fact that the women's game was less developed there saw her again often training with men's teams and playing sevens. Whilst in the Caribbean, she was determined to try and spread the popularity of the game, working in a rugby camp and then as a development officer and coach.

After her time overseas, she returned to Prince Edward Island, where her big sister persuaded her to come back to playing 15-a-side for the first time in three years. She was asked to take part in a trial for the Ontario provincial team, and when playing for them was spotted by a national rugby coach and asked to join up with a senior development camp. The autumn of 2004 would see Moyse not just starting a master's degree, but also making her International debut against England and scoring her first International try.

I spoke to Moyse on video from her home on Prince Edward Island, and she was an engaging, fun and honest interviewee. I asked her what she remembered of her debut:

> Not very much! I never remember specifics of games. There are some people I've played with that ask me if I remember what happened in the nineteenth minute, or moments with a particular player, and I'm like, "Nope, sorry!" I think against England I went around the outside and scored on the right of the pitch. But to be honest, what I recall most is the feeling of relief. I was playing at a different level with a new team, and when I scored that try, I proved I was good enough to be there.
>
> I was also ignorant about the world of rugby: I didn't know who was meant to be really good. I never went into games with preconceived, sabotaging thoughts of who I was up against. They were always just another group of girls. I didn't realise England were meant to be better than us. Scoring, to me, was just doing my job.

Establishing a spot in your national team's XV as a pacy and hard-running full back would be the peak of 99.9% of people's sporting careers, but not for Moyse. In 2005, she was invited to take part in some recruitment testing for the Canadian National Bobsleigh Team, by a coach who had been impressed by her sprinting and strength abilities in her college track and field days. Despite Canada being a winter sports superpower, Moyse had had no previous interest in bobsleds, and – like most of us – would admit that what little knowledge she did have stemmed from the movie *Cool Runnings*. She went into the week-long camp without any expectations but broke at least one testing record and, just four months after first getting in a bobsleigh, via a Canadian championship win, she would be competing at the 2006 Winter Olympics in Turin. Remarkably the rookie Moyse and her partner, Helen Upperton, came fourth in the final of the two-woman bobsleigh event, missing bronze by an agonising five one-hundredths of a second.

Then it was back to rugby and the 2006 Women's Rugby World Cup, hosted by Canada, where Moyse scored a tournament-leading seven tries in their run to the semi-finals. She would continue to juggle work, education, International rugby and bobsledding, and in 2010 would compete in her second Olympics, in Vancouver.

This time there'd be no heartbreak. Moyse and her partner, Kaillie Humphries, stormed to victory in front of a home crowd, becoming the first Canadians to win an Olympic gold medal in the women's bobsled event. She became a household name in her home country, appearing on the front cover of *Hello! Canada*, among other media attention.

Though Moyse might now be a famous bobsledder, her commitment to rugby remained. Just two weeks after winning gold at the Olympics, Moyse began training for that year's Women's Rugby World Cup:

> I took those two weeks of kind of letting my body relax a little bit, and then right back into it, because my endurance was next to nothing. When you're coming off a bobsled season, everything is about short, explosive speed for five, six seconds max.
>
> So I turned my entire attention towards building my endurance, getting my hands back on the ball again. I just did hill sprints over and over and over that whole transition. And then they had that spring training camp that ended off with a couple of games against the US. And it was a hard camp for me, not just physically but also mentally and emotionally.[46]

The hard work paid off, as she would again be the (joint) top try scorer at the 2010 World Cup.

The story takes another twist now, as a serious ankle injury in Canada's final game of that World Cup saw Moyse take up track cycling as part of her rehabilitation. Soon enough, the national coach saw what she was doing and invited her to train with the national team. Her times were good enough to see her selected to race for Canada at the Pan-American Track Cycling Championship in 2012. Despite having no experience, she came fifth in the 500 m sprint and fourth in the match sprint, and if a few things had turned out a little differently, could have been going to the 2012 London summer Olympics as a cyclist.

The following year came yet another championship: the Rugby World Cup Sevens in Moscow, where her Canada team won a silver medal.

Juggling the demands of different high-level sports did not come without its challenges. Bobsled and rugby both had their own unique requirements, and neither were awash with cash to support their representatives. The pressure came from different angles.

Firstly, there was time management. Moyse told me how she eventually found a solution to balancing her schedule:

> The World Cups were always the same year as the Olympics. So I would just say to my rugby and bobsled coaches, "Here are each other's email addresses: you guys talk and sort it out. Tell me where I need to be and when, and I'll be there." That's how I managed it. I was like, "I am not going to choose; you guys figure it out!"

Then there were the sponsors. Moyse would recall one conversation with a sponsor who was looking to invest in the bobsled team, but was concerned about her playing rugby because of the injury risk and wanted her to quit until after the next Olympics.

> I told him I understood his concerns, but Bobsleigh Canada had recruited me as a rugby player, and I wasn't willing to give that up. I loved rugby. He started to explain the finances... I have no idea where I found the assertiveness and the strength to respond the way I did, but through an emotional tightness in my throat, I said, 'But... high risk, high reward.'
>
> The businessman just stared at me, then slowly cracked a smile (just a little one). There was nothing he could really say. I told him that if they thought I was too much of a risk, I would understand and would find my own way. For me, rugby was not negotiable.[47]

Then there's the pressure from within. The feeling that once you are at the top, you need to stay there, and everything else that comes from elite-level sport. Now imagine that times three in totally different sports. Moyse couldn't have achieved what she did without supreme mental strength, but also an awareness of the challenges that this pressure can create. Today she works as a motivational speaker, drawing upon her many varied experiences to talk to audiences all over the world, and is the author of an excellent memoir-cum-self-help book, *Redefining 'Realistic'*, which honestly and accessibly deconstructs, assesses and offers learnings from her life.

In her book, she talks about the online criticism she received following her selection for the 2010 World Cup squad. Instead of dwelling on it, she acknowledged she had her own doubts whilst being interviewed on a TV show. For Moyse the results of this were clear:

> Announcing to the world that I, too, had had doubts worked to disempower them in my own mind. They no longer had control... Internally acknowledge the pressures and expectations that you are feeling, from others and yourself, ask yourself why you are feeling that pressure and then put it all into perspective.[48]

Then there's the pressure from teammates, which Moyse opened up to me about:

> Because I was often absent for winter tours for rugby, with the Olympics, I'd come back into the squad for the spring training camp. And there were always some players that made it hard for me to feel I was properly integrated into the team. I think they believed I was going to come back into the squad and take their place, and that because I hadn't always been in the squad, I wasn't fully committed. There was a feeling from some that I was getting in because of my performance at the Olympics. It was often people I hadn't played with before, and who didn't know me as a person. All they knew was Heather Moyse, this

> elusive person who's going to suddenly show up and, they thought, just walk back onto the team. But I wasn't walking into any team – I was coming to training camps and working the same as everyone else.
>
> This was hard for me. I'm a relatively emotional person. You can hear something and then have that comment worm away in your brain, and you start questioning yourself, you start doubting yourself, you start wondering, 'Why am I here? What if I don't deserve to be here?', and all that stuff. And so I very quickly had to trust that the coaches know what they're doing and that I'm here for a reason. I had to just let it go. But it took a little while. There were many who were always super stoked to have me back on the team and knew what I could do, but this was definitely the hardest part of moving between the sports.

And finally, there are the injuries. In rugby she's fractured her radius bone, wrist, spine and shoulder, destroyed her right ankle with the cartilage crushed, suffered micro-fractures in four ankle bones and a completely ruptured anterior talofibular ligament, and towards the end of her career required separate surgery on each hip due to overuse from training for so many sports. And this is not to mention all the minor sprains, strains, cuts, bruises and black eyes regularly received in training and in matches.

The balancing act would continue at the Winter Olympics in Sochi in 2014. She won her second straight Olympic bobsleigh gold with pilot Kaillie Humphries, coming from behind in the final heat to become the first women's bobsleigh team to successfully defend an Olympic title.

Moyse turned 35 shortly after winning silver at the 2013 Women's Rugby World Cup Sevens in Moscow, and having recently undergone hip surgery, turned down the opportunity to be part of the programme preparing for Rio 2016, when rugby returned to the Summer Games. Moyse told the *Between the Lines* podcast:

> I was exhausted. I was just tired. I was not wanting to move away and live, like, [my] priorities just shifted. After being on the road for almost two years straight, I think had I been given that opportunity to [stay closer to home], then it would have been maybe a different choice. But I chose what I needed in my life then, and what was important to me.[49]

Her International rugby playing days might now be over but in 2016 came a huge honour when she was inducted into the World Rugby Hall of Fame: the first Canadian woman and the second Canadian overall (after Gareth Rees) to be included. It was an extra special ceremony as it also marked the Hall's first-ever physical location in Rugby, England. She was in fantastic company, joining fellow ex-Blackrock College player Brian O'Driscoll, Wales star Shane Williams and England legends Jeremy Guscott, Maggie Alphonsi and Jonny Wilkinson, to name just some of the 12 greats inducted that day.

Even without her, Canada would win silver at the 2014 Women's World Cup and bronze in the sevens at the 2016 Olympics, and her fellow Hall-of-Famer Gareth Rees, inducted in 2011, saw the sport as still feeling the Moyse effect:

> She had a bit of star power and that's always needed. She's an incredible finisher. Incredible pace... She's representing all her teammates, that whole generation. She really took women's rugby to a new level with her teammates.[50]

Moyse had one more tilt at elite sport left in her. At the age of 39, and not having done any competitive bobsledding since the Sochi games in 2014, she rejoined the Canadian Winter Olympics team in 2017. This time things were a little different. The comeback was triggered by an email from Alysia Rissling, a young member of the team seeking help in navigating the mental and physical minefield of elite sport. This proved an intriguing link between Moyse's old passion of bobsleigh and her new role as a motivational speaker and author.

> At first I was just like, "Well, I'm kind of done. I love what I do now." My business is all around empowering other people and helping other people achieve their goals. But when I started saying it out loud, I was like, "Coming back and helping Rissling or other development drivers or whomever on the team, that *is* empowering other people, that *is* coming back and investing in the next generation and pushing future athletes." I'm not motivated to go back and just try and win another Olympic medal, but I am motivated by the idea of helping someone else win their first.[51]

Together they would qualify for the 2018 Winter Olympics – Moyse's fourth and Rissling's first – although sadly there would be no fairytale ending. They came sixth, 1.18 seconds off the gold medal-winning time.

Today Moyse is completely retired from all sports, and back living on her beloved Prince Edward Island. Although she is still setting herself challenges: she recently climbed Antarctica's highest peak, Mount Vinson, as part of an expedition to support the members of the Canadian Armed Forces and raise awareness of PTSD. She is also kept busy with her motivational work – drawing upon her life as a high-performance multi-sport athlete, allied with her qualifications and work in occupational therapy, to help individuals, groups and organizations shift their perspective and maximise their potential.

Towards the end of my chat with Moyse, I asked her what her idea of a maverick was.

> I thought you might ask me this! I think it's very easy to be swayed by other people's definitions of success. Even winning Olympic medals or playing for your country, you can be in society's eyes successful, but if you aren't doing something you love or want to do, you're literally chasing someone else's definition of success and not your own. A real maverick knows what they want, focuses on the things that they love to do and is not swayed by other people's opinions.

In this book, we've covered mavericks who, whilst wildly talented, never fully harnessed their potential, and others who became overwhelmed by their abilities and what they brought. Their spirit made them great, but also either held them back or destroyed them.

When it comes to Heather Moyse, her spirit made her achieve more than most athletes, male or female, have ever done. Four Olympics and two gold medals, two Rugby World Cups – highest try scorer at both – and entry to the Rugby Hall of Fame, International cycling, overcoming double hip surgery and serious ankle injuries, frequent travel, attending university and working at the same time as training in three different sports – I could go on... she really did choose her own adventure! And now all this experience is being channelled into the next generation. There'll never be another Heather Moyse, but it's certain that her influence will be felt for years to come.

FINN RUSSELL

"Let's have a bit of fun then."

FACTFILE

Full name: Finn Alastair Russell

Born: 23 September 1992, Bridge of Allan, Stirling, Scotland

Positions: Fly half, Centre

Representative teams: Barbarians, Scotland, British & Irish Lions

Clubs: Stirling County, Falkirk, Ayr, Lincoln University (New Zealand), Glasgow Warriors, Racing 92

Nicknames: White Chocolate, Finnsanity, The Muscle

NOT LONG AFTER the 2021 British and Irish Lions tour of South Africa, I met up with my friend Pete, a big rugby fan of the Irish persuasion. Our talk quickly turned to the tour, but after a minute or so, we realised that we couldn't actually remember many specifics of what had happened just a month before. Sure, we'd had a pint or two, and he had his impending wedding and I had another baby on the way, so we had a few more things on our minds than before, but we could recall details from 1997 and 2001, and the previous tour – the pulsating drawn series against New Zealand in 2017. This one? Not so much. It was a deeply underwhelming tour, heavily impacted by Covid-19 and played in front of empty stadia. There seemed to be little buzz, with no raucous travelling fans, undercooked warm-up opposition, none of the usual off-field activities for the players, and, well, quite simply it was just not that much fun. Then we remembered Finn Russell.

The Scottish fly half, on as a substitute after just 11 minutes of the third Test, did more than anyone to inject a much-needed shot of adrenaline into the tourists' stodgy trudge through South Africa. The Lions had won the first Test 22-17 before the home team levelled the series with a 27-9 win in the second. So it all came down to the decider in Cape Town.

Waiting to come on for the injured Dan Biggar, Russell was seen on camera laughing away on the touchline, the most relaxed man in the stadium. Jogging onto the pitch, he told scrum half and fellow Scot Ali Price, "Let's have a bit of fun then." As soon as he entered the field, it was less a changing of the gears for the Lions and more a release of the handbrake.

Within minutes, he'd slotted a penalty: the first of eleven points he'd bank. A precise cross-field kick found Josh Adams on the right wing; his kick to the corner led to Ken Owens' pushover try; there were missed passes and long passes in his own 22. No one seemed to have told him he couldn't do these things against the world's best rush defence. Or maybe they had and he'd simply ignored them.

But still, it wasn't enough. In a remarkable echo of the 2009 Test series defeat, Morné Steyn – having not played for South Africa in five years – would kick a late penalty to win the game 19-16 and take the series win, 12 years on from having done precisely the same thing. The great rugby scriptwriters in the sky deemed it would be the 37-year-old Steyn who secured the glory and the headlines, rather than the mercurial Scot. But Russell, playing his first match in five weeks following an Achilles injury, and making his Lions Test debut, ensured that the Lions at least lost with a defiant roar rather than a mere whimper. He certainly set social media ablaze, with plenty of discussion about the 'what if's, had he started, and several

YouTube videos made with 'evidence' that he was the missing link the Lions needed to achieve a series win.

"I'm happy I got the chance to show the style of rugby I would have played against South Africa," said Russell, post-match. "It was pleasing to have actually got on and chucked it around a little bit. I just went on knowing we had to move them around a bit and play some expansive rugby. I just went on and played my style of rugby. That showed in that performance tonight."[52]

It does, though, have to be noted that it was a Russell mistake – a knock-on in the closing stages – that gave the Springboks the platform to win and kick the winning penalty. Which was something Lions coach Warren Gatland was to mention in his post-match comments:

> He was good. We talked about moving the ball and the ball went through his hands a lot, which was good.
>
> He'll be disappointed that he's dropped a ball in the air which he would probably normally take. He was a bit unlucky on the [Kolbe] tackle, and the left-foot kick down the middle of the park wasn't one of his best moments.[53]

Russell would, on his return home, make some of his own criticisms of Gatland, telling the *Scottish Rugby Podcast*:

> I thought that in all three Tests we should have played more rugby and gone at them a little bit more. The first two Tests, we played off nine for two phases and I kind of felt that played into their defence. We weren't doing much out of the back of it. We were keeping the attack narrow instead of having a wide attack. The first ten minutes of the third Test, there was still quite a bit of kicking and a lot of play off nine. There wasn't much rugby that actually got played.

So in this Lions cameo, he displayed some blistering skills, made a high-profile mistake, saw social media explode on the matter, then exchanged criticism in the media with his coach. In many ways, this is the whole of Finn Russell's career in microcosm.

His life would have been so very different, however, if he hadn't taken another risk – in 2012, when he swapped his trade for a crack at professional rugby career.

Finn Russell was born into a sporty family. His father Keith is a former Director of Domestic Rugby for the Scottish Rugby Union (and the 'former' aspect is something we will revisit later), his grandparents played International badminton and both his brothers are rugby players, with his youngest, Archie, a try scorer for Cambridge University in a Varsity Match win over Oxford in 2017.

After school, Finn took an apprenticeship as a stonemason, pocketing £300 per week whilst playing club rugby first for Stirling County and then for Falkirk, and he never seriously thought he'd become a professional player.

For three years chisels and hammers, and not boots and balls, were the tools of his trade.

He looked back on this period as a tradesman a few years into his professional career:

> On rainy days it could be pretty miserable. It was for a company in Thornhill near Stirling and I worked out of a wee shed. It could be tough but I enjoyed it. I'd be making windowsills, door frames, fireplaces – even building walls. But compared to playing rugby, it's night and day.
>
> If I ever have a bad day at training, I think back to what it was like working in that cold shed. When I got offered my academy contract with Glasgow three years ago, I wasn't sure if I should accept it. But I looked around and thought: 'Do I want to be here all my life or do I want to give rugby a crack?' Now I just sit and think how blessed I am that it has all paid off.[54]

The path from the shed to the Lions has been a far-from-straightforward one, however.

He played (at centre) for Scotland at the World Rugby U20 Championships in 2012, then joined Glasgow Warriors as a development player whilst playing for Ayr, with whom he won a domestic league-and-cup double in 2012/13. In turning professional he took a risk, quitting his stonemasonry apprenticeship (with a year to go to completion) for a rugby one, and taking a pay cut. His parents had to help him keep up his monthly payments on his car.

He took advantage of Glasgow's top players being away at the Six Nations to make his professional debut in February 2013, but his career initially failed to ignite at Glasgow. Then he received the John Macphail Scholarship. This was created in memory of ex-Scottish International and businessman John Macphail, with previous beneficiaries including John Barclay and Jonny Gray, to name just two. It gave Russell the chance to spend 15 weeks in New Zealand from March 2013, playing for Lincoln University and scoring 151 points in 14 games, as well as receiving specialist coaching at the Canterbury Rugby Football Union international high-performance unit.

Billeted with a local family and given a bike to cycle to training, he would later tell the New Zealand press how he benefited greatly from his Kiwi sojourn:

> It was a really good standard of rugby for a non-professional league. It was the way they played: expansive rugby and a really fast-flowing game. It was brilliant to play, not so much fun when you are defending against it, but good to be playing with the ball. Three months over there really brought me on and gave me that extra bit of confidence.[55]

The following season he became a regular starter for Glasgow Warriors, and he made his International debut for Scotland against the USA in the summer of 2014. His career might have been slow to start, but once it picked up some speed, it quickly became meteoric.

He became Scotland's first-choice Number 10 during the 2015 Six Nations and would take part in that year's World Cup, hosted by England, playing a role in the agonising 35-34 quarter-final defeat to Australia.

In a professional game which had become increasingly dominated by well-drilled defences and granular game plans, the appearance of Russell – someone who is never afraid to throw huge missed passes, attempt audacious grubber kicks, offer flicks and tricks and, yes, make mistakes – was a breath of fresh Caledonian air. He was a reminder of the kind of rugby we'd play in the schoolyard or the garden with our friends – the fun type!

If you want one perfect example of Russell's ability, it's to be found in the Calcutta Cup match of 2018. Scotland are 10-6 up against England after 30 minutes and have a scrum just outside their own 22. Russell receives the ball, glances right and sees that the England defensive line is broken: Jonathan Joseph has come too far forward and has created a hole behind him. Russell hurls a huge pass over Joseph's head – if the Englishman catches it, he's straight under the posts for a try. But he doesn't. It floats high in the air, tantalisingly close to being forward, before it lands in the hands of Huw Jones, who scythes his way through the gap and motors downfield.

Jones is brought down but Scotland keep hold of the ball, going through the phases across the pitch, about 15 yards away from the line. Russell gets the ball: again he glances and again he sees a gap. England wing Anthony Watson, covering two Scottish attackers, hedges his bets and stands between them. This time a small, subtle pass is needed. Russell delicately passes the ball over Watson's head and into the hands of Sean Maitland, who goes over in the corner. From one end of the pitch to another, two risky but perfectly executed passes from Russell, decided upon in milliseconds, had created the try and set Scotland on course for their first victory over the Auld Enemy in 10 years.

It's hard to speak highly enough of this try. Head over to YouTube and look up 'Alternative Highlight Sean Maitland try' and you won't be disappointed.

Russell's exploits for Glasgow (whom he helped win their first-ever PRO12 Championship in 2014/15) and Scotland caught the eye of French giants Racing 92. Historically a somewhat eccentric outfit, being owned by a Swiss real estate billionaire has changed their reputation hugely and Russell reportedly signed on for a salary of approximately £600k a year when he joined them in 2018. The fact that he was brought in to replace the retiring Dan Carter speaks volumes for his status in the game.

Unlike many other British or Irish players, he has thrived in France, receiving a European Player of the Year nomination in 2020 and forming a particularly strong relationship with a fellow flair player, Ireland's Simon Zebo. Indeed, it was Zebo who coined one of Russell's nicknames – 'White Chocolate'. It initially perplexed fans, but Zebo explained it was the nickname of NBA player Jason Williams, who reminded him of Russell:

> Williams looks like Finn: on the pitch, he had incredible individual technique and made crazy moves, blind passes, between the legs... And like Finn, 'White Chocolate' always played with a smile.[56]

Russell and Zebo would play a big part in Racing 92's thrilling 2020 Heineken Cup Final against Exeter. It was classic Russell, with some fantastic moments of skill and some high-risk play. A sumptuous pass from the middle of the park to Zebo on the wing, allowing the latter to dive over in the corner for a first-half try, was his highlight, but later on a loose pass in his own half saw Exeter's Henry Slade score what would prove to be the decisive try in a 31-27 win for the English side.

Another remarkable moment in the Russell portfolio came for Racing against Munster in a Heineken Cup game in Limerick. Receiving the ball just inside the Munster 22, he shapes as if to pass out wide but then sends a delicious, deft grubber kick through the legs of his onrushing opponent (who is so perplexed he slips and falls over), picks it up and pops over the line for a try.

Whilst Russell's career was going so well in Paris, his relationship with the national team – and in particular its administrators and coach, Gregor Townsend – would begin to take a nosedive.

In 2020, on the eve of the Six Nations, he was told he had not been selected to face Ireland in Scotland's tournament opener, after what the Scottish Rugby Football Union described as a 'late-night drinking session'. He had arrived in Edinburgh on the Sunday after travelling from London, where'd he been playing for Racing 92. He spent the evening drinking in the team hotel, but when asked to stop by both backroom staff and teammates, he refused and instead went to his parents' house.

He wasn't at training the following morning but did arrive in the afternoon. When he was told he was not going to be considered for the Irish game, but was welcome to stay in the squad, he left and returned to Paris.

Russell had a different view of events. He stated that the players were permitted two beers with dinner, and he'd ordered a third – hardly a 'late-night drinking session'. He told *The Times*:

> This whole situation with Scotland has been made out to be about me wanting to have a drink, when in actual fact, it's about control, respect and trust, on and off the pitch. I want the best for Scotland and so I've questioned the environment to try and make it better. We (he and Townsend) have clashed quite a lot, him saying one thing and me saying another. It's come to a point where I'm saying, 'You can be you and I'm going to be me. That's how this relationship is going to be.' Well, it's not really a relationship.[57]

Russell wouldn't play for his nation again until October 2020. But in the 2021 Six Nations he started at 10, delivering a virtuoso performance in an 11-6 victory over England Scotland's first win at Twickenham since 1983. A year later, a late Russell penalty saw Scotland retain the Calcutta Cup with a 20-17 win. The following week he delivered a far more uneven performance with several mistakes and a sinbinning, seeing Scotland falter in Wales and once again fail to build on the momentum of strong start to the tournament.

The fallout from the 17-36 home loss to France in 2022 would prove a disaster for Russell. Yes, they were up against the eventual Grand Slam winners, but he put in a low-energy, lackadaisical performance and a post-match Twitter video from rugby analyst Brett Igoe – highlighting, among other things, Russell's poor work rate – would be viewed almost 100,000 times.

Ireland and Lions winger Shane Horgan would lambast Russell on Irish television, animatedly stating as he watched the Scot trot back while his teammates scrambled to get back into defensive alignment for the first French try:

> That is actually pathetic, for your top player, your talisman. Five minutes into the game. He doesn't have an injury. He's not fatigued... you've got your best player performing like that. There's no way any team can win consistently if you've got players doing that.

Worse was to follow.

As another disappointing tournament came to an end, there was another explosive clash with Gregor Townsend.

Along with captain Stuart Hogg and four other Scottish players, Russell was disciplined for breaching team protocols when they visited an Edinburgh bar after returning from Rome, where they had just beaten Italy. Russell was demoted to the bench, only featuring in the last 14 minutes of a dismal

26-5 defeat to Ireland. And that was the end of the 2022 Six Nations and possibly Finn Russell's Scottish career, at least under Gregor Townsend.

Now, as anyone reading this book will be aware, falling out with authority figures is not a rare occurrence for a maverick spirit. But for Russell there is an extra aspect to consider – how the Scottish Rugby Football Union treated his father. Keith Russell took up the role of Director of Domestic Rugby in 2015, but was summarily dismissed in 2017. He took the SRFU to an employment tribunal, which in 2018 found the dismissal to have been 'both procedurally and substantively unfair'.

This was a high-profile story in the Scottish media and it would prove to be a challenging time for the whole Russell family. For Keith, the damage was significant: "It is so disappointing to realise that the guys at the top are not good guys and do not represent the values and culture of rugby."

Finn's mother Sally would also comment on the impact this case had:

> To end up with one of our sons [Finn] standing with the ball out in the middle of the pitch at Murrayfield... it is great for us... And when we used to go it was like a dream because he's had a rocky road to get there ... but now it is forever tainted.[58]

SRFU Chief Executive Mark Dodson, who was responsible for dismissing Keith Russell and was censured in the ensuing tribunal, remains in his position.

As of September 2022, Russell sits at a key point in his career: still a key part of Racing 92's squad, his position in the national team remains uncertain. He's been linked to moves to English clubs and is exactly the kind of player that would be wanted in Japan, but I'd suspect he'll stay in France, at least until it hosts the 2023 World Cup.

Still only on the cusp of his thirties, he has some good years ahead of him. Perhaps we will start to see the development of a more rounded figure, focusing more on dictating the play than needing to conjure up magic – although it would be a shame to lose any of that natural exuberance which makes him such a rare and compelling figure in the modern game. With so many players now coming through a very specific pathway, Russell made his own way – from the stonemason's yard to club rugby via New Zealand – to fame and fortune. Like Liam Williams of Wales, who had a similar trajectory, there's a certain element of flair and rawness that comes from emerging out of the real world rather than the regimented routes that most of their teammates have trodden.

I'll give the last word to Ronan O'Gara, whose comments I found fascinating when rewatching the coverage of the 2021 Lions tour:

> Simply, he is the best man to pick apart a rush defence. Why do I say that? Because he is probably the most instinctive player in Europe... Do not be fooled by his smiley, lazy, laid-back approach. I know Mike Prendergast, who coaches him at Racing, and he says he is hugely diligent, highly involved in studying the game inside out. His capacity to execute is better and he just has an extra zip in his pass.

Let's hope there are many more years of looping passes, speculative grubbers and, yes, the odd mistake to come from Finn Russell. And I'm sure when he does hang up his boots, he'll be a superbly provocative pundit.

WAISALE SEREVI

"Rugby makes people happy. If given the opportunity, I like to make people happy."

FACTFILE

Full name: Waisale Tikoisolomoni Serevi

Born: 20 May 1968, Suva, Fiji

Positions: Scrum half, Fly half, Full back

Representative teams: Fiji B, Fiji XV, Fiji sevens, Barbarians, World XV, Fiji

Clubs: Nasinu, Rewa, Nabua, Suva (all Fiji), Mitsubishi (Japan), Leicester Tigers, Stade Montois, Stade Bordelais, Staines (England)

Nicknames: The Wizard, The King of Sevens, Maestro

OFFICIALLY THE FIRST Rugby World Cup took place in 1987 in New Zealand and Australia, but there's a good argument that the first truly global rugby tournament actually happened 11 years earlier in Hong Kong. In 1976, teams from Indonesia, South Korea, Australia, New Zealand, Tonga, Japan, Sri Lanka, Malaysia and Fiji headed to the Hong Kong Football Club in Happy Valley, in a tournament sponsored by Cathay Pacific and Rothmans Tobacco. It was a marketing manager at the cigarette company who got the ball rolling, so to speak. He was originally keen to sponsor a pan-Asian 15-a-side tournament, but after extensive discussion with the chairman of the Hong Kong Rugby Football Union, A D C 'Tokkie' Smith, who had recently returned from watching the Melrose Sevens tournament, it was agreed the shorter variant of game would be cheaper and easier to set up. Initially the traditional rugby-playing nations were invited, but when England declined, the HKRFU switched its focus to Pacific and Asian sides.

That first Hong Kong Sevens would prove to be a revelation. It showed the game was more than just Commonwealth countries plus France, Ireland and Argentina, and the raft of commercial sponsors gave a glimpse into the world of professionalism. Tokkie Smith would describe it as "the most colourful day of sport that I have ever seen. One that put Hong Kong on the International sporting map." He wasn't wrong. From these small beginnings, the tournament would grow into one of the most beloved and lively events in the rugby calendar.

Bill McLaren, in his autobiography *Talking of Rugby*, would write glowingly of how the tournament has developed:

> I remember a big South Sea islander saying that, in his view, the Hong Kong Sevens were really the Olympic games of Rugby Union. Certainly, the Hong Kong event encapsulates all the really good things that the game has to offer – splendid organisation, wonderful sporting spirit, universal camaraderie, admirable field behaviour, the most enjoyable crowd participation, the chance for emergent rugby nations to lock horns with the mighty men of New Zealand, Australia, Fiji, Wales, Scotland and the Barbarians. There is, too, scintillating running and handling, which is what the game is supposed to be all about.[59]

No country has been more successful at sevens than Fiji, and the Pacific island's success is synonymous with one man: Waisale Serevi, also known as the King of Sevens. The undisputed best in the business when it came to the short game.

The Serevi story begins in the Fijian capital, Suva. The third of five children, he grew up in a strongly Christian family, giving him a faith that would be an important guide through his career. Rugby first made its mark on the young Serevi in

1977, when Fiji defeated the touring British and Irish Lions 25-21. Although he didn't watch the game, he recalls it well, writing in 2014:

> I was in my school uniform in Fiji, and then people were all happy and shouting and I asked my mum, "Why are these people happy?" She said, "Oh, Fiji has just beaten the British Lions, and rugby makes people in Fiji happy." So, I thought, if I have an opportunity to play for Fiji, I'll try and make people happy.[60]

Growing up, it was mainly touch rugby he played, using a coconut shell or plastic bottle as a makeshift ball. He maintains that these games helped make him the player he'd become, learning to step quickly thanks to needing to avoid potholes, which required him to change direction suddenly and sharply.

This step would become his trademark, and he'd explain further how he perfected it as a youngster:

> I would try to slow down to make people think I was tired, but no, it was a trap! I was slowing down and looking at them, and as soon as they tried to sprint to get me, I'd apply the goose step as I left them for dead.[61]

A talented young player, he joined his first club, Nasinu, in 1985. Unfortunately, at first his height (5' 7") was held against him, and though training most days, he spent most of his time as the unofficial kit man, busier handing out shirts and socks than scoring tries. But eventually, in 1987, he got his chance and soon began to light up the Fijian club scene, playing the 15-man game. In 1988 he was selected for Fiji B, and the following year he got the call to play for Fiji at the 1989 Hong Kong Sevens.

The trip would prove super exciting. Before this, he had only seen planes on video, but he was not overawed by the experience of swapping island life for the buzzing metropolis of Hong Kong. And although New Zealand would win this tournament, beating Fiji 12-10 in the semi-finals, Serevi – with his blistering youthful pace – was named Player of the Tournament, and it would begin his lifelong love affair with the short game, and the Hong Kong event in particular.

The following year he'd be back. Although there was now a major buzz around him, there was still a distinct lack of glitz around his travel arrangements, as he recalls in his book, *Waisale Serevi: The King of Sevens*.

> By tradition, two players roomed together for each tournament but in 1990 the inclusion in the touring party of the coach's father, Ratu Ilisone Ravoka, made space a valuable commodity.
>
> As the baby of the party, Serevi was assigned to a room with his half back partner Pauliasi and his uncle Vesi, eight years his senior. With just two beds servicing three adults, Pauliasi had to make a tough call. He looked Serevi up and down and claimed the bed closest to the window. He then assigned Vesi the bed closest to the door. If the 1989 Hong Kong Sevens MVP [Most Valuable Player] thought he was owed special treatment, he was sadly mistaken. Pauliasi handed him some spare sheets. Serevi would be sleeping on the floor this year.[62]

He may have been sleeping on the floor of the Hong Kong Hilton, but it didn't stop Fiji gaining revenge over New Zealand in the final and winning the tournament, their first of three consecutive titles.

In total he'd appear in 15 instalments of the Hong Kong Sevens, winning seven of them and picking up five Player of the Tournament awards. In 1997 and 2005, the tournament expanded to double up as the Sevens World Cup, and in both Serevi captained Fiji to success, each time procuring a day's national holiday back home. Wayne Pivac, the Fiji coach in 2005, was glowing in his admiration for Serevi: "Waisale is the eyes for the other guys, he brings the others into the game and puts players into gaps."[63]

Serevi also picked up two Commonwealth Games silver medals and one bronze, two golds at the World Games and countless other medals, cups and trophies at sevens tournaments around the globe.

Fiji might have been the star attractions at sevens tournaments all over the world, but they still found the logistics a challenge.

When they travelled to Scotland in 1993 for the inaugural Rugby World Cup Sevens, the Fijians had grossly underestimated the cold of Edinburgh, as he would later recall in his book:

> No Fijian player owned a jacket, so each stacked on several layers of cotton jerseys hoping they would suffice for that moment of truth when they stepped off the team bus for their first training session. At first it seemed like someone was throwing rocks or gravel at them. After a hasty reconnaissance seeking out any mischievous Edinburgh youths, it suddenly dawned on Serevi that these small stones were actually falling from the sky.
>
> The Fiji team was on the precipice of a full-blown hailstorm. The boys beat a hasty retreat back to their bus to wait out the storm and dispatched the team manager to find some more suitable cold weather gear for the next excursion into Scotland's freezing conditions.
>
> Somewhere along the line that communication got horribly scrambled. When the team returned to their hotel that evening, the manager presented them with his solution to their problem. The players were crying out for solid waterproof athletic wear to seal out the cold and damp but instead were handed 12 dinner suit jackets, resplendent in a maroon finish. With no other options, the Fijian squad soldiered on through their 'dinner party' training session the next day wondering how on earth they had finished up in this 'formal' predicament.[64]

Whilst these kinds of situations lead to amusing anecdotes to relay in magazines and books such as these, they do highlight a major problem in world rugby – the disparity in resources between rugby-playing nations.

It is hard to overstate how popular and important rugby sevens is in Fiji. The game dominates both the front and back pages of the two main newspapers and making it as a player internationally not only offers a source of pride, but also the opportunity to earn money to alleviate the often grinding poverty that blights the island. After sugar, rugby players are the second biggest export from Fiji, and combined with their Pacific neighbours, Samoa and Tonga – combined population of around 1.3 million – provide almost 20% of the world's professional rugby players.

This staggering statistic highlights a system of colonial-style exploitation of cheap labour from these small island nations to Europe, Australia and New Zealand, with little done to support the domestic structures within Fiji, Samoa and Tonga. A powerful documentary, *Oceans Apart: Greed, Betrayal and Pacific Island Rugby*, presented by the former Samoa forward Dan Leo, cast a powerful spotlight on this area in 2020 and things are beginning to change.

In 2021, World Rugby amended the rules to allow players to represent a different country after a stand-down period of three years, if it's where they, a parent or grandparent were born. A player can only switch allegiance once. The change, in force since January 2022, was enthusiastically received by Pacific Island players and coaches, who can now significantly strengthen their squads for the 2023 World Cup and beyond.

To give just one example, Charles Piutau, the current Bristol full back, was born in New Zealand to Tongan parents, and between 2013 and 2015 picked up 17 caps for the All Blacks. But as this last appearance was over three years ago, he is now able to play for Tonga, whom his brother Siale had captained. Using the same principle, though far more unlikely, Danny Cipriani – last capped in 2018 – would now be entitled to pull on the jersey of Trinidad and Tobago.

Allowing the likes of Piutau to play for teams where they have a strong heritage, plus the allocation of greater financial resources and the addition to Super Rugby of two Pacific Island teams – an established club side, Fijian Drua, and the newly created Moana Pasifik, with players from Samoa, Tonga and other Pacific Islands – will hugely strengthen 15-a-side rugby in the region.

Serevi himself also played as a 15-a-side International, winning 38 caps, scoring 221 points and featuring in three World Cups. He played in Japan, had two spells in the second tier of French rugby, one season at Leicester and briefly at the end of his career turned out for English amateur outfit Staines RFC. But compared to his superhuman heroics in the sevens game, it remained a curious sideshow.

In truth, he struggled to fully adapt his game for the 15-a-side version. Whilst still explosive in attack and accurate from the kicking tee, his defence and positioning was often exposed in tight matches.

But reading Leicester fans' recollections of his one season there in the late 1990s, there's a warmth towards him and an acknowledgment that they were lucky to see a true great of the game in the famous green, red and white. His finest moment for the Tigers was in a Heineken Cup game in 1997 against French giants Toulouse, where he first served up an outrageous try by chipping over the full back's head, rounding him, catching it before it bounced then offloading to Will Greenwood to go over. He then got in on the points himself with an outrageous dummy that fooled everyone and left him in acres of space to cruise over.

Two other stories, possibly apocryphal, seem to come from his time in the English Midlands. One is that after being selected at scrum half against a particularly physical opposition, he wore two scrum caps. And the other is that he forgot to lock up his house in Fiji when he moved to Leicester and it remained unlocked for the whole season, but when he returned it was entirely untouched. Considering his reputation in Fiji, this second tale is the more likely of the two.

Serevi probably underachieved in 15-a-side, but it's hard to maintain a balance between playing on the globetrotting sevens circuit and the grind of weekly training and matchday performances required in a demanding professional team. Certainly if you look at stars of the England sevens team such as Ben Gollings, Dan Norton and Simon Amor, the short game dominated their career, with modest spells at 15-a-side teams squeezed in between tournament commitments.

This balancing act meant Serevi did miss out on even more appearances for Fiji, when playing commitments in Europe stopped him attending training camps back home and meant he was dropped from some squads.

Following their second World Cup win in 2005, Serevi was appointed player-coach of the Fiji national sevens team. In his first year, they won the IRB Sevens Series, victorious at the South Africa, New Zealand, Singapore and London tournaments, and became the first team other than New Zealand to take the series. Following this triumph, the Fiji Prime Minister said of Serevi: "You have set an example of what we can do as a country through vision, sacrifice, hard work, discipline, and making the best use of our gifts and talents." A song, *'Na Noda Laione'*, was written in Serevi's honour.

After a disappointing season in 2007, Serevi was dismissed as Fiji manager. He would return a year later but would leave again in 2009. After this came a turbulent year-long spell as sevens coach of Papua New Guinea.

Such major disappointments after such a glittering career hit Serevi hard. Throughout his career, he had always sent money home to support his large extended family. With his playing days behind him and no managerial position on the horizon, he received a further blow when he was subject to a tax audit and was forced to borrow money from a friend to clear a debt. With financial worries mounting and his pride having taken a serious battering, he slipped into depression and alcoholism.

In those dark days, Serevi felt that only God remained, calling this his own "valley of death." His Christianity has played a major role in his career, and he used to write 'Philippians 4:13' – a verse from the Bible: 'I can do all things through Christ who strengthens me' – on his wrist and his boots when he played. This verse now has a deep connection with Fijian rugby.

Change was to be found in the most unusual of places: the north-east corner of the United States. Invited to play in a friendly sevens tournament in Seattle, he was offered the opportunity to stay and begin a new life. His wife and three children followed, and he is now based in North America, spreading the word about rugby through coaching and rugby schools in the USA and Canada as well as advising teams in Russia and Jamaica. He has even shared his insights with the NFL team Seattle Seahawks. A lively and energetic coach, he is very popular with his young players, with one – Karl Keane, who could be on his way to International honours himself – telling journalists: "He's a really humble man. He was this big superstar, a World Rugby Hall of Famer, but you'd see him in Seattle running touch at a game in the park, teaching people how to play."[65]

The Serevi story is a remarkable one. It's no exaggeration to say that he is the biggest figure in the whole of sevens history, and his explosive playing style and the following he and his team built played no small role in welcoming sevens into the Olympics in 2016. And the winners of the men's gold medal? Fiji of course.

Quite simply, he brought a whole new dimension to the game – the little Fijian magician was always the centre of attention. His presence at a tournament would sell tickets and boost viewing figures and the successful teams he was a part of helped created a production line of Fijian talent that remains consistent to this day. And in Hong Kong – a venue that fellow mavericks David Campese and Zinzan Brooke would also light up, not to mention Jonah Lomu – there was no bigger star.

Even on the International stage, he might sometimes have looked almost like he was playing in a park or on a beach with his mates, but underpinning such skills came a backbone of hard work and discipline. For him, showboating was part of the game, but never the whole game: he wanted to win as well. And he was the same player back in 1989 as he was when he retired in 2007. I have no doubt he had coaches that recommend changes, but if they did, they weren't heeded.

The clips of him playing really do show rugby joy in its purest form. And as a global debate rages over the many concussions, fractures and worse being delivered more and more often on the rugby pitch, watching Serevi is a reminder that avoiding contact can be a beautiful thing.

As he said himself, talking about his new life teaching American kids:

> I always tell the kids it's how I survived 21 years of rugby. Using the space and making the big boys look funny on the field. The kids always like that – and so that's what we try to do.[66]

MARNIE CUNNINGHAM

"Here was one of the most remarkable people I had ever met, turning his back on his career and sporting life at just 22..."

FACTFILE

Full name: Martin 'Marnie' John Cunningham
Born: 23 June 1933, Cork, Republic of Ireland
Died: 31 May 2000, Salford, Greater Manchester, England
Position: Flanker
Representative teams: Irish Universities, Barbarians, Ireland
Clubs: University College Cork, Cork Constitution, Munster, Lancashire, London Irish, the RAF

"A CITY UNIQUE in Ireland, where rugby cuts across all social barriers," wrote *The Irish Times*. An anonymous official said that Limerick's rugby support, "dockers and bank clerks, like in Swansea or Cardiff, made them more likely to respond to protest aggressively." The *Limerick Leader* predicted widespread disorder, with reports that thousands of outsiders, many of them "extreme left wingers", would descend on the town, intent on causing trouble. 400 Gardai were to be placed on duty, and nine clubs would provide stewards at Thomond Park itself as barbed wire was run across the walls surrounding the ground. The *Leader* added that it was "sick of the modern kid-glove method of toleration and we are fed up of the fanatics featured on RTE", and gave its blessing to a tough response.

Limerick on Wednesday 14 January 1970 was a powder keg ready to explode.

The Springboks were in town. And the city was divided.

In the chaos surrounding the ground pre-game, one former Munster favourite and full Irish International had just arrived from England. He was not in Limerick to watch the game and catch up with old friends and teammates, though many would greet him warmly. No, his purpose was to protest the welcoming of a team that he saw as representing an immoral regime. When he played, he was known as Marnie Cunningham, but now he was Father Marnie.

And he wasn't happy.

Cunningham would tell an *Irish Times* journalist part of the reason for his anger: "I have a friend in South Africa who is as good as any man on this Springboks team, but he cannot even watch a match there now because he is 'Coloured' [the South African term for someone of mixed ethnicity]. I would love to watch the match, but I cannot support racialism."

The same journalist counted at least 25 clergymen entering the ground as spectators. Cunningham would be the only man of the cloth protesting.[67]

His story begins in Cork, 37 years earlier. Born Martin John Cunningham. he was known to all as Marnie (though his name has widely appeared posthumously as Marney, this is not how he spelt it). Educated at the city's Presentation Brothers College, a school with a strong rugby heritage listing many who have played for their country as former pupils – Ronan O'Gara, Peter Stringer and Simon Zebo, to name just a few – Cunningham first came to playing prominence whilst at University College Cork, whom he helped to win the Munster Senior Cup in 1955. From there he went on to play for Cork Constitution, which his father Jack had previously captained, before being selected for Munster (as would his brother Joe).

Marnie received a call-up for Ireland at the age of just 21 and made his debut in a 3-5 defeat against France in January 1955. A fellow debutant that day was Tony O'Reilly, who would shine for Ireland and the Lions before a remarkable business career that would see him become Chairman of food giant Heinz (the first non-Heinz family member to hold that position) and CEO of Irish media conglomerate Independent News & Media (INM), before going bankrupt in 2017.

Back then O'Reilly was just a callow teenager, whose indecision led to the decisive try for France. He remembers well the no-frills instructions that debutants were given, having to bring their own "trainings togs, clean white knicks, towel and soap" and be sure that their boots were in a "playable condition".[68]

Also lining up with Cunningham that day was another special player, Jack Kyle. He made 46 appearances for Ireland, then a world record when adding in his six Tests for the Lions, and was a member of the Grand Slam-winning side in 1948. In 2002 he was voted the Greatest-Ever Irish Rugby Player by the Irish Rugby Football Union. Few who saw the scenes of him congratulating Brian O'Driscoll in Cardiff in 2009, when Ireland ended a 61-year wait for another Grand Slam, will forget them. The torch was truly passed on at that moment. But like O'Reilly, and indeed Cunningham, it was his post-rugby days that he became most known for. A doctor, he spent the years 1966 to 2000 serving Chingola, a mining town in Zambia, where he became a hugely important and beloved figure.

Cunningham would play seven times for his county, with his last appearance being a try-scoring one in a famous win 11-3 over Wales at Lansdowne Road in 1956, a triumph which deprived the visitors of a Grand Slam. A report at the time stated, "our forwards were rampant and most outstanding of the lot, Cork's Marnie Cunningham, broke through two tackles for the try, which put the issue beyond doubt."[69] Many considered him unlucky not to have been selected for the Lions tour of South Africa in 1955, although he did represent Irish Universities and the Barbarians.

It wasn't form, or injury, or even rugby league that ended his International career at the age of just 22. No, it was a higher calling – the Catholic priesthood.

I spoke to Paul Cunningham, Marnie's nephew and also an ex-Munster and Ireland A hooker, and asked if this move was something the family had been expecting.

> Absolutely not. The family would attend Mass but weren't hugely religious. He told everyone he had some news, but people thought it was about a job, or perhaps a girl – but no, it was becoming a priest. I don't think there was a particularly dramatic event that made him decide this, but he never, ever regretted it. And his sister Marie would later also enter religious service, becoming a nun in the Dominican order.

Marnie's good friend Michael Kiely would later recall a similar surprise, writing for Cork newspaper *The Echo* that shortly after his heroics against Wales, Cunningham sought him out:

> "Mick, I am making a change and I want you to pick which option I am going to take: I am going to play professional rugby, I am going to marry a blonde air hostess, I am going to take big job as an engineer in Glasgow, or I am going to be a priest."
>
> I replied he could cross the last one out for sure. He laughed and said, "You are wrong, I am going to be a priest." I was stunned. Here was one of the most remarkable people I had ever met, turning his back on his career and sporting life at just 22…[70]

A few years earlier, Tom Gavin – or to use his full title, Monsignor Thomas Gavin – in playing twice for Ireland in 1949 fuelled a ferocious debate among archbishops as to whether priests should play International rugby, before a Cardinal finally ruled that he could. Gavin, recalling those games years later, remarked that his teammates were unfazed by the presence of a dog collar in the changing room: "Ireland changing rooms are pretty eclectic places and priests are very much part of everyday life in Ireland. They certainly didn't tone the language down on my account."[71]

Gavin remains the only ordained Catholic priest to play International rugby.

Cunningham had qualified as an engineer at UCC, but now moved to a seminary in England – St Joseph's College in Upholland, Lancashire, where he captained the football team. He was ordained in 1962.

The Cork Examiner reported that he had turned down a £1,000 a year job to join the priesthood, but Marnie showed no regrets, telling the newspaper: "There is more satisfaction and happiness in serving the Church than in playing rugby or working as a civil engineer. I don't think I will play rugby again; I have not played for six years because of my studies for the priesthood."

However, he couldn't ompletely shake his old habits. Just a few months later it was reported that he had been selected for Lancashire in a county championship match, in 1965 he'd be recorded as playing for London Irish, and whilst serving as an RAF chaplain in Asia, he represented them in a game against the Army.

At first he worked in a church in Cork and then, after his time with the RAF, he served for the rest of his life as a parish priest at St Charles in Swinton, Greater Manchester.

If he had stayed in the game, he was expected to have been long a fixture in the national team, and no doubt Lions selectors would have taken a look at him too.

But it would be 1970 before he would be back in the rugby spotlight again.

Whilst the 1960s had brought many major social, cultural and sexual changes, in South Africa, the apartheid system – institutionalised racial segregation which ensured that the country was dominated politically, socially and economically by the nation's minority white population – remained firmly and increasingly brutally in place.

Despite this, South Africa teams (almost always entirely white) competed freely in International sports during the 1950s. But as we entered a new decade, this began to change. FIFA suspended South Africa in 1961 and the Olympics followed suit, barring the team from sending a team to the Games from 1964 onwards. It was becoming clear to opponents of apartheid that sport could play a major role in putting international pressure on the South African government.

This became clearer with the 'D'Oliveira Affair' in 1968. Basil D'Oliveira, a cricketer who would be categorised as 'Coloured' under the apartheid system, was called up to join the England cricket team to tour South Africa. Teams of "mixed race" were explicitly banned from playing white teams under apartheid, and with the addition of D'Oliveira, this is what England became, in the eyes of the apartheid government. Whilst South African Prime Minister B J Vorster had a level of pragmatism when it came to sport, he viewed the selection of D'Oliveira as based on politics rather than on form and announced that the England team would not be allowed in if he was included. A huge storm erupted, the tour was cancelled, and South Africa didn't play Test cricket for another 23 years.

So by the time the 1969/70 Springbok tour of the UK and Ireland came around, the issues of sport and apartheid were inextricably intertwined. Rugby was the national sport of the white minority and was followed with a fervour comparable at the time only to that found in New Zealand and south Wales. At the official farewell to the tour, Prime Minister Vorster spoke to a squad who were largely naïve as to the reception they'd be receiving. The South African vice-captain, Tommy Bedford, who had studied at Oxford University, tried to warn the team they were going to have a tough reception but was shouted down as being unpatriotic.

On 30 October 1969, as the team touched down at Heathrow, Nelson Mandela was on Robben Island, five years into his 27-year sentence. Even an optimist like him probably wouldn't have expected this tour to have such an impact on not just rugby, but his country as a whole. 26 games across three months stretched ahead of them, and the banners at the airport would have given them an indication of what was ahead – with 'Don't Scrum with a Racist Bum' the most eye-catching.

On the drive from the airport to their hotel they will have seen 'No to Boks' scrawled in prominent spots along their route. And an evening reception at the South African embassy in Trafalgar Square ended with the squad huddling in the foyer, unable to leave due to protestors and waiting for the police to rescue them.[72]

Their first game, against Oxford University, had to be switched to Twickenham for security reasons. Two weeks before the match, 'Oxford Rejects Racism' had been written on the pitch with weedkiller, in letters five feet high.

On the day of this fixture, Wales and Lions flanker John Taylor announced that he would no longer play against the Springboks. A teacher by profession, he recalled:

> I was a young schoolteacher at a huge comprehensive in Putney – 2,000 pupils, a very multi-ethnic and multi-racial intake – and I wanted to look them in the eye. Although I already had misgivings about the apartheid regime, I desperately wanted to play for the British Lions, so I went on the 1968 tour with some reservations. By the time I came home from the tour, those misgivings had turned into absolute convictions. I decided I was not going to play against South Africa as a matter of conscience.[73]

For his troubles, Taylor received criticism from some archaic rugby committee men, and a file was opened on him by the South African security services.

The fourth game of the tour, against Swansea at St Helens, saw a 2,000-strong demonstration – chanting, among other things, "Paint 'em black and send 'em back", "Jack in the Boks" and "Swansea Shame". The city had (and still has) a strong left-wing element, and feelings ran high. The protests soon turned into a riot. A battle with police went on for over two hours, with protestors attacked and beaten and over 100 needing treatment for their injuries.

One protestor, Fred Fitton, recalls what he saw that day:

> This was the most violent demo that I have ever been on and since that time I worked on three miners' strikes... the police did not appear to care what they did and I was amazed that no one was killed that day.[74]

In an enquiry afterwards there was a particular focus on the special 'stewards' that the police had hired that day, who seemed to have had carte blanche to deal with protestors however they liked. The government told police chiefs not to use them in future, but fell short of criticising the police.

The tour had become a siege.

The locks on players' doors in their London hotel were glued up and had to be broken down. On the morning of the fixture against England, one activist managed to slip into the team bus and chain himself to the steering wheel before driving off with half the squad on board. The players panicked and managed to get their hands round his neck and wrestle him out of the driver's seat, but not before he'd smashed into six cars. There were 5,000 anti-apartheid protestors outside Twickenham that day, facing off against the National Front (British fascists), who were now travelling to actively support the Springboks. Inside the ground, two protestors disrupted the game by running onto the pitch and handcuffing themselves to the posts.

Much of the opposition to the tour was organised by the Stop the Seventy Tour Committee (STST), which was formed in 1970 to generate a mass movement of non-violent civil disobedience to disrupt the matches. The chairman of the STST was the

19-year-old Peter Hain, an anti-apartheid activist who had grown up in South Africa and would later become the Labour MP for Neath, a Cabinet member and then Lord Hain. He recalls:

> Over Christmas, two months into the tour, the players had taken a step inconceivable in the annals of Springbok history and voted to go home. The management, under political pressure, ordered them to stay... For the first time the Springboks, accustomed to being lionised as perhaps the leading national rugby team in the world, had been treated as pariahs.[75]

In the new year, the Springboks headed across the Irish Sea. A match against Ulster that had been scheduled earlier in the tour had been cancelled – adding anti- and pro-apartheid protests into the rising violence of the Troubles was viewed as too combustible.

The game against Ireland in Dublin on 10 January 1970 was described by Hain as "the biggest and best demonstration of the whole tour." Ireland at this time would not have been known for its radicalism – the deeply Catholic arch-conservative Éamon de Valera, at 87, still had three years to run as President – but the Springboks would enjoy no relief from the protests that had dogged them in the UK.

A hundred clerics from the seminary at Maynooth were the first to protest, then the Irish Rugby Football Union's headquarters was daubed with slogans and the goal posts at University College Dublin, which hosted Springbok training sessions, were destroyed. Unlike in the UK, trade unions took a lead, with attempts made to disrupt transport, phone and mail services. A conservative he may have been, but de Valera declined an invitation to watch the fixture, as did the Taoiseach. No member of the government attended.

On the day of the match up to 10,000 marched to the ground, led by a host of prominent Irish figures such as writer and politician Conor Cruise O'Brien and Republican activist and MP Bernadette Devlin, who had travelled from Northern Ireland. Also in the protest group that day was an 80-year-old veteran of the 1910 Lions tour and 17-cap Irish International, Alec Roulston Foster. A teacher by profession, he worked in elite Protestant boys' schools throughout his career, but frequently clashed with the authorities over his more radical, nationalist beliefs. In his later years he committed himself to both anti-apartheid protests and the burgeoning civil-rights movement in Northern Ireland.[76]

The game, an 8-8 draw, went ahead on a pitch cordoned off by barbed wire.

The Irish hooker that day, Ken Kennedy, recalled being hit by a bottle aimed at a Springbok and afterwards being shouted and spat at on the street. His teammate Fergus Slattery described it as "an odd day. You had thousands outside protesting, so the ground wasn't full. The pitch was covered in straw because of the frost and it was like we were playing in a meadow."[77]

That night the Springboks went out for dinner with heavy police protection, under a hail of bottles, eggs and stones.

Next up was Munster, in Limerick.

The Springboks were met on arrival by a large Garda presence and an even bigger set of protestors. The team trained far away from the public gaze and stayed not at the hotel visiting teams usually used, but one next door to a Garda station.

This is not to say that all of Limerick was opposed to the Springboks being in town. The picture is more complex. The team were warmly welcomed by local Labour Party TD and Mayor of Limerick Steve Coughlan, who had initially vowed he would not meet with the South African team, but would soon begin claiming that "revolutionary communist groups" would use the Springbok visit as an excuse to "stir up trouble".

Many locals were happy to see a team of such repute arriving to play their beloved Munster, and were appalled by some of the scenes they'd seen in Dublin the previous week and at many of the matches on the British leg of the tour. Unlike many other cities in Ireland, rugby was the most popular sport in Limerick, cutting across class and religious divides, and there was concern from some that the issue of the Springbok visit would drive a wedge through this unity.

South African diamond firm De Beers, who sponsored the Springbok stay in the mid-west, also had a major facility in Shannon, 20 minutes up the road from Limerick, which may also have gained some local favour.

But protests still came, with Father Marnie Cunningham at the head of them. His sister Marie, a nun in the Dominican Order, served in South Africa and worked in the townships, providing a direct insight to her brother into life under the apartheid system. In an era when the rugby establishment mostly ignored the issue, he had flown back from England to make his view clear: apartheid is morally wrong, and a team that represents it shouldn't be welcome in this corner of Ireland. It took a priest to pull back the establishment's comfort blanket of conformity. And I wonder how many on their way to the game that day saw the protest, recognised Cunningham as not just a priest but a former International and felt a twinge of unease or even guilt that, yes, there were some who loved the game, but weren't prepared to separate sport from politics.

Alongside him was another Labour politician, Jim Kemmy, who was so disgusted with the welcome that Coughlan and other colleagues gave the Springboks that he quit the party and became an Independent TD instead. The weather was wet and cold but around 350 anti-apartheid protestors arrived at Thomond Park with their banners, slogans and songs.

The Irish Times reported that Cunningham's leading of the protest was "one of the most remarkable aspects" of the day, that he "exchanged greetings and gentle banter with former teammates going into the ground" and that Noel Murphy, the former Ireland captain and a fellow Cork man, greeted him warmly. At one point one player called out to him, "I'm surprised at you!", to which the unflustered priest replied, "Everyone to their own thoughts."

The uneasy atmosphere around the game that day had an impact on a Munster team proud of its performances against visiting International teams. One report describes the atmosphere inside the usually feverish ground as "eerie" – the Springboks, in their 21st game of the tour, were by now used to such frosty receptions and won at a canter, 25-9. Another notes one Munster fan, a Limerick doctor, commenting coldly, "Even the damn protest is more exciting than this."[78]

The Cork Examiner said that "Munster's deep-rooted rugby pride took a rude jarring when the Springboks produced a crunching victory in a one-sided and, therefore, desperately disappointing game."[79]

The Springboks would move on: there were four more games, with over 5,000 protestors for the International versus Wales, then they limped home.

Limerick, shaken by an international spotlight and the imposition of hard choices, had a lingering hangover. The fear of a "hard left" invasion of the city might have been groundless but there followed a panic of about Maoists – believers of a particular type of socialism advocated by China's Mao Zedong. A priest claimed there were 200 in the city, and they were threatening the city's churches. In fact there were at most six, working mainly in a socialist bookshop.

The red flag never flew over Limerick.

And the apartheid regime would last in South Africa until 1994, when the first multiracial elections took place. But the British and Irish response to the tour shook the country deeply and hastened the period of sporting isolation that it would be locked into. Isolation that, it has to be added, was far from complete – the Lions toured in 1980, as did France; a year later Ireland visited; and in 1984 England did the same. But the 1986 Lions tour was cancelled, and the Springboks were excluded from the first two Rugby World Cups in 1987 and 1991.

Tommy Bedford recalls the immediate reaction back home, following the tour:

> We knew that no other country could afford a tour like this. That was the catalyst for change in a radical way. When I got back to South Africa from the UK, I took time out. I went to a deserted part of the country and I thought about Peter Hain, Bernadette Devlin and all those anti-apartheid people who put us in this laager [camp]. I came to the conclusion that maybe they did have a point.

Father Cunningham returned to his parish in England.

But his strong sense of social justice would remain steadfast. In 1981, despite significant opposition, Ireland would tour South Africa. Cunningham wrote a powerful letter to *The Irish Times*, directed towards those players who would be selected to tour, in which he deftly emphasises the moral aspect to the choice of whether or not to accept the invitation. He is wise to the complexities of the issues, though is firm on the "evils" of apartheid and "the unnecessary human suffering that results from it".[80]

He highlights the danger of "uncritically accepting the statement that rugby and politics must remain separate" and asks those who do tour to go to South Africa with the idea of supporting change, and to "speak out in public and private when you see apartheid at any level". The letter is signed off with an appeal to all involved to "please reflect deeply on what you are about to do".[81]

Ireland did send a squad to South Africa, though three of the first-choice team – Hugo McNeill, Tony Ward and fellow maverick Moss Keane – declined the invitation and a number had to resign their posts when their employers refused to grant them a leave of absence. The tourists would play seven matches, of which they won three, and lost the test series 2-0 in an undignified chapter for Irish sport.

A man of humility and kindness, deeply popular with his parishioners in Salford, Father Cunningham suffered ill health late in life, battling a debilitating disease for seven years before dying just before his 67th birthday in 2000.

Nephew Paul recalls the closeness Marnie had with his family and those friends from his previous life:

> He was great fun, still loved his sport and had a great sense of humour. But he was always very humble about what he had achieved. It was lovely that just three days after he was ordained, he was able to fly back to Cork to officiate at my father Joe's wedding. That was very special for the family. He also remained great friends with Tony O'Reilly, despite their lives going in such different directions. He officiated at his wedding too, and would be close to him all his life.

Cunningham might be the least well-known player in this selection, but in addition to being an excellent player, he was clear on his beliefs, even if they took him away from the game. First into the priesthood, then back to Munster to protest the Springboks' visit. Whilst many in the game buried their heads in the sand on the issue of apartheid and some even offered their tacit support, Father Marnie did no such thing.

He did the right thing at the right time, and not everyone can say this.

DAVID CAMPESE

"You can't work on it, it just happens."

FACTFILE

Full name: David Ian Campese

Born: 21 October 1962, Queanbeyan, New South Wales, Australia

Positions: Wing, Full back

Representative teams: Australia sevens, Barbarians, World XV, Australia

Clubs: Queanbeyan Whites, Australian Capital Territory (ACT), Petrarca Padova (Italy), Randwick, New South Wales, Amatori Rugby Milano

Nickname: Campo

THE SILENCE IN the Australian changing room was deafening. A few groans, some sighs, the clatter of dirty boots dropped to the floor as they were eased off tired feet, but no talk. Through the walls, the ecstasy of the Lions could be heard clearly – the singing, the shouting and the distinctive clink of beer bottles. For the tourists, it was the start of a big night; for the hosts, the end of a bitterly disappointing Test series.

David Campese sat looking at his teammates. They were only snatching glances at him amidst the sullen silence.

Speaking to me on the telephone from Australia, Campese recalled that no one spoke to him for a full ten minutes after the final whistle, and only when his captain Nick Farr-Jones came over to sit next to him was the silence broken. In his typical sardonic style, Campese related the rest of that evening to me: he skipped the official dinner, got a speeding ticket on the way home, and then received a phone call from St Helens, with an offer to switch codes.

The world had looked very different for the 26-year-old flyer just an hour before.

The 1989 Australia v. British and Irish Lions Test series was finely poised at that point. The tourists had been well beaten in the first match, 30-12, but had battled back in the second to grind out a 19-12 victory.

It came down to a decider in Sydney, and the Wallabies were leading 12-9 early in the second half when Rob Andrew's attempted drop goal from just outside the 22 drifted wide. The Lions fans groaned as the ball was gathered by Campese behind the posts and I doubt there was a single person in the stands who didn't expect him either to dot the ball down for a 22-metre drop out or to take it forward a few steps before utilising his fine boot to clear the danger far from the Australian tryline.

Campese, however, had other ideas. He turned and began to run, seeing that the Lions defence on that side of the pitch was undermanned and there was a real opportunity for a counterattack. He ran forward but Ieuan Evans, the Lions winger, blocked his path. Campese threw a loose and high pass to full back Greg Martin, who clearly hadn't been expecting it, and it went agonisingly behind his outstretched arm.

The ball bounced backwards into the corner of the pitch – now known cruelly as 'Campo's Corner' – and Evans and Martin jostled each other as they fell onto the ball at the same time. Today it would go to the Test Match Official (TMO) and agonising minutes of multiple replays would ensue. Not in 1989, though. The French referee gave the try, and although this wasn't the end of the game, the Lions didn't relinquish their lead, winning the game 19-18 and taking the series. The Australians hadn't won a Test series against the Lions since

1930 and they would have to wait until 2001 until they'd get their next triumph.

The opportunity to score a decisive length-of-the-pitch try might have been there, but the risk was immense. There's a fine line between genius and madness: David Campese was usually the former, but at this moment the latter had taken hold.

Even viewing the footage as a Lions supporter, it's a tough watch, especially with the Australian television commentator Chris Handy angrily exclaiming:

> This is the classic shocker. David Campese had to drop that ball down... you don't do this on your own line. You don't wear the green and gold jersey to pull out that sort of Mickey Mouse rugby.

As Campese walked off the pitch, a fan shouted, "Hey Campo, that's another Test you've lost for Australia!" Campese's fragile state of mind was not helped by the post-match snubbing from his teammates.

What followed was extraordinary, even by the standards of a sports-mad country like Australia. Even decades later, Campese vividly recalls the vitriol he felt in the weeks following that final Lions Test.

> How the press treated me after the Lions game was brutal. It was a mistake, but that's how I played. Life is about making mistakes. A lot of people didn't accept me: I was Italian, I didn't go to private school. If you are different, it makes it difficult. That's carried on through my career, and is why I wasn't given a proper chance at coaching in Australia. But you learn from mistakes and two years later I won the World Cup.

The criticisms aimed at Campese were unrelenting, not just in the days that followed but all through the remainder of 1989. It wasn't just journalists that went to town on him, but former Australian players as well.

The views of former teammate and captain Andrew Slack proved particularly stinging, with Campese later writing:

> [He went] leaping into print about what a mess I'd made of things and why I'd done it. My rugby in Italy was dragged into it and blamed – ridiculous! For one mistake? When I played alongside Slacky, I thought he was a great guy, but I have to say the scenario in which a former mate can take you to the cleaners in the papers just because he's joined the journos' ranks isn't the most appealing to me... What the hell happened to the notion of old mates sticking together?[82]

I suspect it was Slack's description of Campese as playing "spaghetti rugby" that most upset him.

Such was the abuse continuing to roll his way that Australian captain, the erudite and talented lawyer Nick Farr-Jones, wrote a letter to *The Sydney Morning Herald* in support of his colleague:

> Not only as captain of the national team, but as an Australian, it disturbs me to hear and read the constant and at times vilifying attacks by rugby followers and the press on one of our greatest sportsmen, David Campese. Campo's blunder was careless and costly. But few of the Australian players would be satisfied with their performances, including myself.

Yes, it was a bad error from Campese, but no one wins or loses a game on their own and the Lions pack had the better of their Australian counterparts from the first whistle – as the Lions Head Coach that day, Ian McGeechan, remembers:

> It has probably gone down as one of the most horrendous defensive acts in Test history, and I am sure that it came about because of the pressure we had put on the Wallabies, restricting the ball to Campese, so when it did finally come to him, he felt he had to try and make something happen.[83]

Clem Thomas, first a Wales and Lions player and then a fine journalist of the game, neatly encapsulates the situation, writing in the official Lions history:

> The Australian media pilloried Campese without giving any regard to the years of artistry, skills and match-winning with which he had blessed them.[84]

Clem was right. Lesser men might have quit, and it did cross Campese's mind, but from the nadir of that July day in Sydney, the best was yet to come.

Campese was born in the small New South Wales city of Queanbeyan in 1962 to an Italian father, Gianantonio, and an Australian mother, Joan. The family moved to back to his father's native village – Montecchio Precalcino, in the north-east of Italy – when he was two and stayed for two years. Just two years after making his International debut, Campese would return to Italy in 1984 to play for Petrarca, about 40 miles from where he spent part of his childhood. He later spent ten happy and productive winters at Amatori in Milan, in the off-season from his club Randwick back down under in Sydney.

This unique arrangement, whilst criticised by some, never had any negative impact on his ability to switch up a gear when returning to the higher standard of International rugby. It also offered some other advantages, as recalled in his very open, honest and entertaining 1991 autobiography, *On a Wing and a Prayer*:

> I mentioned the good lifestyle a rugby player can enjoy in Italy and I'd like to expand on that. I do not deny, for example, that I have got something financially out of going to Italy – how else could I have lived there? But it has been done through promotional work, which I am entitled to do as I have no other occupation. I work sometimes for a travel agency, Five Viaggi, which is a company associated with Silvio Berlusconi [later Italian Prime Minister]. I have an allowance as well as expenses..."[85]

Remember that rugby union would not become 'open' – that is, turn professional – until 1995, but in the early 1990s Campese was viewed by many as the sport's first professional, declaring, "I'm still an amateur, of course, but I became rugby's first millionaire five years ago." This is just one of many controversial quotes from him, and we'll get to some of the others shortly. Yes, his arrangement with Italian clubs was unorthodox, particularly at Amatori, but his professional attitude towards fitness, training and diet was years ahead of most in the game.

Campese might have pushed the amateur status to its outer limit, but this kind of attitude wasn't rare at the top end of the game. Stars across the UK and Ireland, and in the Southern Hemisphere, would often be set up with a pseudo-job in marketing, public relations or sales where there was very little expected of them, or with a club sponsor, where their main function would be to attend functions and impress clients at meetings. Even those in seemingly less flexible jobs such as teaching, the police or the military were given extra time to train and attend matches – the view being that having a high-profile rugby player attached to your school, force or regiment was a positive. Then there was the famous 'boot money': cash that would be placed into boots after the game.

Whatever the reality of those hazy last days of the amateur era, David Campese was a true superstar, and relished playing at a time when it was acceptable to try things and take risks without the pressure the modern professional game brings.

Between the ages of 12 and 17, he only played a handful of Union games. Campese recalled those early years to me:

> My dad's Italian, and never played sport in his life. It was rugby league that was my first focus, playing it between 8 and 16 – in between golf, Aussie Rules and cricket. I was a good League player, and played in a Grand Final as a youth, but we lost. And the coach blamed me. Plus, there was a big drinking culture, and I wasn't into that. So I quit, and with my newly found free time

> went to watch a 4th-grade rugby game. The team lost, and after the match, I went up to the coach and asked if he wanted a full back. He said yes and I played the following week. I didn't know too much about the rules or the history of the game, so just ran! I loved it and never really looked back.

Within two years of committing to Union, aged just 19, he was selected at full back for the Australian U21 side, and in 1982 he would make his full Wallabies debut on the wing in the most challenging fixture possible: away to New Zealand.

Campese would be coming up against the veteran Kiwi wing Stu Wilson, and prior to the first Test in Christchurch a journalist asked the young Australian how he felt about facing a far more experienced opposite number. His seemingly offhand reply was "Stu who?" Campese told me that he had so little knowledge of the game that he genuinely didn't know who Stu Wilson was, but Wilson was incensed at the attitude, and admitted he went into the game wanting to "serve it up" to the youngster.

In the event, it would be Campese doing the delivering. His first touch was a goose-step – a specific half-jump with high knees whilst running that changes the speed of the run, enough to disrupt the timing of the defensive players but not enough to significantly slow the speed of the ball carrier – which completely flummoxed Wilson. Campese would score his first International try in this match and Wilson ended up having a poor series, despite the All Blacks ultimately coming out on top.

The goose-step would become something of a trademark for Campese, yet he is perhaps uncharacteristically coy about its use, telling me that it has been "blown out of all proportion" and that it "has been part of my game for some years, since I was eight years old and playing in Yass [a town in New South Wales]. Two kids came at me, I did it and they bumped into each other and knocked themselves out. I never practised it. You can't work on it, it just happens."

Campese first came to major prominence in the Northern Hemisphere during the 1984 Australia tour of the UK and Ireland, a wildly successful expedition which announced the return of the Wallabies as a world-class rugby-playing nation. The team was packed full of stars. There was the remarkable fly half Mark Ella, who was the first overseas player to score tries in each Test of a full series against the four Home Unions. Outside him was Michael Lynagh, as cool an operator as you'd find in the centre, but always on a hot kicking streak. The captain was Andrew Slack, still some years away from his journalistic days and the wise old head among some callow youths. Getting the backline moving was the livewire scrum half Nick Farr-Jones; locking up at the back was Roger Gould, safe under a high ball and with a huge kick; and then on the wings you had a classic, strong-finishing winger in the shape of Brendan Moon on one flank, and on the other, of course, David Campese.

This illustrious group achieved a Grand Slam of victories over the Home Nations, winning by a total margin of 100-33, and by doing so became the first and – so far – only Australian side to achieve this feat.

This was no whistle-stop tour of the north, either: they played 18 games, with matches against a Combined Services XV, South of Scotland and Pontypool, among others. Campese played in eleven of the tour matches, including all four Tests, scoring 24 points in the process.

The Wallabies even had time to meet the Queen at Buckingham Palace, where they also made a major impression. At the royal reception, back-rower Chris Roche perched on the edge of an antique table, which – clearly not used to having a hefty Australian flanker pressing down upon it – promptly collapsed. A red-faced and crumpled Roche was rescued by Prince Phillip, who, in his typical style, coolly remarked, "Don't worry, we have plenty more of those in the storeroom."

Campese was unimpressed with the standard of opposition that he and his teammates faced on the tour:

> The Brits were kicking mad, even to the extent of trying to drop goals from the halfway line rather than attempting to score tries by moving the ball. It has always been my deepest belief that to win the rugby game you must score tries... when we left Britain, we had set an example of how to play running rugby... it was perfectly possible to win and entertain at the same time.[86]

As the 1980s progressed and the game began to take its first steps towards professionalism, a first World Cup was organised for 1987, co-hosted by Australia and New Zealand. The Wallabies started with a Campese try in a convincing group-stage victory over England, before the wing scored further tries in straightforward wins over Japan and the USA. Ireland were beaten in the quarter finals and they faced France in the semi-finals.

The game took place in Sydney and proved to be an absolute cracker. Australia were the favourites and at one point led 9-0. Campese had already touched down with his usual try but with moments left, the scores were tied at 24-24. This time, however, it would be another mercurial back, Serge Blanco, who would get the glory – finishing a move that had begun deep in French territory, with the ball going through the hands of 11 French players before he splashed down in the corner and Australia crashed out.

Campese was phlegmatic about the defeat, writing some years later:

> Running the ball very nearly beat the French team that day, so I don't think our tactics can be criticised heavily. In the end, an extraordinary try, which was made possible because the French players refused to let the movement die, won the match.[87]

Australia might have fallen short at the 1987 Rugby World Cup, but Campese continued to score tries at an amazing rate. By the time he retired, he had scored 64 in 101 Wallaby appearances, in consistently dazzling performances.

So much so that Australian coach Alan Jones called him the "Bradman of rugby" – likening the winger to Don Bradman, the cricketer described by *Wisden* as "the greatest phenomenon in the history of cricket, indeed in the history of all ball games." Bradman is an icon in Australia and this praise was well documented in the media, ultimately having a detrimental effect on Campese, leaving him "stunned". It was reported that when he did make mistakes, the phrase would be thrown back in his face by Jones: "I told people you were the Bradman of rugby and now you have let me down."

A Bradman or not, four years later at the 1991 World Cup Campese would reach dizzying new heights. The second edition of the tournament would be co-hosted by England, Scotland, Wales, Ireland and France, but it would be Australia who would leave with the trophy. They strolled through their group, with Campese getting three tries in as many appearances, then edged Ireland 19-18 in a tense affair in Dublin, before facing the old enemy New Zealand in the semi-final.

As the All Blacks lined up to perform the haka, the Australian team stood in a line to face it. Except, that is, for David Campese, who stood behind the posts practising his kicking. The Australian coach had given instructions to the players to do what they wished whilst the New Zealanders performed their famous pre-match ritual, and Campese, always his own man, did just that. It set him up for probably his greatest-ever performance.

He scored the first Wallaby try after just six minutes, drifting in from the wing to the centre, and taking quick ball off a ruck. He ran diagonally across the Kiwi defence, turning John Kirwan inside out in the process, before touching down in the corner.

Five minutes before half time, he gathers a kick from Michael Lynagh, flummoxing Kiwi full back Kieran Crowley, who ends up falling helplessly to the floor without laying a hand on the winger. Bearing down on the try line, Campese draws the last two defenders and is about to be wrapped up by scrambling Kiwis Graeme Bachop and John Timu when he flicks a 'no look' pass back over his right shoulder and into the arms of a chasing Tim Horan, who has the space to cross the line unopposed and score the try. It takes a few rewinds on YouTube to see how he does it, but it's a thing of beauty.

Mark Ella wrote of that pass as being "the ultimate of its type. I cannot think of another player in the world who could have managed it."[88]

The neutrals were blown away by the performance too. Former Ireland fly half Tony Ward, writing in *The Independent*, said of Campese:

> He is the Maradona, the Pelé of International Rugby all rolled into one. You cannot put a value on his importance to our game. He is a breath of fresh air and I think perhaps the greatest player of all time. Without being too soppy, it was an honour to be at Lansdowne Road just to see him perform.[89]

Campese warmed up for the final against England in typical rambunctious style, criticising the English style of play in the press as "boring" and a "good way to destroy the image of the game", before going on to state that "England would never beat us in the World Cup because they are a bunch of toffs, and we are convicts."[90]

His performance in the final at Twickenham was less explosive, and he was lucky not to give away a penalty try late on when he knocked on the ball from a dangerous English pass, but it was enough to see the Wallabies win 12-6. Along with his winner's medal, Campese picked up the title of Player of the Tournament.

His exploits in the 1991 World Cup made David Campese a global star, the biggest until Jonah Lomu announced himself at the next instalment of the tournament in 1995. He would go on to play for Australia in the brave new world of professionalism and keep scoring the tries until he retired from International rugby in 1996. Running parallel to his performances in the 15-man game was a successful career playing sevens: winning the famous Hong Kong tournament three times, reaching a World Cup Final in 1993 and picking up a bronze medal at the 1998 Commonwealth Games.

Along with the tries, Campese is best known for his outspoken, brash nature, and for a man who was one of the greatest-ever entertainers to grace the field, he was far from universally popular. It's probably for the best that Twitter didn't exist during his playing days.

There is a steady stream of stories that people tell about him: some real, some imagined, some recycled yarns about other players.

There's the story of when his club team were invited to the Melrose Sevens tournament in Scotland. It was a particularly rainy day, and the locals were rubbing their hands at how this superstar would get on in a mud-bath. Turns out he loved it. His team – Randwick – won the tournament, and he scored a try against the home team in which he slithered, kicked ahead, slithered again, kicked it through, and scored. "I wouldn't have scored that bloody try," he said, "if it hadn't been so sticky."[91]

His teammate Michael Lynagh once said of him, "One of the great joys of Campese's play is that he never knows what he is going to do next, so neither does the opposition."[92]

Whilst former Wallaby coach Bob Dwyer once said Campese had "a loose wire between his brain and his mouth", devoting a whole chapter of his autobiography to explaining (or trying to!) what makes this unique character tick.

Perhaps my favourite quip about him comes from Mark Ella, who, whilst in Israel playing in a sevens tournament, went with the Australia team to visit Bethlehem to "see where Campo was born."

His name has also passed into the vernacular in Australia, with the phrase 'easy Campese' now meaning 'no worries'. Then there's the filet Campese, the special steak dish named after him, available in Australian restaurants.

David Campese occupies a unique place in rugby history as one of the last amateur superstars and one of the most famous names in the new professional era. He was unusual in not coming from what was then the traditional Australian rugby background of private school and university. In an era when standards of fitness were more mixed, he was meticulous in his physical preparation. He took a wider viewer of the game too, challenging the establishment and pushing the argument that the game risks "dying" if not expanded into new geographies and demographics. Indeed, many of his points in *On a Wing and a Prayer* – caps through residency, supporting smaller nations, the role of touring, and worry about the dominance of kicking – are as valid today as they were when it was written 30 years ago.

On the pitch he was a revolutionary as well, changing the role of a winger – not just waiting patiently on the flank for the ball and an overlap but instead coming into the pitch, looking for work, and scoring tries from the kinds of positions that defences wouldn't expect a winger to come from.

To conclude my time with the affable and open Campese, I ask if he would like to have played today:

> It's just a job for people now. Today, the guys are massive. Jonah was unique at the time, but since then that size has become normal. The game is a bash fest now. There's no idea about how to play the game if the coach doesn't tell you. It's robot rugby. The players can't change the game. There are few individuals with that ability now. Think back to the last World Cup, when Japan beat Ireland. Even when they were behind and the plan wasn't working, the Irish weren't able to change what they were

> doing. I was very fortunate to play the game when I did, and in such great teams. Winning the World Cup was great, but there were so many highlights and a real freedom around the game then.

David Campese permanently altered how the game was played and appreciated. His genius, most visibly manifest in his outrageous goose-step, captured the imagination of not just Australia but the world. The rigid, coaching-focused rugby of today's professional game would, I suspect, have been incapable of accommodating a player of such dash and daring, and the game is all the worse for it.

NON EVANS

"I didn't hear the final whistle because everyone jumped on top of me and all I kept saying was, 'Has the whistle gone, has the whistle gone?'"

FACTFILE

Full name: Non Evans MBE

Born: 20 June 1974, Pontarddulais, Swansea, Wales

Positions: Centre, Wing, Full back

Representative teams: Wales sevens, Wales A, Wales

Clubs: Cardiff UWIC, Cardiff Harlequins, Clifton RFC, Tylorstown

Nickname: Nonny

FOR MANY OF us growing up in the 1990s, a childhood Saturday teatime will always be synonymous with *Gladiators*. The energetic and exciting dose of family-friendly television, imported from the USA but filmed in Birmingham, refereed by a gruff Scot, featuring a pantomime villain in Wolf and presented by Ulrika Jonsson with first John Fashanu and then Jeremy Guscott, felt very British. Each week four members of the public would compete against the Gladiators, a group of super-fit athletes clad in lycra, with names like Jet, Hunter, Zodiac and Rhino, across a series of physical events. In an era of just four terrestrial channels, it was hugely popular and

Cobra's visit to my school is something that still comes up in conversation with my friends, 25+ years on. Such was the impact of *Gladiators* that even when you are a rugby legend who has also competed internationally in three other sports – judo, weightlifting and freestyle wrestling – anyone interviewing you is still keen to learn about your appearance on the show.

Evans would be chosen from 26,000 applicants to appear as a contestant on the show in 1997. She would recall in 2021:

> It was massive just to get on it. It's all filmed in two weeks and you ache in places you've never ached before… I was against a girl called Audrey Garland; I'll never forget her name. I had a five-second head start and I kept my lead and, just before the travelator, there's two see-saws. You have to keep your foot behind the yellow mark so you don't jump off it too early. But as I was going on to the second see-saw, [referee] John Anderson called me back and said I'd missed the mark. I knew I'd touched it, to this day, and as I got called back, Audrey catches up, goes past me and wins. She won the whole series – and I'd been beating her easily.[93]

The whole episode is on YouTube and watching the interview afterwards, in which contestants usually just thank their families, she demanded to see a replay. When a fresh-faced Evans is presented with a silver medal, her polite smile can't hide that she just can't wait to take it off.[94]

Evans can laugh about it now, but even 25 years after this experience, the incident clearly still rankles. This little snippet of a remarkable sporting life says a lot about her quest to be the very best in every sport in which she competed.

The Non Evans story begins in Pontarddulais, near Swansea, in 1974. She grew up the middle child of a Welsh-speaking family. Speaking from her home in Mumbles, she tells me:

> I was born with the umbilical cord wrapped three times round my neck, and my mum always jokes I've not stopped moving

> since. I was walking at nine months and running at a year. I was pretty hyperactive as a child, so spent most of my time on the go! I remember pulling my sister along with her trike tied behind my bike, and telling anyone who would listen I wanted muscles!

In an attempt to harness this energy, at the age of 10 she was taken to a judo class and began winning competitions almost immediately. She would become first Welsh then British Champion, before participating in the 1992 Commonwealth Judo Championships – where, at just 16, she was the youngest competitor. Evans was quite small for a judoka (5' 3") but was faster and had a lower centre of gravity than most, and picked up a silver medal. She would go to the Commonwealth Judo Championships again in 1996, winning another a silver, before the sport was admitted to the full Commonwealth Games and she represented Wales there in 2002.

Evans would first pick up a rugby ball when she went to university, at what is now Cardiff Met. This famous institution – which boasts among its alumni Welsh rugby legends Sir Gareth Edwards, J J Williams and Ryan Jones, and more recently several current members of the England rugby squad: Alex Dombrandt, Luke Northmore and Tom Pearson – would be the perfect place for Evans to begin her rugby journey.

Judo, rugby and studying for a degree was still not enough for the young Evans, who at 18 started weightlifting. She would win the World Youth Powerlifting Championship at 21 with a 120 kg deadlift. But as powerlifting wasn't in the Olympics or Commonwealth Games, she switched to weightlifting, becoming Welsh Champion, winning a silver medal at the British Championships, and then going to the 2002 Commonwealth Games – where, by also taking part in the judo competition, she became the first woman to compete in two sports at the same Games.

She excelled at rugby, making her International debut at 22 against Scotland, and quickly made the Welsh full back jersey her own, winning 87 caps between 1996 and 2010. The era in which she played was often a difficult one for the Welsh team, with the women's game still in its infancy. Wales Women didn't play an official game until 1987 – before then, Welsh players were selected to represent Great Britain. Even after 1987, fixtures weren't all that regular, and often against England, and they'd have to wait until 1993 for their first victory.

Evans recalls how it was in these early years:

> I remember reading the small newspaper match report of my debut match versus Scotland, and the reporter likened our standard to that of an U13 boy's game. The media coverage was very limited. Normally our coaches were just using us as a stepping stone to jobs in the men's game, so didn't care too much and moved on pretty quickly. Everything was a battle before we even got on to the pitch.

This period saw the men transition from amateur to professionals when the game went open in 1995, but Welsh women would remain firmly amateur. From 2004 to 2006 a policy of selecting only players based in Wales resulted in a series of poor results – and failure to qualify for the 2006 Women's World Cup. Evans, alongside many of the Welsh national team, had been playing for Clifton in Bristol, so she switched to Tylorstown in the Rhondda – with many of her International colleagues – and the team duly dominated Welsh domestic rugby. The policy was reversed in 2006, and the team immediately delivered their best Six Nations performances, beating Scotland, France, Spain and Ireland in 2006 and Ireland, Scotland and Italy in 2007.

Evans was at the heart of everything good for the team in this era, having also taken on the kicking duties:

> I wasn't a particularly good kicker but it frustrated me for years that we'd lose games by one or two points because we didn't have a goalkicker, so I thought, 'Right, I'm going to practise. My boyfriend at the time was Mark Perego, a flanker – he played for

> Llanelli and Wales and he was so talented, he could kick off both feet, and we just used to go out in the field and kick and kick and kick. I wasn't the best in the world and didn't have any coaching, but we did win quite a few games because I could kick, at least better than anyone in the past.[95]

Her abilities and coolness with the boot came to the fore in the 2009 season, when Evans came back into the team after an horrific leg break during a game against France. Such was its severity that it didn't begin to heal and required an external fixator – a procedure usually reserved for motorbike accidents – where pins are nailed into the bone to keep it in place. It was a long road back, but she made it, and was a key part of the Wales team that secured a Triple Crown and a first-ever win over England. She recollected:

> England were winning 15-13, the clock had gone red, and we had an attack in their 22 and we got a penalty. There was no time to go for the corner so it was either tap and go or go for the posts. It wasn't a particularly difficult kick, but it was what the kick meant, and I was obviously the goal kicker, so I went for it and thankfully it went over and we won 16-15. I didn't hear the final whistle because everyone jumped on top of me and all I kept saying was, "Has the whistle gone, has the whistle gone?"

Wales have only won once since against the old rivals.

It might have been a huge moment for Welsh women's rugby, but the celebrations were muted:

> It was absolutely unbelievable. It was Valentine's Day and the girls had tickets to go to the men's game afterwards, but there weren't enough tickets for everybody so I just went home. It was such an anti-climax: the girls got changed to go and watch the men's game – there was no drinking or anything as we were playing again the following weekend. I remember sitting in my flat with a cup of tea and a Cadbury's Creme Egg, watching the men's game on TV. It was a great victory, though.[96]

This anecdote is the perfect example of the realities of International rugby for most women. Female Internationals have typically had to balance a working week with rugby for club and country – those with families having an extra layer of responsibility to juggle. It was only in 2019 that the England women's rugby team became the first in the world to provide their players with full-time professional contracts, worth £30,000 a year. Since then, France, Ireland and Scotland have offered varying degrees of financial commitment, while Italy's women only get paid expenses.

In 2021, the Welsh Rugby Union announced that it would be offering its female Internationals full-time contracts – well, 12 of them at least – for 12 months, plus between 9 and 15 development contracts for up-and-coming young players. The move came after 123 former International players, including Non Evans, signed a petition in September 2021 calling for the WRU to take action on the issue, among other development points for the women's game.

Wales captain Siwan Lillicrap said of the announcement:

> As players, we feel this is the best model for us at this stage. It's a structure that gives us an opportunity to prepare for the Rugby World Cup in a better place. It will allow some of our players to commit to being professional athletes and also take charge of certain tasks on behalf of the team, for example around analysis, and others to make decisions around their personal circumstances that will allow them to train and recover in a more manageable way, so that we can make strides forward as a group.[97]

The contract was reported by the *Telegraph* to be worth around £19,000 a year, approximately £10,000 below the average annual wage for a woman in Wales. Whilst many players have relished the opportunity to focus on their rugby playing, even just for a few years, the salary and length of contract is still problematic.

"I wouldn't have taken it," former Wales International Alecs Donovan told ESPN. A yoga instructor with her own company, if she'd taken a contract like this, it would have jeopardised the business she'd spent years building.

> You sacrifice so much for the women's game. People haven't gone for promotions in the past, [or] quit their jobs to do a tournament. It's not unheard of – people giving up a lot for women's rugby. Some girls have dropped their wage by half to take these contracts.

She would recall her own experience of trying to balance the challenges of work and elite rugby, after a Wales game in Cardiff: "I think the game finished at 4 p.m. and then I had to drive to teach a yoga class by 5.30 p.m."

For Evans, there would never be any professional rugby contract coming her way. She worked first as a teacher, then as a medical rep for Pfizer, alongside media work in both Welsh and English. Playing largely in England for Clifton, she would train on her own each day and with her team twice a week, and then travel to games at the weekend. She would save all her spare cash to pay for her expenses and keep all her holidays from work to be able to attend training camps and tournaments. This is without mentioning the other sports she was competing in at International level.

Evans recalls her life at the peak of her sporting career:

> I'd get up in the morning, put my bobble hat on, and do my running session on the pitch, my kicking practice or my weights. I'd go to work and then, after work, I'd be training – judo, wrestling, doing my weights or rugby training in the evening. Then I had to do my computer work in the evenings as well, so my life was just packed from the minute I got up to the minute I went to bed. At the weekend it was either judo training or wrestling training, rugby training, matches or competitions.[98]

Danny Cipriani at Wasps in 2009

Ray Gravell prepares for battle of a different sort!

A relaxed Sonny Bill Williams, snapped during the 2011 Rugby World Cup

Geoff Trotter/Wikimedia Commons, CC BY-SA 2.0

England's Andy Ripley is tackled by France's Jean-Pierre Rives in the 1975 Five Nations

PA Images/Alamy

Heather Moyse in full flight at the 2006 Women's Rugby World Cup

Paul Seiser Photography

Finn Russell smells blood! Scotland v. Australia, 2017

www.davidmolloyphotography.com/Wikimedia Commons, CC BY 2.0

Waisale Serevi celebrates winning the 2005 Hong Kong Rugby World Cup Sevens with his son

Bobby Yip/REUTERS/Alamy

Literally hanging up his boots as he enters the seminary: Marnie Cunningham

Courtesy of the Cunningham family

David Campese scoring one of his most celebrated and spectacular tries at the 1991 Rugby World Cup

Ross Kinnaird/PA Images/Alamy

Fellow Wales legend Sir Gareth Edwards presents Non Evans with her 50th cap

Zinzan Brooke leading the haka for the All Blacks in 1994

Neal Simpson/PA Images/Alamy

Christophe Dominici (front) rocks the pink shirt of Stade Français in 2007

www.fabiendany.com/Wikimedia Commons, CC BY-SA 2.5

A rare quiet moment for Dai Bishop in the famous red, white and black of Pontypool

Jeff Morgan/Alamy

The ever-elusive Prince Alexander Obolensky (with ball) turning the Richmond defence inside out for Oxford University in 1936

PA Images/Alamy

A giant even among his teammates: Moss Keane (centre) for Ireland in 1981

PA Images/Alamy

Sergio Parisse on the charge for Stade Français, 2014

Fanny Schertzer/Wikimedia Commons, CC BY 3.0

The official 1972 tour photo of Keith Murdoch

Keystone Pictures USA/Zumapress/Alamy

Jean-Pierre Rives showing off his *Casque d'or* in 1978

S&G/PA Images/Alamy

The emotion is plain to see: James Small during his country's anthem in 1997

Neal Simpson/PA Images/Alamy

No chicken: David Pocock with Alys the Rhode Island Red in his backyard in Canberra, 2016

Emma Pocock/Wikimedia Commons, CC BY-SA 4.0

There was also the media work, with Evans proving a talented and engaging presenter both in Welsh and English. There's one particularly memorable clip which I'd encourage you to seek out on YouTube, where Evans is interviewing an elderly Aberavon fan, Mrs Mainwaring, for S4C. She gives enthusiastic answers to Non's questions but at the end of each take asks, "Any good?", forcing the interview to be reshot several times. Mrs Mainwaring's accidental comic timing couldn't be better, and Evans' patience and politeness is impeccable.[99]

Non Evans retired from rugby in 2010 with a remarkable 87 caps and an amazing 64 tries – a record for the women's game, the same total as fellow maverick David Campese and topped only by Springbok legend Bryan Habana with 67 and Japan's Daisuke Ohata on 69.

Yet, having called it day with the oval ball, there would be no slowing down. Towards the end of her rugby career she also started wrestling, and quickly began placing in championships. She qualified for the 2010 Commonwealth Games in Delhi, becoming the first athlete to compete at the event in three different sports. She would just miss out on a bronze medal by a point.

The following year a career-ending injury, in which her hamstring became detached from the bone, stopped her competing in all sports, and put paid to her dreams of making the 2012 Olympics in London. Evans would, however, find some consolation in 2011 when she was appointed a Member of the Order of the British Empire (MBE) for services to sport, the first-ever female rugby player to receive this award, and was also inducted to the Gorsedd of Bards at the National Eisteddfod (alongside another rugby trailblazer, Nigel Owens). The following year, she was inducted into the Welsh Sports Hall of Fame.

But when Evans finally retired from all elite sport, as for many other athletes, fresh and far more troubling challenges would appear. The gap left by the end of her sporting career was exacerbated when Covid-19 struck. Her life began to unravel after losing her job and her focus, and she began to drink heavily and suffer from depression.

When I said to Evans that coming off the escalator of constant training and performing she'd been on since childhood was always going to be difficult, she laughed and – with a nod to her *Gladiators* days – suggested that a 'travelator' would be more appropriate, but she did agree:

> I've always wanted to be the best at whatever I'm doing, whether it's sport, work, even this interview! And I have a bit of an addictive personality, and this helped me achieve in my career, giving me the focus and motivation to do what I did. But when the sport fell away, there was an emptiness, and other things came in its place. I was never really a drinker, but I did begin to drink to combat the anxiety I was increasingly feeling: I did it just to feel normal. I hit some big lows. And they have been well publicised. But I sought help and have come through them now.

Evans isn't the first player featured in this book to endure some tough times on retiring, and her response when I asked what her definition of a maverick is was telling:

> That's an interesting question. I think deep down a lot are a little insecure. They need to prove something. To someone or themselves. The other two Welsh ones you've written about, Ray [Gravell] and Dai [Bishop], both had this side to them. And I think I certainly have. And my own maverick heroes? Well, Ieuan Evans when I was growing up – he was from the same place, and as there were no female players to look up to, I loved watching him play. Plus Mark [Perego], who helped me a lot when it came to my game, but was also a free spirit himself, and also Alan Jones, my old judo coach – who is still competing now, well into his seventies!

Today, the future is looking bright for Non Evans: living a stone's throw from the sea in Mumbles, working for a large media company and still determined to help inspire others with her commitment and love of sport and healthy lifestyle. She is still coaching, training and offering advice to those looking to be fitter and healthier, and has worked with many top rugby stars and athletes, such as Shane Williams and Jamie Baulch, who turned to Non to help keep them in shape as they gave up full-time professional sport.

As we finish up our discussion, I ask Evans – who was a lively and warm interviewee – if she'd have liked the opportunity, if things had been different, to focus just on rugby and be paid for it:

> To be honest, no. I wouldn't have wanted to miss the opportunity to do different sports. I sometimes joke that if I was a man, I'd be a millionaire. But despite all the juggling and organisation needed, I always enjoyed it, have so many memories and wouldn't have had it any other way.

The women's game is looking forward to a stronger future too. Yes, there are still great inequalities within it, both compared to the men's game and within its own competitions, where there are frequent mismatches, but its progress is clear.

The 2022 Women's Six Nations was run on a separate calendar to the men's, now has its own title sponsor (social media giant TikTok) and, with each fixture broadcast live in participating countries for the first time, enjoyed record-breaking viewing figures as well as attendance numbers. Fresh from the roll-out of professional contracts for some of the squad, Wales finished third in the Championship, their highest-place finish since 2009.

The almost superhuman drive required to compete at an elite level of sport is rare, but Evans summoned it up for five different sports – rugby, judo, wrestling, weightlifting and powerlifting – for over 20 years. All whilst remaining amateur and juggling competing with first her studies, then full-time work. If a man had done all this, he'd be one of the most famous athletes in the world. And yes, this single-minded streak did feed into some of the struggles following the end of her career. And no, she may not have won on *Gladiators*, but there are few warriors in the world of rugby stronger than Non Evans.

ZINZAN BROOKE

"I knew I could do it, so I just did."

FACTFILE

Full name: Zinzan Valentine Brooke

Born: 14 February 1965, Waiuku, New Zealand

Positions: Flanker, No. 8

Representative teams: New Zealand Māori, New Zealand XV, New Zealand sevens, Barbarians, New Zealand

Clubs: Auckland, Lazio, Casale (both Italy), Auckland Blues, Harlequins, Coventry, Windsor (England)

Nickname: Zinny

YouTube is an absolute treasure trove for the rugby fan. And an even more invaluable resource for the rugby writer. Thanks to that site, I've been able to hear what long-departed players sounded like, see fantastic tries once thought lost to history and sample a little of the feverish atmosphere at places like Pretoria, Pontypool and Limerick. It's such a good resource that it can be hard to navigate away – there's always another try, red card or 'you won't believe this' moment available at a click of button. I've watched a LOT of rugby on YouTube. But I doubt there are many more joyous videos than that of Zinzan Brooke scoring a drop goal at the World Cup in 1995.

In the final moments of a tight game, when a team is losing by just a few points and on the attack, the idea of the drop goal always springs to mind. It's a way of cracking even the meanest defence and doesn't require the opposition to make a mistake. But there's a finality to them: score and you will win, miss and the attack is likely to be over and the game is probably gone. Perhaps as a result, they are decreasing in popularity. In 106 International appearances, Johnny Sexton has scored just four. Dan Carter was a little more prolific but still had only eight in 112 games, Owen Farrell has slotted three in 99 appearances, whilst fellow maverick Finn Russell has none in 57. Johnny Wilkinson, perhaps unsurprisingly, is the leading drop-kicker in the history of International rugby, with 36 in 97 games for England.

If drop goals are already a rare treat for the rugby fan, there's an extra frisson of excitement when the scorer isn't a back but a forward – and it's even further enhanced when it's popped over from a long distance in a huge game.

This was the case in 1995 when Brooke scored the first of his three International drop goals in a World Cup semi-final against England. This game will always be remembered for the four tries scored by a 20-year-old Jonah Lomu, but there was one other moment of All Black magic. The moment began with a searing kick downfield from Brooke's younger brother Robin, a lock with a similar skillset, into the England 22.

Will Carling boots it clear but fails to find touch and the ball bounces about 10 metres inside the Kiwi half. Brooke the elder catches it, takes a few steps forward and, with Lomu on his left flank, the already shellshocked England defence back off a little. But instead of passing, he looks up and unleashes a huge kick towards the posts from about 45 metres – or as legendary Kiwi commentator Keith Quinn measures it, "a million miles out". It sails through the uprights, a beaming Brooke lifts both arms in triumph as he jogs back into his defensive position and his team would canter to a 45-29 win.

The moment has gone into rugby folklore, and Brooke would recall it in his typically confident style:

> That was a day when everything went right for us... take my drop goal, although when people tell me that No. 8s aren't supposed to do that sort of thing, I reply, "Then why did I spend all that time with Grant Fox before all those training sessions in Auckland having kicking competitions?" You practise these things and if the chance comes along, you have to have confidence in your own ability. Mind you, Graeme Bachop and Frank Bunce were inside me shouting, "No, Zinny, don't do it..."[100]

He would add, when asked about how this fitted into his reputation as a notorious risk taker, "I thought: 'How can I upstage Jonah?' I knew I could do it, so I just did. I knew it was going straight through the sticks. Jonah scored four tries, but everyone remembers the drop goal."[101]

A year later he would do it again, at an even more significant moment in a far tighter match versus South Africa at Loftus Versfeld, Pretoria. The All Blacks won the first Test in the series 19-23, and late in the second Test the score is 30-26 to them when Brooke is passed the ball in midfield, about 30 metres out. He glances up and calmly slots over a drop-goal for a 33-26 lead. Despite intense pressure for the rest of the match, the All Blacks hold firm and seal their first-ever series victory in South Africa.

He added a third drop goal for good measure against Wales the following year at Wembley, their temporary home whilst the Millennium Stadium was being redeveloped – enabling him to claim the honour of being the only rugby player to have 'scored a goal at Wembley'. Comfortable kicking with both feet, his trio of drops gives him a higher tally than illustrious Kiwi kickers Carlos Spencer, now retired (0), Aaron Cruden (1) and Beauden Barrett (2 so far).

Brooke would also score 17 tries in 58 International appearances for the All Blacks, and is considered one of their all-time-great No. 8s. He combined the power and precision of a forward with the running and kicking skills of a back, which made him an extremely mobile and effective fixture in the team. In total he would score a remarkable 161 tries in first-team games.

Bill McLaren wrote of him: "He could have filled any position in the All Blacks side and would not have looked out of place. Scrum half or full back, either would have been meat or drink to him."[102]

Born on Valentine's Day in 1965, his original name was Murray Zinzan Brooke, but he changed it by deed poll to Zinzan Valentine Brooke whilst still in primary school. His unusual first name has a long history in the Brooke family, though its precise origins are uncertain. He is related to another notable New Zealand sporting family, Test cricketer Parke Gerald Zinzan 'Zin' Harris and his sons – both also International players – Chris Zinzan Harris and Ben Zinzan Harris. In various articles I've seen the name described as being of Indian, Albanian or Italian provenance. Chris Zinzan Harris told journalists a story of its origins being found with an adventurer called Zingario, who travelled from Italy (where *zingaro* means 'gypsy') in the sixteenth century, became an equerry in the court of Henry VIII and changed his name to Zinzan.

He is not the only illustrious forefather in the clan. There's also a Brooke family heirloom, an old silver service, given to another ancestor, a sea captain, and inscribed with the passengers' gratitude for his fighting off Chinese pirates.

There's certainly a little bit of magic in the Brooke family. In addition to their mysterious European heritage, they are also proud to have Māori blood, and Brooke is a member of the Ngāpuhi *iwi* (the word *iwi* means a 'people' or 'folk' and though it can be translated as 'tribe' or 'clan', it can also refer to a larger grouping of tribes). I've already noted one brother, Robin, who played lock for Auckland and New Zealand Māori and won 62 caps for New Zealand – 39 alongside Zinzan – and another, Marty, was also a fine player who turned out for Auckland, Southland and New Zealand Māori. In the next generation, Zinzan's 20-year-old son Lucas, born and raised in England, has been at London Irish since he was 13 and has won caps for the Red Rose at U20 level.

Born in Waiuku, a rural town in the Auckland region in the North Island, Brooke grew up on a farm. It was there, in the paddock, that he first began playing rugby with his brothers. As he would recall, his rugby origins were modest:

> I played for the local village team. It wasn't much to talk about. Dad would shake a tree and whoever fell out would end up in the side. Most of the pitches were farm paddocks and we often had to clear sheep off the pitch or fish out balls from the river. I can't say I thought too much then about being an All Black. I just wanted to work on the farm, become a shearer.[103]

He began to excel at the game while in high school at Mahurangi College, originally as a prop, and it wasn't until he was selected for New Zealand U17s and started working his way up through the All Black youth teams that he began to imagine he had a big future in the game.

Brooke would begin making a name for himself playing No. 8 for Auckland. After fewer than ten games for them, in addition to representing New Zealand at sevens, it was a surprise to many when he was selected to make his full All Black debut against Argentina at the 1987 World Cup. He was just 22, and would not only score a try, but being the only Māori in the side, was asked to lead the haka.

It would, however, be his only appearance at this World Cup, which the All Blacks would go on to win on home soil. The legendary Wayne 'Buck' Shelford was ahead of him in the pecking order, alongside A J Whetton and Michael Jones in a high-class back row, and Brooke had to wait until 1989 to win his second Test cap. And not until 1990, when Shelford was sensationally dropped after leading New Zealand in 14 Test matches undefeated, did Brooke get his chance as the new first-choice All Black No. 8.

Taking the place of a legend is always a difficult, and few legends were bigger than Shelford. An ultra-physical hardman with a different, more direct, style to Brooke, he was beloved by All Black fans, who began a national campaign to 'Bring back Buck'. Shelford would never play another Test, but signs urging the All Blacks management to reinstate him would appear for years to come. And not just at rugby matches, but also at cricket, soccer and even the Olympics. Look carefully at major events where New Zealanders gather and even today you might see one.

The 1991 World Cup in England would prove a disappointment, with the New Zealanders looking stodgy in a semi-final loss compared to the quicksilver Australia side of another of our mavericks, David Campese. Their attempts to retain the Webb Ellis Cup weren't helped by the absence of their influential flanker Michael Jones, who missed three Sunday games, including the semi-final, due to his religious beliefs, nor by the departure of some big names, such as Frano Botica, to rugby league. Brooke himself was also linked regularly with a change of codes to the Manly Sea Eagles but never did make that switch.

When Laurie Mains took over as the New Zealand coach in 1992, he wasn't initially enamoured with Brooke, with doubts over his work ethic. One of the selectors of that time, Peter Thorburn, would neatly articulate it when he said, "Laurie was not the sort of coach that openly accepted forwards who were a bit fancy."[104] Zinzan certainly was a bit fancy at times. And when he was late returning to an All Black camp from a spell playing in Italy, he was dropped for Arran Pene.

But Brooke would soon win over his dogmatic new coach. Thorburn recalled:

> It was a matter of timing. Zinny was always going to be a very, very good All Black because of the skills he had and his competitive nature. He was tough. He might have shown his

> pain a bit more than Buck did, but he was as tough as old boots. You don't last that long at the top level if you're not hard.

From 1992 to 1997, Brooke was the best No. 8 in New Zealand, and probably the world. In a book from this era, Wayne Shelford would write. "(I) admire him greatly even though he is my rival… Always entertaining and lively off the pitch."[105]

Another New Zealand great, Sir Colin 'Pinetree' Meads, was also impressed with Brooke:

> I was lucky enough to be manager for a time when he was playing. Zinny was one of the great tourists. He'd have been great in my day. His sheer competitiveness, allied to the mercurial things he could do around the field with the ball.[106]

Zinzan would score a try in the famous 1992 'Return Test' victory over a South African team playing their first game since their post-apartheid readmission to International rugby. It was classic Brooke: New Zealand had been awarded a penalty and as the Springboks turned their backs expecting a kick, he saw a chance, tapped it and ran through a bewildered defence to cross for the first try of the match. His ability to shape a game in his own image was rarely better than in this historic fixture, after which the local press labelled him the 'Colossus of Ellis Park'.

In a match against the South of Scotland in 1993, he scored four tries in 84-5 win, the kind of result that would herald the end of these kind of fixtures for tourists but saw him described by Scottish great John Rutherford as "the most skilful forward in the world." The following year he'd be named New Zealand Player of the Year and be a part of a team that secured a series win over South Africa.

In 1995, he'd score that drop goal against England, but World Cup glory would remain elusive. Whilst he avoided the sickness bug that struck the All Blacks squad before the final against South Africa (with rumours persisting that they were intentionally poisoned, perhaps by a betting syndicate), the emotional tide of the Springboks would wash away their chances. He would, however, gain an element of revenge in 1996, when his drop kicking again came to the fore in securing an historic first series win on South African soil.

His fine form continued through 1997, with two tries in his 50th Test match – against Australia – slotting a third and final International drop goal against Wales and then making his final All Blacks appearance in a pulsating 26-26 draw with England at Twickenham.

As rugby entered its brave new world of professionalism, Brooke was the kind of talented and eye-catching player that the modern game increasingly demanded. In the last years of the amateur era, Brooke was part of a fantastically successful Auckland team that included John Kirwan, Grant Fox, Sean Fitzpatrick and Olo Brown, to name just a few.

He also, like David Campese, had regular spells in Italy during the New Zealand off-season. As the game went open and money began to legitimately flow into it, he signed off his domestic career by leading Auckland to consecutive Super 12 titles in 1996 and 1997, before heading to London to sign for Harlequins and catch a late-career payday. After that, he would have a spell as a coach at Quins before playing for Coventry and at amateur level for Windsor.

Father of six Brooke settled in Windsor, just outside London, when he retired, for a while running a boutique bed and breakfast with his wife Ali. He is now CEO of a successful recruitment business for the construction industry, and an established part of the community – the Windsor and Eton Brewery brought out a 3.7% Red Bitter called Zinzan's World Cup Drop in 2015 to mark the World Cup coming to England. Slightly randomly, a successful racing greyhound in Australia was also named Zinzan Brooke.

His unconventional spirit returned during the Covid-19 pandemic, when he reactivated a largely dormant Twitter account to regularly comment, share and like Tweets casting doubt on the official response to the pandemic. He has retweeted posts claiming that "masks can harm children in schools", criticised the speed of the vaccine roll-out, placed suspicion on the role of 'big pharma' and shared support for the use of hydroxychloroquine – a drug touted by Donald Trump as a possible cure to Covid-19 – among other views.

Brooke's previously unknown interest in epidemiology made the news in New Zealand, where leading microbiologist Associate Professor Siouxsie Wiles suggested that he "should stick to what he's good at", before questioning whether he had any expertise to make his claims or support those of others, adding, "You wouldn't ring me up and ask me about the strategy of the next All Blacks games."

Kiwi epidemiologist Michael Baker sympathised with Brooke but was concerned that it is "potentially harmful" when high-profile people spread disinformation: "Zinzan Brooke has always struck me as a decent person. Many people use their positions responsibly – I think of John Kirwan and mental health. It's a huge opportunity to be a force for good, so I hope sports people do recognise that and take that opportunity to be real leaders."[107]

In response to the coverage from New Zealand, Brooke tweeted on 7 March 2021:

> Wow haven't I stirred the pot! I thought you'd forgotten about me. But guess what, like all of us we have a voice and Ali and I have learnt a lot through this last year of madness. I've read some strong opinions, yes I've retired but you never lose that fight, so bring it on...

But we've all heard enough about Covid-19 for one lifetime – let's come back to rugby.

Zinzan Brooke was a special player, in a strong era of mavericks. There was something about beginning in the amateur game and finishing in the professional era that yielded a bumper crop of free spirits. That mix of real-world experience and then the money, time and exposure that being a full-time player brings created some very memorable characters.

He scored and created tries (and drop goals), was an enormous physical presence in defence as well as attack with a huge spin pass, and as a great reader of the game was able to dictate terms against even the toughest opponents. Whilst primarily a No. 8, he was also capable of playing anywhere in the back row. His strength would pour cement across the back of his own scrum and his tackling ended many a promising attack by the opposition.

Legendary commentator Bill McLaren described him as the "most skilful forward it has ever been my good fortune to see in action" and named him in his all-time XV – though, with immense credit to Brooke's flexibility, he selected him at No.6, with Mervyn Davies taking the No. 8 spot. Let's give McLaren the final word, with his own recollection of a particularly memorable demonstration of Brooke's abilities:

> It was the Hong Kong Sevens, New Zealand were behind to their arch-rivals Fiji with time almost up and were first to the touchdown to prevent an opposition try that would have sealed it. Touching down quickly, Brooke grabbed the ball, ran to the 22 and, left footed, placed the restart kick with such pinpoint accuracy in behind the Fijian defender, he was able to gather the bounce, run through and score the clinching try at the other end... Sometime later when I congratulated Zinzan on his astonishing skill level he just laughed and then said, "Yeah, bloody great kick, wasn't it?"[108]

CHRISTOPHE DOMINICI

"If I had been happy, I would not have played rugby and I might have done a lot more stupid things."

FACTFILE

Full name: Christophe Philippe Didier Dominici
Born: 20 May 1972, Toulon, Provence, France
Died: 24 November 2020, Saint-Cloud, Paris, France
Position: Winger
Representative teams: Barbarians, French Barbarians, France
Clubs: Solliès-Pont, La Valette, Toulon, Stade Français
Nickname: Domi

THE FAMOUS FRENCH daily sports paper *L'Équipe* has always had an eye for a striking front cover, and never more so than the one they published the day after Christophe Dominici died. The picture that filled the page is of Dominici, lined up for the anthem before a World Cup match in 2003. He has his arms tightly intertwined with two far bigger teammates: they dwarf him, and we see only their shoulders. His shirt is bright blue and sponsor-free, with your eye drawn to the golden cockerel on its red shield. Dominici looks skyward, a smile forming on his handsome face, which enjoys a soft glow from the light directly upon him. There's more than a hint – intentional, I am sure – of the religious in the picture, as if his image might inspire a stained-glass window, or at another time have been painted by Caravaggio or Michelangelo, or one of the Pre-Raphaelites.

The day that this edition of *L'Équipe* was published, another superstar, Diego Maradona, died. The Argentinian graced the cover of another special cover the next day, this time in *Le Parisien*: like Dominici, Maradona is at a World Cup and again he is looking straight up, bathed in light. But the Argentinian is crying, and alone.

Dominici, with his teammates flanking him, looks small but unbowed, looking up into the sky.

This is how we remember him: as being something different, within some wonderful teams.

He often was. Until he wasn't.

But let's start with the man at his very best – let's travel to Twickenham on Halloween 1999.

It was the Rugby World Cup semi-final, between France and New Zealand. In the June of that year, a French team that included Dominici had been beaten 54-7 in Wellington. Earlier in the tournament, the Kiwis had beaten Italy 101-3, in a grisly mismatch.

The All Blacks – boasting the likes of Jonah Lomu, Christian Cullen, Andrew Mehrtens, Josh Kronfeld and Taine Randell – were firm favourites pre-match and had galloped into a 17-10 lead by the end of the first half.

Lomu had already scored a trademark try, but in the changing room at half-time, it was Dominici who urged his colleagues to believe that despite what the scoreboard said, they had the All Blacks on the ropes.

"I have looked into the eyes of Jonah Lomu," he told the team. "They are shit scared of us."

Now, let us remember that Dominici, at 5'7" and 12st 12lb, was positively impish when compared to his opposing wings that day: Lomu, who loomed large at 6' 5" and nearly 19st, and Tana Umaga, a mere 6' 2" and 16st.

Two rapid drop goals followed by a pair of penalties, all from Christophe Lamaison, brought France within two points – at which point Dominici turned his big half-time talk into action. France turned the ball over on the halfway and he read a long kick by Fabien Galthié perfectly. There's a moment of hesitation between two All Blacks as it fizzes between them, then Dominici whizzes forward, taking the ball one-handed on the bounce, sprinting out of a desperate tackle, zooming down the left wing then turning inside and touching down. He pops up on his knees, his happy face looking around, as one of the French substitutes warming up behind the posts runs over, ruffles his hair and gives him a very Gallic kiss on the forehead.

The French floodgates would open, with two more tries rounding off a stunning 43-31 win in a game widely viewed as the greatest the World Cup has ever seen. As the ESPN report breathlessly concluded:

> France looked down and out in London, trailing by fourteen points early in the second half, only to come off the ropes and hand the All Blacks the mother and father of pastings. After today, future generations of New Zealand children will be sent to bed with the warning, "or else Benazzi/Magne/Lamaison/Galthié will come to get you." France caused an upset of titanic proportions... In doing so, they confounded the bookies, the press and the All Blacks, who will never again believe all they read in print.[109]

To think that Dominici had what he would later understand to be a panic attack on the morning of the match. This, though, gave an indication of what would befall him a year to the day after this semi-final epic, when on 31 October 2000 he was put into an induced coma, having stayed awake for 25 days straight.

> I couldn't sleep any more. I had no appetite for life. I'd had a lot of problems with my ex-partner. When you are hungry, you want to devour life, but I'd lost that desire. I had been overtaken

> by emotion and stress, but I didn't want to take medicine so that was the only solution.

The emotional problems were fuelled in part by a burnout from France's World Cup run (they would eventually lose in the final to Australia) and the ensuing attention: "It was a euphoric period, and I didn't know how to say no; I never had a break."

By autumn 2000, the rigour of the professional game was also taking its toll: "You don't play for yourself, you play for a club. It's a business and it's your work unless you get ill; sport is not the priority like it should be."[110]

And finally, what led the 28-year-old Dominici to breaking point was a tragic and overwhelming chain of events in his personal life. The death of his older sister, Pascale, in a road accident when he was 14 would forever haunt Dominici. He opened up about how it had affected him in his autobiography, *Bleu à l'Âme* ('Blue to the Soul'), published in 2007:

> When she died, I went into self-defence. I resented the whole world. Pascale helped me with my homework and taught me to dance.
>
> The blues of my childhood always caught up with me. I feel like I am naked, helpless. I plunge into melancholy. I give free rein to my self-destructive ideas. I think I am going to die, suffocated or crushed under an invisible weight. I cannot stand up. I stay in bed for days, curled up like a foetus.[111]

Shortly after the 1999 World Cup, his best friend since childhood was killed in what was rumoured to be a gangland murder. Then another close friend, his psychologist Pierre Cesano, died of an illness and not long afterwards his partner of 12 years walked out on him. In his autobiography, he also revealed that he had been abused as a child, "brutalised" being the word he used in the book.

These problems all came together and pushed Dominici into a deep depression followed by a full nervous breakdown. He would come out of the medically induced coma and return to play for France within a few years, but the damage this episode did would remain. He said in his book:

> When I woke up, I felt good physically, all my physical potential had returned, but psychologically it was hard to come back. In that situation you hang on to little things, little turning points, like the day when you feel you are getting speed back.[112]

Christophe Dominici was born in the rugby-mad city of Toulon, to a Corsican family who ran a flower and vegetable business. He had an often troubled childhood, with sport being a key outlet for his energies – although it was football, not rugby, that was his first focus. Such was his footballing talent that he trained with one of France's premier clubs, AS Monaco. There he met future World Cup-winner Lilian Thuram, with whom he forged a lifelong friendship.

Rugby would in the end win out over football for his affections, but not without some help from a typically unorthodox quarter:

> My mother saw a medium and the clairvoyant told her that her son had a gift. My mother convinced herself that this 'gift' was rugby. She kept telling me: "You will be in the French team, my son."
>
> "But, mom, you made me a dwarf! Why do you want me to be in the French team with my 1.72m [5ft 7ins] and my 68 kilos [10st 10lbs], when there are guys who have arms like thighs and thighs like trees?"[113]

Although he would often be the smallest, lightest man on the field, it never held him back. He started playing club rugby for Solliès-Pont at just 17, before joining second-tier RC La Valette on the Côte d'Azur two years later. There he was often playing at fly half or centre, but when he moved to his home-town club of Toulon in 1993 at age of 21, he switched to the wing.

He spent four years lighting up the pitch for Toulon, but then in 1997, as the game shifted to professionalism, he asked for a salary increase and was refused. So in the newly found spirit of free enterprise that was now swirling around the game, he and a few teammates decided to call Max Guazzini, a radio station tycoon and president of the newly promoted Stade Français, who was dedicated to making the club the greatest in France.

The call went well, and Dominici would soon be heading north to the capital. In his first season they won the French championship – the first of five he would win with the Parisian giants, alongside two Heineken cups, as Stade Français became one of the most famous clubs in world.

Guazzini's approach to the game matched Dominici's, particularly when it came to their eye-catching and unique kits. Typically bright pink, they have featured garlands of flowers, David Bowie-esque lightning bolts, hippy-style swirls and one inspired by Andy Warhol with bold, bright pop art-style multicoloured images of Blanche de Castille – wife of Louis VIII and mother to the saintly Louis IX. You have to Google this one to believe it!

Along with the garish kits came nude calendars of the players, huge spectacles at their home games and a steady stream of trophies. French rugby was typically orientated around the south, with clubs like Toulon, Toulouse, Clermont Auvergne and Castres all proud of their tough regional identities. Stade Français, newcomers to the top table and based in the capital in the north, embraced their own identity and flaunted it in the faces of their more-established rivals.

Dominici made his International bow in the 1998 Five Nations with a try-scoring debut against England, and would play for the national team for the next nine years. The following year would be the heroics against New Zealand, in the first of three World Cups that he'd illuminate. In 2003 he scored four tries, before France were outfought in the semi-finals by England. Four years later, on home soil, they'd beat New

Zealand in the quarter finals in another breathless encounter, but would again fall short against England in the semis. The defeat to Argentina in the Bronze Medal decider of this 2007 World Cup would be his final match for France.

Although the World Cup thrice eluded Dominici, he had a glittering International career, scoring 25 tries from 67 caps and winning four Five/Six Nations titles, including Grand Slams in 1998 and 2004.

A winger of considerable flair, he loved entertaining the crowd – and occasionally this would lead to a mistake, the most famous of which came against Italy in a 2004 Six Nations game. With France 13-0 up, he receives the ball not far into the Italian half, bursts through the defensive line and his pace takes him round the remaining opposition. He crosses the try line and, at speed, tries to place the ball casually down with one hand. But instead, he drops it and tumbles awkwardly off the pitch, the ball trickling limply after him. He pops up, slightly blows out his cheeks and glances at the touch judge. He knows it's no try, as do the 80,000 in the ground.

The Irish commentator would say, "He's dropped it! Well, I think in our part of the world, the word is Eejit," before adding, "Well, that's straight to bed with no supper for him."

French coach Bernard Laporte was apoplectic post-match:

> It was unacceptable and an imbecilic thing to do. It's a lack of respect for the team, for all the work that has been done during the week and for himself. It's a professional fault but you cannot ban a player for life because of a mistake, however stupid...[114]

France went on to win 25-0, however, on their road to a Grand Slam, so no harm was done in the end!

In 2008, the year following his International retirement, he hung up his boots for the final time. Shoulder and ankle injuries were taking their toll and he felt it unlikely he'd make the next World Cup in 2011.

His first job post-retirement was as an assistant coach at Stade Français under Ewen McKenzie, but they were both relieved of their duties after just over a year following a disappointing start to the 2009/10 season. He would then become a pundit and commentator on French TV and radio. Several rugby luminaries have appeared on the BBC's *Strictly Come Dancing* – Gavin Henson, Ugo Monye and Martin Offiah, to name just a few – and Dominici followed suit and competed in *Danse avec les stars*, the French version. Watching his tango to Queen's 'Bohemian Rhapsody' on YouTube, you can see a strong level of focus but he is far from relaxed, and we see none of the flair he'd displayed on the rugby pitch. He and his partner, French model and dancer Candice Pascal, were the first to be eliminated in that series.

Dominici's life took a significant turn for the worse when he became involved with an Emirati consortium bidding to buy Béziers, a once proud and successful club, then suffering serious financial difficulties. Exactly what happened is still unclear, and will probably never be fully known, but Dominici became the face of this very public bid. Plans were discussed to bring in a host of French Internationals and elite Southern Hemisphere talent. But after extensive work, the plans turned to dust when French rugby administrators doubted the validity of the bid and blocked its progress. The UAE money walked away, and Dominici was left bereft:

> It is an obvious lack of respect. We wanted to make this club the biggest in Europe. We suffered an injustice, an offence. I have been on this project for two and a half months, day and night. I wanted to build a great team with national and International players, to make this club the largest in Europe.[115]

He'd spoken to a host of his former teammates, including Rodrigo Roncero, Juan-Martín Hernández and Frédéric Michalak, to get them to agree in principle to become involved with the relaunched Beziers.

One can imagine how difficult the follow-up conversations must have been.

The Mayor of Beziers, Robert Ménard – previously supportive of the project – blasted Dominici in public:

> By making believe things of which he did not have the beginning of a proof, Mr Dominici did a terrible harm to this club and to this city... He is no longer welcome in this town hall... He was a huge rugby player but he should have stuck to that reputation.[116]

Dominici's mental health went into a rapid decline. A bizarre and unpleasant incident at a hat shop in Sanary-sur-Mer on the French Riviera in July 2020 gave a worrying indicator of his state of mind. Entering the store shirtless, he asked to try on the "most expensive hat in the store" and after finding a Panama to his liking, asked the shop assistant to let him take it away and return to pay later. When she declined, he pushed her to the floor and the police were called, although no charges would be brought.

On 23 November 2020 he told his partner he was going out to buy some cigarettes. She would never see him alive again.

Shortly before three o'clock the following day, he climbed to the roof of the abandoned Sully army barracks in Paris' Saint-Cloud Park, the home of Marie Antoinette's famous rose garden. From the roof he'd have seen the River Seine and panoramic views across the capital, a city where he had made such amazing memories for club and country and where he was deeply loved. It would be the last thing he'd see. No one saw him fall, but his body was found on the ground, and he would be declared dead from his injuries shortly afterwards.

Christophe Dominici was 48 years old.

He left behind his partner, Loretta, and two daughters, Chiara and Mia.

His tragic and untimely death was met with shock and sadness across the rugby world.

"He left his mark on a whole generation of rugby," the French Rugby Federation said. "Today the rugby family has brutally lost a legend, an emblematic player."

Former teammate Frédéric Michalak, who played in two World Cups with Dominici, described to *L'Équipe* his huge influence on young Internationals breaking through:

> He was a bit like our big brother. He had a strong character while being sensitive at the same time. He was always there for us, reassuring us. I shared many good times with him.
>
> He had exceptional qualities as a player, you could see in his eyes how determined he was. As an opponent, Domi was formidable. He was hard, he sacrificed himself for the jersey he wore. Thanks to his aura, he'd send the others to get stuck in.

Fellow wing, the South African Bryan Habana greatly admired Dominici's style: "For me he represented all of the good things about rugby. He had so much energy and was so positive whenever we had a conversation. Rugby has lost a legend."

Jonny Wilkinson, who played against him for England in two World Cup semi-finals, included him in his own World XV: "His opportunism, his flair, his game reading, his sheer explosivity is something that sticks in my mind."

The tributes would flow for weeks from all quarters of French society. Robert Ménard, the mayor of Beziers, would now strike a different tone after the death of the man he had so publicly hung out to dry:

> He was an endearing boy. Someone complicated, with unease. He represented people who lied to us and who may have lied to him. We will forget that and remember that he was a boy who could seduce or exasperate, but who left no one indifferent.[117]

French rugby, which I think could have done more to help Dominici in life, has acted quickly to ensure he will not be forgotten in death. The stadium where Stade Français train has been renamed the Christophe-Dominici Stadium and the Paris outfit have allied with Toulon – the other club which he represented professionally – to create a trophy in his name, which they will play for each time they meet each other. A popular youth tournament has also been started in his name.

In a country that has always had players to light up the game, Dominici shone particularly brightly. Quick, elusive and charismatic, he proved a counterpoint to the growing giants of the modern game as typified by Jonah Lomu, showing the world there was still space for someone of his build at the top of the sport. The famous win over New Zealand in 1999 continues to be talked about as the greatest-ever World Cup game, and his medal haul for club and country was extraordinary.

But with the ups came the downs, and a lifelong battle with his mental health. The title of his book, which translates as 'Blue to the Soul', references both the national shirt he wore with such pride, and his depression. Despite the challenges, he will always have a place in rugby fans' hearts, and it's impossible to watch the compilations of his tries (yes, even that fumble v. Italy) without a smile on your face.

It's players like Dominici that remind you that rugby is still just a game and should be fun. Seeing someone play the sport at the highest level but with the same childlike enthusiasm many of us had when we first picked up a ball is a rare treat. I hope there's still a place for the Dominicis of the game, and I hope they are better looked after.

Of all the tributes I've read to Dominici, it's one from Thomas Lombard, his former Stade Français teammate, that stuck most with me. He sums up his loss poignantly: "Life is more monotonous without Christophe."

Even if he did go too soon, we were lucky to have him.

DAI BISHOP

"He always went his own way and he absolutely never stuck to the approved script."

FACTFILE

Full name: David 'Dai' Joseph Bishop

Born: 31 October 1960, Cardiff, Wales

Position: Scrum half

Representative teams: Wales, Great Britain (rugby league), Wales (rugby union)

Clubs: Cardiff, Ebbw Vale, Pontypool (rugby union); Hull Kingston Rovers, Salford, London Crusaders (rugby league)

Nickname: Bish

STATUES ARE A bit controversial right now. Who is depicted? Who isn't? How much should we say about their lives? Once up, should they stay up? I could go on. But whilst there's a reassessment of many sculptures, there are two in Cardiff that I doubt will ever come down. One is on Queen Street, looking towards the castle – the fact that he sometimes has a traffic cone on his head is no indication of a lack of respect. This is, of course, the statue of Aneurin Bevan, a man who went down the mines at 13, but would in 1948, as Labour Minister of Health, found the National Health Service.

The other is arguably the other great icon of twentieth-century Wales, Gareth Edwards, whose statute is situated incongruously by the Primark in St David's Shopping Centre. Erected in 1982, just four years after he retired, it depicts Edwards in bronze, replete with shaggy mid Seventies hair, looking keenly up and about to deliver a bullet pass into the arms of a teammate. It captures his presence well and provides a permanent reminder to Cardiff shoppers of what a classic scrum half looks like, or at least the Welsh idea of one.

Edwards remains the template for what the Welsh public think an International scrum half should be – quick, sharp and with a pass out of both hands. Terry Holmes did a solid turn in the unenviable job of filling Edwards' huge shoes. The two Roberts, Howley and Jones, regularly excelled but often in poor Wales teams. Dwayne Peel and Rhys Webb have their supporters and the Lions tours to argue their case. Mike Phillips – despite his caps and medals (not to mention self-confidence) – never clicked for some, who were unable to accept his more abrasive and physical style of play, however effective it might be. Looking at the current crop of Welsh No. 9s, I don't think it's unfair to say that (at the time of writing, at least) they are yet to truly capture their public's imagination.

There is another Cardiff boy, however, who came through just as Edwards was finishing. Whilst he will never get a statue, he has a huge place in the affections of a particular corner of Wales. A sometimes troubled maverick, his talent was matched only by his self-belief and the scorn with which some of the Welsh rugby administration regarded him.

The late John Billot of the *Western Mail* called him "the best scrum half in Welsh rugby since the Second World War". Ex-Neath rugby supremo Brian Thomas called him the finest player in the northern hemisphere. Former England scrum half Richard Hill said he was, for a period in the 1980s, not just the best in the British Isles, but in the whole world.

Most people know him as Bish. I of course mean David 'Dai' Bishop, one of the biggest and most controversial figures in Welsh rugby in the 1980s.

There are plenty of great stories to tell about one of the truly great characters of Welsh rugby, but perhaps we can begin on 23 January 1988, at Pontypool Park for the Schweppes Cup third-round fixture against Swansea RFC. Bishop lines up alongside another livewire, Mark Ring, in the half backs, with the late, lamented Eddie Butler – not yet fully swapped from pitch to commentary box or newspaper pages – also part of a fearsome Pooler pack. The visitors have brought a typically strong line-up, with two Moriarty brothers among the pick of the forwards and a Lions axis at 9 and 10, where Tony Clement and Robert Jones are pulling the strings for the All Whites.

The world of professionalism and regional rugby is still years away, and the rain-soaked ground is packed with around 12,000 fans. Golfing umbrellas, shell suits and moustaches abound as the camera pans across the packed bank. Many of the sponsors don't exist anymore – whither Hunter's Bitter? And some of the men watching would still have done a shift down the pit before a quick shower, a splash of Old Spice and heading straight up to Pontypool Park.

It's a big game, and with the Five Nations approaching, the commentator makes a point of highlighting by name some of the Welsh selectors in the crowd. Rewatching the game, it's a tight, physical, slightly niggly affair – with the mud soon rendering the kits useless, making it near impossible to see who's who, particularly during some of the frequent dust-ups.

Bishop is at the heart of everything creative for the home team and, one long-distance penalty in the bag, gets another chance late on. The kick is awarded after Bishop scoops the ball up one handed and as he tries to circumnavigate the Swansea defence is clattered in the throat and barged off the pitch by Paul Moriarty. Today it would be a red card, but then just a shake of the head from the referee, a bit of lip from an irate ball boy towards the Swansea man and the indication of a penalty.

The pitch is by now an absolute mudbath: there's no grass to be seen, let alone any markings. Just inside his own half,

Bishop points towards the post and then starts digging into the sodden ground with his boot. He must do this a dozen times to find a solid-enough nest for the ball. He takes around 10 steps back, and then runs full pelt at the ball, mud splashing as he does, and thwack, he bangs the ball high into the darkening sky and down between the posts.

The Pontypool fans go wild as this makes the game safe for the home team, and a mud-splattered Bishop, the black and red of his kit barely visible, runs over to the grandstand (where the selectors are seated), puts both hands in the air and wiggles his backside as he does a little dance before triumphantly clenching his fist in jubilation.

Post-match, Bishop is asked by the TV reporter about the dance: "That was just a little thing for the supporters... it's all enjoyment in the game, we play for the enjoyment, and if the footballers can do it, so can we."

Asked if he had a point to prove, following speculation as to whether he would be selected for Wales ahead of the Swansea scrum half that day, Robert Jones, he answers: "No, that's not true, the press have been building it up all week about me and Jones, and I wish him all the best. It's not his fault. I'm playing my rugby – I'm enjoying every minute of it."

However, he goes on to add moments later: "I think the boys wanted to prove a point as well, because as far as the East of Wales is concerned, there's no players getting selected. And, deep down, it's hurting the boys. And I think they had a point to prove to the selectors and West Wales as well, that we can still play rugby here."[118]

The skills may have been undeniable, but the attitude would prove irrevocable, and the Welsh selectors would remain unmoved. Robert Jones would be the Wales scrum half for that year's Five Nations.

Bishop would later recall that after the cup win over Swansea:

> Coach Ray Prosser went up to two of the Little Five, as I call them [they were actually known as the Big Five: the panel who picked the Wales team] to ask about me. He was told that while they were in charge, I'd never play for Wales again. It broke Pross's heart when he came to tell me. Let me tell you this: at one point I said to myself, "If I play as well as I can, they cannot not pick me." But they just kept leaving me out.[119]

Although the 1987/88 season was the most successful in Pontypool's history – they lost only two games all season – at the end of it, Bishop would turn his back on Welsh rugby and head to league and Hull Kingston Rovers. In an era of poor International performances, one of Welsh rugby's few world-class players was gone.

The David Bishop story begins on Halloween 1960 in Cardiff, where he grew up as the eldest of six children. Educated at St Illtyd's College and Rumney Technical College, he came through the ranks at his hometown club, coming on as a replacement for Brynmor Williams to make his senior debut at the age of 17 against Penarth. A talented all-round sportsman, as a youth he had boxed for the Welsh amateur team and played baseball for Wales. But his career at Cardiff came to an end after a discipline breach on a pre-season tour of Italy. And then came an incident on a night out in the Welsh capital which saw Bishop charged with GBH.

These eventful few years for young Bishop would take another turn when, whilst on bail and in his dad's pub, he was told a woman and baby were in trouble, having fallen into the swollen Taff – the river that runs through the heart of Cardiff. As Bishop arrived, they were clinging onto the bank of the fast-moving river, and whilst there was a crowd watching, no one seemed to be doing anything. Quick as a flash, he got into the water with her, grabbed the baby and passed it to safety, then as she began to slip into the water, he climbed out, grabbed her hair, and hauled her to safety. For this he would receive an award for bravery from the Royal Humane Society. Though he was presented with it in prison, at the start of his stretch inside for GBH.

Amidst all the upheaval and after a few games for Ebbw Vale, Bishop would find a home in Pontypool and made the first of his 241 appearances in an 18-15 home win over Aberavon on 21 October 1981. In the return fixture five weeks later, he broke his neck. Initially diagnosed as just ruptured ligaments, once the severity of the injury was realised, surgeons had to drill into his skull while he was conscious to fit a brace and take a chunk of bone from his hip to wedge into his neck.

The surgeon who operated on him offered some stark advice to the 21 year old when asked if Dai could return to playing rugby, as Bishop told *WalesOnline* in 2020:

> He scolded me like I was a naughty schoolboy. "Get out of here," he said. "You're lucky to be walking. There are two things you can't do: dive off high boards and play rugby — don't even dream of playing rugby." The first thing I did when I got back was go to the Empire Pool. I went in off the top board.

Making a big splash would, however, only get Bishop get so far. He needed medical clearance for insurance purposes if he wanted to play rugby again, so sought a second opinion. This doctor told him his neck was probably stronger now than it had been in the first place, but added a major caveat: if he broke it again, he wouldn't just be paralysed – he'd be dead.

"I said, 'That's fine. Just sign there, Doc,'" recalled Bishop. "That was it. I played against Maesteg and against Gloucester the next week."

His father, however, wasn't as enthusiastic that he was making a return to the game that had nearly paralysed him:

> When it came to the comeback, Dad was distraught and wouldn't talk to me for a couple of weeks but Mum knew I needed to play to keep my sanity, really. We were a strong Catholic family

> and the first thing she did was march me off down to Father Maguire's for a blessing. Then she would get this Holy Water from Lourdes and bless me every time I left the house to play. And I took some Holy Water everywhere I went and developed my own routine.[120]

Bishop wouldn't suffer a major injury again. And his 11 months out in recovery did nothing to reduce either his abilities or his appetite for the game.

In the 1970s Pontypool had built a global reputation on their flinty toughness and forward prowess – in particular, on the famed Pontypool Front Row of Charlie Faulkner, Graham Price and Bobby Windsor and the coaching expertise of Ray Prosser.

The recruitment of Bishop by Prosser, who loved a rough diamond, transformed the team – as Alun Carter, a teammate of Dai's, would later write:

> The big point of difference between the Pontypool sides of the '70s and '80s was undoubtedly one man: David Bishop. We never had a player of such talent in the position – or one that could exert such complete dominance over the game. It would be no exaggeration to say that 'Bish' added a gilt-edged quality we'd never had before or since.[121]

In his first season back, Pontypool won the Whitbread Merit Table (a precursor to the league system), and Bishop would be Man of the Match when Pontypool won the Welsh Cup for the only time, in 1983. The following year came a call-up to the national team to face Australia in Cardiff.

After a few splashes of holy water, he ran out at the Arms Park for the first and only time in a Wales jersey. The home team were outclassed by a crack Australia XV – containing another true maverick, David Campese – which would be the first and, to date, only Wallaby side to achieve a Grand Slam tour and defeat all four home nations. Wales would lose 28-9, but Bishop did himself proud with a sensational late try, acrobatically juggling the ball as he crossed the line. It was the only Test try the Wallabies conceded on that European tour.

Aged just 24, we'd never see him in a Wales jersey again. He would later tell Brendan Gallagher of *The Rugby Paper*:

> You know the film *Trading Places*? I'm the Eddie Murphy character. He got to be a stockbroker for a day and I got to be a Wales rugby player for a day. And then they took it away from me. During the week of that Australia Test all the 'big Five' – as the selectors liked to be known – came up to me at one stage to say they had been voting for me over the last couple of years.[122]

There was one positive of that day, however: one of Bishop's brothers placed a £30 bet at 17/1 that Dai would score a try, pocketing the equivalent of around £1,800 in today's money.

In 1985 the first-choice Wales scrum half, Terry Holmes, made the switch to rugby league, and many expected Bishop to be the man to take his place. Instead, that year, in a fiery Gwent derby against Newbridge, he punched Chris Jarman in an off-the-ball incident, and broke his jaw. In a highly unusual move, Jarman brought a private prosecution against Bishop, resulting in a suspended jail sentence and an 11-month ban from the game from the WRU.

Bishop admits hitting Jarman, but not breaking his jaw:

> But the reaction was out of all proportion – and remember there was no video or footage, no citings: what followed was all based on various people's accounts of what they saw or thought they saw. You would have thought I was Jack the Ripper. All the time the civil case rumbled on, Wales wouldn't look at me, and then on top of that I got an 11-month rugby ban. In fact, I couldn't even go in a public park. All for a punch![123]

Whilst Bishop was kicking his heels, the smooth-passing and squeaky-clean Robert Jones took over the position as Wales' first-choice scrum half and went to the inaugural World Cup in 1987. Bishop was Player of the Year for Pontypool in the 1987/88 season, but by the end of that year, the writing was on the wall. He'd never play for Wales again and missing out on that first World Cup devasted him so much, he decided it was time to join many other Welshmen of this era and head north to rugby league and professionalism.

He signed for Hull Kingston Rovers in July 1988 for around £120,000. He'd almost joined St Helens, who had to cancel his signing press conference when he failed the medical – the club having been unaware he'd broken his neck a few years earlier. He apparently left the ground in a car boot to avoid the press.

Bishop arrived up north with a big reputation, and the locals were keen to test exactly how tough he was. "Targeted? I felt like I was a dartboard! I got battered, I really did," Bishop said in an interview with *Hull Live*.

In his first-ever game of rugby league, against Salford, he was carried off the pitch having torn all the ligaments in an ankle, broken his nose and lost three teeth. But despite the brutal start, further injuries and regular punch-ups, Bishop thrived in the new code, being voted Hull KR's Player of the Year by the fans for two years running and remaining a firm favourite to this day. He would then go onto play for Salford and the London Crusaders (now London Broncos).

Though he had been ignored by the WRU, their rugby league counterparts had no qualms in capping Bishop four times. He was part of a team boasting a fantastic crop of union exiles, like Jonathan Davies, Dai Young, Paul Moriarty, Allan Bateman and John Devereux, to name just a few. And a further honour was to be gained in 1990 when he was selected to play for Great Britain on their tour of New Zealand.

Bishop may have been older when playing for Great Britain but the maverick streak remained, as assistant coach Phil Larder would recall, remembering him failing to sing the national anthem before a match:

> The others were giving it plenty, but not David. So I buttonholed him afterwards, "David, why didn't you sign the national anthem?" He replied, "I can't sing that crap, it's not my anthem..." So, for the next game, I gave him a set of headphones – I think it was a Sony Walkman. What people don't know is that David was listening to '*Hen Wlad Fy Nhadau*' while everyone else was singing, 'God Save the Queen'. And what's more, he was singing it too! I guess that's David to a tee. He always went his own way and he absolutely never stuck to the approved script.[124]

When rugby union went professional, Bishop returned to Pontypool as a player-coach, playing his last game for Pooler in 1999 and retiring with a remarkable record of 241 appearances, 171 tries, 80 conversions, 17 penalties and 21 drop goals for a career total of 981 points.

But on finally hanging up his boots, the anti-establishment spirit that had been the driving force through his career was channelled into darker places. He sank into a world of drug addiction, depression and domestic difficulty. Speaking to the *Central Club Podcast* in May 2022, he opened up on his challenges in typically candid style:

> Drug addiction just rules and dominates your whole life. Unless you have been down that street, it's difficult for people to understand. The lowest point was when I started begging for money off friends and good friends of mine were turning me down. My ex-wife left me with the kids and I just went on a worse pattern.
>
> You get so many lows. You turn up in places which are rat holes. And you know you shouldn't be there. "What the fuck am I doing in here?", you know. But you've just get to get it [the drugs], got to get it, got to get it. And as much as you think it's a secret, everybody knows. You have to hit rock bottom to come up, and there are only a few who make it.[125]

These challenges will always be part of his life, but he now acknowledges them: "Depression is something I've found difficult to talk about, but I don't mind doing so now. If well-known people don't talk about traumatic times and keep sweeping them under the bed, the issues will never come out."[126]

A welder and sales rep during his union playing days, he is now a doting grandad who runs an eco-friendly heating business specialising in solar panels. In spring 2021 he suffered a stroke, but harnessed the spirit of his playing days to make a good recovery. At 61 years young, he still cuts a spry figure around Cardiff.

Looking at the career of David Bishop, one thread runs through it consistently: both triumph and disaster were never far away. From brushes with the law, breaking his neck and being frozen out by the Welsh selectors, to saving the life of a woman and baby, taking Pontypool to new heights and building a second career in league, to his post-playing battles with depression and drugs, you can never accuse Bishop's life of being straightforward. It's probably fair to say that the only predictable thing about him is his unpredictability.

When mentioning to Welsh friends and family that I was writing about Bishop, their eyes would light up and they would laugh and typically say something like, "Ha ha, plenty to write about there!" Even after all these years, his playing days still bring warm memories. He may have only won one single cap, but his reputation cannot be measured against such an arbitrary yardstick.

He might not be Gareth Edwards, but then David Bishop could never be anyone but himself. We'll give the final word to Graham Price, a fellow Pontypool legend and another player with a maverick spirit:

> The Bish didn't always carry out orders and rarely conformed to expectations of him by others. He was his own man and went his own way, even if that way led to self-destruction. But he was great to play with![127]

PRINCE ALEXANDER OBOLENSKY

"Possessed of splendid physique, attractive by his shock of fair hair, a glorious runner, unorthodox in his tackles, and very fast, he was always most interesting to watch."

FACTFILE

Full name: Prince Alexander Sergeevich Obolensky

Born: 17 February 1916, Petrograd (now Saint Petersburg), Russia

Died: 29 March 1940, Martlesham Heath, Suffolk, UK

Position: Winger

Representative teams: Middlesex, Barbarians, England, British & Irish Lions

Clubs: Trent College, Chesterfield FC, Oxford University RFC, Leicester, Rosslyn Park

Nicknames: The Flying Prince, The Flying Slav, Obo

WITH MINUTES TO go until kick-off against New Zealand at Twickenham in January 1936 Edward, Prince of Wales – three weeks from becoming King – fixed his gaze upon the 19-year-old Alexander Obolensky and coldly asked, "By what rights do you presume to play for England?"

Edward wasn't used to being talked back to, but then it wasn't every day he was speaking to another prince.

Obolensky looked him direct in the eye and replied dryly, "I attend Oxford University, Sir."

Four years later Edward, after a brief spell as Edward VIII, would be in disgrace and under suspicion, idling in the Caribbean as Governor of the Bahamas. Prince Obolensky would die wearing the uniform of his adopted county.

But that's in the future. Today is about rugby, so let's go back to that chilly January at Twickenham.

Obolensky was winning his first cap against the All Blacks, a team that England had never beaten. With two extraordinary first-half tries from the Prince, it is no exaggeration to say it was probably the greatest England debut of all time.

The first is stunning. New Zealand have started strongest, hammering away at the England line, but the home defence is holding firm. From a scrum in the middle of the pitch, England centre Ronald Gerrard makes a break, beats a man, and flicks the ball out to an onrushing Obolensky. He cleanly gathers the ball and swiftly moves right, ghosting past one defender and running towards the touchline to go around a second, before cutting back in and curving a run through open space to outpace the covering full back and score the opening try.

The second is sublime. After absorbing more New Zealand pressure, England again have the ball on the halfway. It's moved across the pitch into the hands of Obolensky, near the right wing in a similar spot to where he received it for the first try. The All Black defence fan across the pitch to try and stop a repeat of what happened earlier.

Instead of doing what 99 out of 100 wingers would do and trying to carve out the same gap he'd succeeded in finding just minutes earlier, he glances into the middle of the park, jinks, and heads infield to a small space the covering defence have just created. He gets into his stride, leaving the All Blacks flummoxed as they twist and turn, trying to readjust. The winger has two men outside him, but the confusion brought by his change of direction means he doesn't need them as he runs diagonally across the pitch. Such is his pace, he is now where the left winger would be – the New Zealand right winger almost gets him, but Obolensky swerves around him.

The Kiwi full back, Gilbert, has a clear view of the rugby chaos happening in front of him but is beaten by the sheer pace of Obolensky. Ball in the right hand, left arm out almost horizontally, the Prince readjusts a little as the space opens up before sliding over for the try and sending the Twickenham faithful into raptures.

England would win the game 13-0. The other winger, Hal Sever, who had run alongside the Prince as he scored his wonder try in Sever's part of the pitch, scored the third and final try.

Legendary rugby writer Wallace Reyburn, who was at Twickenham that day, described it as the "greatest International try of them all… because it was something unique – a right wing, wrong footing all the opposition and running diagonally through them to score a left-winger's try."[128]

The Morning Post described the try breathlessly:

> Runners we have seen before but never such a runner with such an innate idea of where to go and how to get there. His double swerve to gain his first try was remarkable enough but the extraordinary turn-in and diagonal right to left run which won him his second and which drew forth that great Twickenham rarity, a double roar of applause, will never be forgotten by anybody who saw it.[129]

New Zealand, with perhaps the most critical eyes of any in rugby, was equally effusive. Writer Terry McLean stated: "Obolensky's try was a stupendous exhibition of the hypotenuse in rugby." His brother Hugh, who, as a New Zealand flanker that day, had a perfect view of the try, described it as "one that might not come off again in 100 years."[130]

If we are looking for a more modern comparison, we need look no further than fellow maverick David Campese's try against New Zealand in the 1991 World Cup semi-final. In terms of impact, I think that Jonah Lomu's performance against England in the World Cup four years later would be comparable.

Obolensky's second try became instantly renowned, largely due to its spectacular nature against such illustrious opposition, but also because it was captured on film by Pathé News and shown in cinemas across the UK and the Empire.

The film is still available. The England team, tall and slim, bounce out onto the pitch, followed by a squatter, heavier New Zealand, who amble onto the turf. In that nasal, high pitched voice so often parodied now, the film commentator gives his confident opinion from the outset:

> At Twickenham for 70,000 rugger fans it's the high spot of the season, when England come out for their first International match against the All Blacks. England is playing in white. And standing in the middle is Obolensky, destined to play such a great part in this match. Many at first thought the All Blacks unbeatable, but their recent whacking by Wales has given England new hope. And today if they don't put up a good show, his Royal Highness the Prince of Wales, and 70,000 others, will want to know the reason why.[131]

So there's the try itself, the opposition, it being caught on camera, and then there's the remarkable man who scored it.

He was born in 1916 in Petrograd (which would soon become Leningrad and later St Petersburg), the son of Prince Sergei Alexandrovich Obolensky, an officer in the Tsar's Imperial Horse Guards, and his wife Princess Lubov Alexandrovna Naryshkin. The Obolenskys were part of the Rurik dynasty, a noble lineage that weaves its way back through Russian history all the way to 862. The days of palaces, privilege and countless servants would, however, end abruptly the following year, when the Bolshevik Revolution swept away the old order. Prince Obolensky senior, as an aristocrat and member of the imperial bodyguard, had little choice but to flee or risk the same fate as the Tsar and his family.

The Obolensky family hurriedly scattered across Europe and America. One member of the clan, Prince Dimitri, went from being a great landowner to driving a taxi in Paris; another Prince Serge went to the USA, where he joined the forerunner of the CIA, married a member of the Astor family and ended up vice chairman of the Hilton Hotels Corporation; whilst a third, Prince Alexis, became known as the 'father of modern backgammon'.

Our young Prince Alexander, however, along with his siblings and parents, ended up in Muswell Hill, an unremarkable if solidly middle-class suburb in North London, where he would soon begin a very British education – all paid for by benefactors as the Obolensky wealth had been left behind in Russia. First prep school, then Trent College boarding school in Derbyshire and finally on to Brasenose College, Oxford to read Politics, Philosophy and Economics.

He was by all accounts a lively figure, sometimes breakfasting on oysters and champagne – a lover of wine, women, theatrical reviews and the dining culture of the time. Between his socialising and rugby, he received a fourth-class degree, which no longer exists, and was generously described as a 'sportsman's degree'.

It was at rugby that he really excelled, though. One account from college magazine *The Brazen Nose*, written a few years after he graduated, recalled his prowess on the pitch:

> He possessed phenomenal speed, which once drew from a mechanically minded spectator the remark, "By Jove, what acceleration! I've got a good mind to sell my Bugatti and buy an Obolensky." But in addition to his speed, he had the true footballer's instinct and anticipation, and there were few reports

> of big matches that did not contain particular reference to at least one brilliant piece of work on his part.[132]

Allied with his blistering pace was a pioneering use of lightweight boots, with him having despaired of the heavy, clumping boots that he was expected to wear.

He would win two Blues (the highest honour granted to individual sportspeople) at Oxford, in 1935 and 1937, with only an injury in 1936 stopping him completing a hat-trick.

When called up for England in 1936, Obolensky was an Oxford student and an explosive runner with an innate knack for scoring tries, so there should have been little debate about him wearing the red rose.

Except that in the eyes of many, he wasn't English.

The debates over nationality in rugby are nothing new. Nearly every major International team regularly turns out with at least a couple of players who qualify by having parents or grandparents from there, or through residency. Visitors to social media during big matches will often see this mentioned, and some of the most beloved players of recent years have been born outside of the country they are representing: George North (King's Lynn in England), Ronan O'Gara (California), Mako Vunipola (New Zealand) and Hamish Watson (Manchester), to give just a small sample.

In 1936 rugby nationality was a talking point too. Obolensky had lived in England since he was a toddler, but was not naturalised as British and used a special stateless person's document called a Nansen passport to travel. When his selection for England was first mooted, some thought that as a clear product of the English system, he should be capped. Others, however, saw the securing of a British passport first as a prerequisite. At a meeting of the Rugby Football Union, the motion that he needed to be a fully naturalised British citizen to be selected was voted down and Obolensky was free to play for England.

Today he would have qualified on residency without any issues at all.

And I think he'd have proved very good value on social media too.

After his explosive debut, he played in a draw against Wales. The Welsh full back that day, Viv Jenkins, sat through hours of cartoons and newsreels in cinemas, waiting to see that Pathé footage again and again, to make sure he was prepared for what he would be facing. It was a 0-0 draw that day in Swansea, and the only time Obolensky received the ball in a dangerous position, Jenkins was waiting. This precursor to the video-analysis sessions that dominate preparation for International games now had clearly worked.

The stalemate against Wales was followed by a loss in Ireland and a win over Scotland back at Twickenham. Obolensky was rewarded for his performances with a call-up to that summer's Lions tour of Argentina.

Now, a brief word on this tour. The British Lions of 1936 (as they were then known – it wouldn't be until the 2001 tour of Australia that the name 'British & Irish Lions' would become official) were not the organised and structured outfit that we have today. The tours were of a more haphazard nature, this one being a prime example. There were no Welsh players, despite Wales having won that year's Home Nations Championship (the forerunner of the Five/Six Nations), and only a smattering of Scots and Irish, with the squad being overwhelmingly English. In some older history books it's not even recorded as an official tour, but it was and Obolensky is Lion #296.

This might be known by some as a 'forgotten tour', but the trip would prove to be a lively one. They played 10 matches, including one Test against the hosts, and won the lot, scoring 339 points and conceding just 12. Obolensky played in six matches, scoring a dozen tries.

Whilst on the tour, our dashing prince was the centre of attention – particularly of the female variety – alongside Jimmy

Unwin, a Rosslyn Park teammate who occupied the other wing. The social whirl of the long sail across the Atlantic and the various welcomes, receptions and dinners that were part of the tour greatly suited Obolensky's approach to life.

He of course enjoyed travelling First Class.

The ship that carried the tourists to South America, the *Andalucia Star*, was sunk by a German U-Boat off the coast of West Africa in 1942. It wouldn't be the only casualty of World War II connected to this tour.

Back to 1936, however, and one particularly remarkable story that comes out of the tour – though I have to say it remains unconfirmed – is that on the way to Argentina, the team played Brazil in Santos, and Obolensky scored 17 tries in an 82-0 victory. The Lions outclassed the more established teams in Argentina, so I have no doubt that they hammered the Brazilians, but 17 tries seem a little unlikely. The official record holder for a Tier 1/Tier 2 match is the wonderfully named Uriel O'Farrell, who scored seven against Uruguay for Argentina in 1952. Three players in the modern era have touched down six times in a single game, including most recently South African Tonderai Chavhanga in 2005, with Uruguay again as the hapless recipients.

But 17?

Well, as the old saying goes: when the legend becomes fact, *print the legend!*

On his return to the UK, Obolensky would continue to shine for both Leicester Tigers and Rosslyn Park and be a regular crowd-drawing feature for the Barbarians.

The Rosslyn Park archive would recall exactly what an attraction he was:

> I am not sure that the Rugby game has had a bigger 'gate' attraction than the late Prince Alexander Obolensky. To include Obo's name in the programme was to ensure a good gate in England, Wales, Scotland and Ireland. A murmur would go

> round when a team that included him came on, everybody saying, "Which one is Obolenksy?" Of course, his name helped a little in his extraordinary reputation... and all crowds love a personality. Possessed of splendid physique, attractive by his shock of fair hair, a glorious runner, unorthodox in his tackles, and very fast, he was always most interesting to watch.[133]

In 1939 he was close to an England recall when a bizarre incident intervened. Obolensky had been a passenger in a car which had run over a dog. He was lying on the ground, trying to prise the stricken hound from under the wheels, when he was bitten. The wound turned septic and he had to endure a hospital stay, and was then, with his arm in a sling, unable to take the field.

The recall would soon come, but tragedy would strike.

Whilst at Brasenose College, he had learnt to fly as a member of the University Air Squadron and so when war was declared in 1939, he was called up to active service by the Royal Air Force. He was training with Hurricanes in Suffolk during the period known as the Phoney War, before Germany invaded France, the Netherlands and Belgium.

On leave in London, he met up with Welsh International and fellow Oxford Blue Viv Jenkins, who congratulated Obolensky on joining up and asked how the training was going. In his usual nonchalant style, he replied, "It's going absolutely fine, great fun. Except I still haven't got the hang of landing."

This would prove sadly prophetic. Just a few weeks later on 29 March 1940, the day after he'd received an England recall, he had just conducted a training flight and was in the process of landing on the turf of the airfield at Martlesham Heath, near Ipswich, when the wheels of his Hurricane snagged in a rabbit warren and the plane lurched violently forward, overshot the runway and dropped down into a small ravine. He'd already loosened his harness and was catapulted out of the cockpit, breaking his neck. He died instantly.

Pilot Officer Alexander Sergeevich Obolensky was only 24.

Obolensky would be the first of over 100 Internationals to lose his life in World War II. Most of the men he shared the tour of Argentina with would see active service. His fellow back, J S Moll, would also die in an accident whilst preparing to be deployed to Iraq in 1942. Irish prop Charles Beamish would finish the war as a Group Captain in the RAF, the same branch that his three rugby player brothers all volunteered for. The tourists' medical officer and referee, Hugh Llewellyn Glyn Hughes, would be the first Allied Medical Officer to enter the concentration camp at Bergen-Belsen and a key witness for the prosecution in ensuing war crimes trials.

On paper at least, Obolensky's rugby career might have been limited – four caps for England, two tries and one Lions tour – but his memory remains incredibly strong. He is buried in Ipswich and in 2009 the town's Borough Council asked his niece, Princess Alexandra Obolensky, to unveil a statue of the Prince – a large Art Deco-style bust of him, bare-chested and holding the ball behind him while thrusting forward, as he did for his great Twickenham try.

There's a hospitality suite at that old ground bearing his name, as well as a bar at Rosslyn Park (one of two named after club legends, the other being Ripley's). His old school, Trent College, in 2008 opened a new events space named after their illustrious former pupil. He also lives on in *Rugby Spirit*, a 2012 book in the popular kids' rugby series by Gerard Siggins, which features the characters meeting a ghostly Obolensky at Twickenham.

From his remarkable origins to his sad, wasteful death, the story of Prince Obolensky continues to enchant. A romantic figure, gone before his image could age or be tarnished, frozen in those last few years before World War II changed so much. Born into a revolution and dying during a world war, his image remains firmly that of that special day at Twickenham against the All Blacks.

There's something irresistible about reading of a man who tumbles out of bed (possibly not his own), enjoys a dozen oysters and some champagne for breakfast before scoring some breathtaking tries.

In the words of his *Daily Telegraph* obituary, he was "A romantic figure capable of doing almost incredible things." It was a great loss that we didn't get to see more of what he might have offered the world.

MOSS KEANE

"The thought of preparing to take on the greatest rugby team in the world by training under floodlights from Cortinas and Ford Escorts gave us a real lift."

FACTFILE

Full name: Maurice 'Moss' Ignatius Keane

Born: 27 July 1948, Currow, County Kerry, Republic of Ireland

Died: 5 October 2010, Portarlington, County Laois, Republic of Ireland

Position: Lock

Representative teams: Ireland, British & Irish Lions

Clubs: University College Cork (UCC), Lansdowne, Munster

CLOSE FOLLOWERS OF Munster rugby might have been a little perplexed at the appearance of a highly promising but previously unknown player turning out for the second team of University College Cork, going by the name of Fenton. How had they missed this huge blond-haired figure, who in just a few years would be described by the late, great Bill McLaren as "18 and a half stone of Prime Irish Beef"?

He'd not been at any of the area's rugby schools, nor any of the province's many famous clubs.

Who was this Fenton?

Well, he wasn't actually Fenton at all. It was a fake name, a pseudonym – a *nom de rugby*, if you will.

Fenton was, in fact, future Irish International and Lions tourist Moss Keane. He'd taken the name from a collie back on his family farm.

So why was Moss pretending to be Fenton?

Well, the answer is that Irish sport, like the country itself in 1970s, had a very different complexion to the present day. As a player of Gaelic football and a member of the Gaelic Athletic Association (GAA), Moss Keane was explicitly forbidden from playing rugby.

This was due to the GAA's Rule 27, which when codified in 1905 stated that:

> Any member of the Association who plays or encourages in any way rugby, football, hockey or any imported game which is calculated to injuriously affect our National Pastimes, is suspended from the Association.

GAA members were forbidden from playing, attending or even watching any event associated with these sports. It was not unusual in some areas for 'vigilance committees' to be sent out to rugby or football matches to look for GAA members in the crowd. The role of a vigilance committee was, as the writer Breandán Ó hEithir charmingly described it, to spot the "straying sheep among the graceless goats".[134] Any illicit spectator found could be expelled from the GAA, though the reality was that the rule was only haphazardly implemented.

Before we continue, it is worth saying a few words on the GAA, as if you are unfamiliar with its history, this may seem like madness. And if you are thinking that the organisation can be compared to other nations' rugby unions or associations, then you are mistaken. It stands for a lot more than just sporting administration.

It was founded in 1884, a time when all of Ireland was still ruled by London, and it can be seen as part of the wave of modern Irish nationalism that would ultimately lead to independence. The aim was to establish a national organisation that would make athletics more accessible to the masses, and to revive and grow indigenous sports and pastimes.

Rule 27 emerged as part of a defence against what was viewed as a creeping Anglicisation of Irish culture, as one commentator writing in *The Nenagh Guardian*, a weekly newspaper in County Tipperary, described it: "There is grave danger of a big land-slide towards West Britonism, as exemplified by the Jazz-Soccer-Golfstick mentality which is on the increase in this country today."[135]

The rule was still in place when Keane was a youngster, as he describes in his excellent biography, *Rucks, Mauls and Gaelic Football* – a charming mix of rugby stories, off-field craic and an often-tender account of Irish family and farming life in the middle of the twentieth century. He recalled:

> We couldn't play rugby and they couldn't play football or hurling. There was even a ban on attending rugby dances. The ban was enforced by vigilantes who roamed the countryside, looking for transgressors. Sometimes they hid behind ditches, and more times they skulked behind girthy trees outside country dance halls.
>
> And, at the time, many of our lads thought the rugby lads might have been looking down on us. The rugby lads were for the most part graduates of the private schools, where Gaelic football was a foreign game, another less-publicised form of discrimination.[136]

I spoke to GAA academic and author Donal McAnallen about what led to the end of Rule 27:

> By the time we got to 1970, the enforcement of the rule was lax in general, though it would vary from county to county and sport

> to sport. In the 1960s there had been several attempts to change the rule but, in the end, it was television that helped bring about the change. TV ownership in Ireland had rocketed, and the 1966 soccer World Cup, and the European Cup wins for Celtic and Manchester United, gave people access to non-Irish sports in way that never could have been imagined before. So the writing really was on the wall for Rule 27.

A rule cast in 1905 could never have factored in such a technology and it now meant that you could be banned for attending a soccer or rugby game in person but could watch them at home to your heart's content. No contortions could disguise this awkward position. The rule could not hold, and someone would soon be the first to take the step from Gaelic football to representative rugby. Enter Maurice 'Moss' Ignatius Keane, an unlikely rugby pioneer.

Keane was born into a farming family in Currow, County Kerry in the south-west of Ireland. He would grow to 6' 5" and weigh in at 16st 10lb in his International days, and gave his poor mum an early indicator of what was to come by weighing 14lb when he was born.

Kerry is renowned for its fanaticism for Gaelic football, with the county having won more All Ireland Championships than any other. Despite that, this small rural village with only around 1,000 inhabitants has given a start to a number of successful rugby union players in addition to Keane: International Mick 'Doyler' Doyle, who would also coach Ireland and the Lions; Mick Galwey, who benefited greatly from the relaxing of the GAA rules in playing for Ireland and touring with the Lions in 1993, after winning the All-Ireland Senior (Gaelic) Football Championship with Kerry in 1986; and most recently J J Hanrahan, a former Munster favourite who joined the Dragons in 2022 from French giants Clermont.

Keane's early years gave little indication of his rugby prowess to come. Gaelic football was the focus for a young Moss, and like most young boys growing up in The Kingdom, as the county is nicknamed, he dreamt of playing for Kerry. He played the sport at school and university, representing his county at U21 level and captaining the University College Cork team.

It was at UCC in 1970, aged 22, where he played his first-ever game of rugby: a novelty match between the university's Gaelic football and rugby union teams. In the first game, Keane struggled a little with the rules, as he recalled years later:

> We Gaelic players took the field with only a rudimentary knowledge of the game. I passed the ball once by punching it GAA style with my fist and I fielded another ball high over my head GAA style again... I spent half the match offside and disgraced myself by calling the referee some choice names, which was fine in football but not in rugby, where you just shut up and accepted the decision. For all the mix-ups, I enjoyed every minute of the game, and we won 6-3.[137]

Following his first taste of the oval-ball game, he combined Gaelic football with games for UCC's rugby team under his dog-inspired pseudonym. The GAA ban on 'foreign sports' was finally lifted in 1971, and Keane played his first 'legal' game for UCC on Easter Sunday of that year, with the local paper waggishly noting that "Fenton was dropped for Moss Keane, the well-known GAA player."

From this debut, his rise was remarkable.

By 1974 he was playing for Ireland.

Three years later he was a Lions tourist.

Quickly establishing his reputation at UCC, the next step was to play for Munster, where he was the first player who came straight from Gaelic football into representative rugby, and he received significant media attention. By now he was juggling his job with the Department of Agriculture, playing Gaelic football and turning out for Munster.

The biggest game of his fledgling rugby career would be against New Zealand in 1973. Up to this point no Irish team

– club or country – had ever beaten the All Blacks, although Munster had come close, losing 6-3 in both 1954 and 1963.

Whilst Keane wasn't steeped in rugby history, the importance of the game and his performance was made very clear to him by Munster coach Noel Murphy:

> Moss, you are no longer an experiment, you are a Munster man picked to play against the All Blacks... Moss, this is very big. Bigger than us all. Just go out and cause mayhem. Disrupt their line-out. Stop them getting quick ball. Stand up for yourself and your team. Kerrymen have more All-Irelands than anyone else – you're afraid of no one. Kerry are the All Blacks of Ireland. That's why we picked you.[138]

Keane was shocked by the haka. He'd never even heard of the famous war dance, let alone seen it. And although a win again eluded Munster – a late, late penalty from New Zealand securing them a 3-3 draw – Keane's performance against such tough opponents saw the Irish national selectors look at him for the first time.

He moved to Dublin for work, helping farmers to implement new EEC dairy regulations, and focussed more on rugby. Whilst still playing Gaelic football, he joined the famous Lansdowne Club and soon after, in 1974, received his first International call-up, to face France at Parc des Princes, Paris.

Keane's rapid journey from playing in a fun student match to facing probably the toughest European team of the time in just four years was a remarkable one, and a key part of the deep affection with which he is held in Irish rugby. Alongside his pioneering place in the game, he was also famous for a nice line in self-deprecating humour and, in an era of big rugby characters, being the teller of some great stories. He played down his abilities on and off the pitch, remarking, "After I left university, I found out had no talent for anything, so I joined the civil service," and "I won 52 caps – a lot of them just because they couldn't find anybody else."

His Munster and Ireland colleague Donal Lenihan told me that he was as popular as he was modest:

> He was great. I roomed with him, and he was great fun and certainly was a different character to most in the squad. Moss had a huge laugh, and everyone would be drawn to him and he'd always make everyone feel very welcome to the squads. But he was also sharp as a razor. He liked to sometimes play the gombeen [Irish slang for a fool] but was very clever: he'd always win the team quizzes and surprise people with the things he'd come out with. On the pitch he was fantastic too. It was a privilege to play with him and I really treasure the memories I have of our time together.

He would lose his first game, going down 9-6 to France, but a draw against Wales followed by wins over England and Scotland saw Ireland win that year's Five Nations Championship. In the seasons that followed, whilst Moss became an established member of the national team, the results proved inconsistent, with the definitive history of the game in Ireland describing the era neatly as "poor performances followed by great and unexpected victories."[139]

In 1977 he retired from playing organised GAA, as the demands of two sports plus a professional career meant that finally something had to give. But a bigger challenge would arrive that year when he was selected for the Lions tour to New Zealand – one of just four Irish players in the original 30-man squad, following a disappointing Five Nations that saw the boys in green pick up a wooden spoon.

The difference between an amateur-era Lions tour and the detail, focus and hype of a modern day one is always surprising. The week of the announcement he was on a lad's holiday in the south-east of Ireland – during which he injured his leg, slipping down some steps going into a pub – as the Lions management tried to find him. It was only on his return to work the following week that he got a call telling him he was in the squad.

The tour would run from 18 May to 16 August and take in 26 games, including four Tests and a match against Fiji on the way home. It was the last of the long tours, and a brutal schedule for amateur players. Keane's initial concerns about taking the time off work were eased when the Minister of Agriculture gave him special leave.

There would be no bags full of branded booty or lavish gifts from sponsors on this tour. Keane was at this point still a bachelor and admits in his book to still relying on his mother (nearly 200 miles away from his Dublin flat) for his washing. His account of arriving at the airport for the first leg of the journey is worth repeating in full:

> I arrived at Dublin Airport with a modest bag, big enough to hold two underpants, four pairs of socks with holes in five, a jumper with no elbows, a pair of jeans, a pants for good wear and three bottles of Lucozade, just in case they didn't sell it in New Zealand. In my kitbag were rock-hard boots (two), unrelated socks (three), togs with a tear up the side of the thigh (one) and jockstrap (one).

Fellow maverick Willie Duggan had with him two suitcases and a kitbag. On seeing what Keane was carrying, he asked, "Where the feck do you think you're going with that small bag? Do you realise we are going to New Zealand for three and a half months and not to London for the weekend? What are you going to do for gear?"[140]

Keane pointed at Duggan's bulging bags.

Duggan's reply was not recorded.

It was a brutal tour, with the Lions going down three-one in the Test series and the club games being characterised by injuries, heavy rain and bouts of bad feeling. Keane suffered a concussion in a defeat to New Zealand Universities. Following the blow, his scrambled brain made him think he was with his club side Lansdowne in Vancouver, where he had played three years earlier. The following day he was groggy in training and vomited. On being told he was selected for the first Test, he pleaded with the management not to play.

His pleas went unheeded and going into the game he was still wobbly on his feet, vomiting up his food, and had blurred vision and a constant headache. Keane was in no fit state to play any rugby, let alone a Test match against New Zealand, and he has only a hazy memory of the 16-12 defeat.

Keane still felt awful when he returned to training on the Monday. He was seeing double and on leaving the pitch saw two changing room doors, guessed wrong, and clattered into a wall. He went to bed and after sleeping for nearly 48 hours, felt fine. This was the end of the concussion, although he does quip that some thought he never fully shook it off.

Concussions can kill, and whilst there's plenty to enjoy from the amateur era, the modern treatment of head injuries – whilst still far from perfect – is a major improvement on what went before.

Keane wasn't selected for the second Test and, in his own words:

> I decided to have a holiday for the rest of the trip ... I lost the run of things, though, and socialised far too much over the next four weeks. It was probably one of the wildest times of my life. I was always grounded by visits to Currow; they steadied me, and I returned to a type of sensible reality with my core values topped up. The trip was too long, and I began to get frustrated with the fact that I was only involved in a peripheral role.
>
> One night I let off a fire alarm and a hotel had to be evacuated. It wasn't a premeditated thing. I was walking down the hallway with Phil Bennett at 4 a.m. and I just reached out and let it off. I was severely spoken to by George [Burrell, the Scottish team manager]... I was lucky to have met such a sympathetic team manager. I heard stories of players who got themselves into bother on tours who weren't picked at International level long after the tour was over.[141]

Keane had some good memories of a challenging trip, but when asked by Nigel Starmer-Smith of the BBC what the highlight of the '77 tour was, replied straight away that it was that Kerry had beaten Cork in the final of that summer's Munster GAA competition.

Whilst the Lions tour ultimately proved a disappointment, the following year Munster would get another crack at the All Blacks. The 1978 game is probably the most famous club game in Irish rugby history.

As we have already mentioned, no Irish team (club or country) had ever beaten New Zealand, and the All Blacks tours of the UK and Ireland were typically processional. Between 1953 and 1977, they won 15 of their 18 Tests, with two draws and a solitary loss to Wales in 1953. On the 1978 tour they played 18 games, winning 17, including all four against the home nations – which saw them become the first team to achieve a Grand Slam on such tour. The only blemish on the record was Munster-shaped.

A ferocious game, played on Halloween in front of a sell-out 12,000 crowd in Limerick, saw the home team triumph 12-0. To give some indication of the scale of this victory, no Irish side would beat the All Blacks again until the national team finally bested them in 2016.

Here's how *The Cork Examiner* began their match report:

> The talented, dedicated and inspired men of Munster stopped the All Blacks dead in their tracks before an ecstatic capacity crowd at Thomond Park yesterday, giving a stunning display of courage, defensive strength and opportunism to become the first Irish side ever to defeat the New Zealanders.
>
> Despite the fact that some 85 per cent of the furiously paced match was played in their half of the field, they shattered the tourists with a dream converted try after eleven minutes and a copybook dropped goal just eight minutes later. Thereafter they coped with everything the despairing Blacks threw at them, absorbing and punishing with such discipline that they never

> gave away a penalty for foul play, and never gave away a kickable penalty...[142]

Few would have fancied Munster's chances prior to the game. But their coach Tom Kiernan was a canny operator. He organised pre-game training in Fermoy, near Cork, where there were no floodlights, so the team's selectors had to rely on the headlights of their parked cars in picking the team. As Keane would remember:

> The thought of preparing to take on the greatest rugby team in the world by training under floodlights from Cortinas and Ford Escorts gave us a real lift. It was a lot of fun too. Brendan Foley would pass remarks like, "Tommy, can you switch to dims? Mossy is having a gawk," or "Turn on the indicators, Mossy is about to turn."[143]

Following this unconventional start to their preparation, they played two warm-up games in London, allying training sessions with nights in the pub, getting hammered 33-7 by Middlesex and scraping a draw against an Exiles team made up mainly of London Irish players.

But by the time the All Blacks rolled into town, they were ready, and a famous win would be delivered. A slick try began with a sweet Tony Ward kick over the top of an onrushing defence and was finished smartly by Christy Cantillon. Munster eventually sealed a hard-fought victory, with Keane playing a pivotal role in winning Munster ball and disrupting All Black possession at the line-out. He was ferocious in the loose, strong in the scrum but also highly disciplined, with Munster not conceding a single penalty in their own half.

The *Irish Independent* match report from 1978 details a match for which the strong and energetic Keane was perfect:

> Munster applied themselves diligently to the task at hand, paid undivided attention to the basics of the game, minimised their

> margin of error and capitalised ruthlessly on the mistakes of the opposition. To a man, they possessed an insatiable hunger for work and a thirst for victory that was unquenchable even in the face of persistent pressure, which decreed that the major portion of the game was contested in the home half of the field.[144]

Since that afternoon, the win has taken on legendary status. Something of a little industry has been created around it, spawning books, documentaries and even a stage play, *Alone it Stands* by John Breen – "the day the underdog bit back" – which has played all over Ireland and toured in the UK, Australia and even New Zealand.

There is no full video footage of the game – only about 10 minutes exist – so there's plenty of room for artistic licence! But what we can see is a packed-out Thomond Park with the crowd almost on the touchlines, and scenes of pure delirium when the decisive try is scored.

Keane, in his own style, played down the victory, describing it as "famous, perhaps too famous" and emphasising that it was Munster's scrum and tackling, plus New Zealand's poor use of the ball, that won it. He didn't even partake in some of the wilder post-match celebrations, skipping the post-match dinner for a few quiet pints with an old friend and new girlfriend Anne, who he would soon marry.

One unpleasant footnote from an otherwise remarkable day was that, alongside teammate Ginger McLoughlin, he picked up herpes from the bandage of All Blacks prop Gary Knight. Writing almost 30 years later, he reported that he still got a flare-up every November as "an ongoing reminder of a memorable day."

Four years later, there would be a foreign challenge of a very different nature – a tour to Romania.

During the 1980s, the game was so strong in the Eastern European country that it and not Italy would be considered the sixth nation of European rugby, with victories over Wales,

Scotland and France in this period. Receiving major support from communist dictator Nicolae Ceauşescu, their leading players were essentially semi-professional, being mainly drawn from army and police teams, and proved a robust challenge to any opponent.

The country itself, however, was struggling with austerity, food shortages and increasing political oppression. The trip made a lasting impression on Moss Keane's Munster colleague, Donal Lenihan: "It was like travelling back in time, and not in a good way."

For one of the games, Moss was rested and took on the role of the designated linesman in a particularly feisty contest, as Lenihan would recall to me, still chuckling:

> I can still see him now. Standing in front of a big open stand that seemed to be packed with soldiers, wearing an old training jersey and his Lansdowne socks. I remember at one stage Tony Ward [Munster, Ireland and Lions fly half] kicking a ball out on the full and Mossie striding up the sideline and putting up the flag, when clearly the ball had gone straight into touch.
>
> The crowd went absolute crazy and started throwing things at him. *The Incredible Hulk* was the big thing on television at the time, and so Mossie turned around and did this impression of your man turning into the Hulk! I can still see the crowd roaring abuse at him. We were all cracking up on the pitch.

Whether playing or not, Moss Keane couldn't help but make an impression.

In addition to doing his best Bruce Banner impersonation to an Eastern Bloc crowd presumably blissfully unaware of American TV shows, he picked up a second Five Nations Championship in 1982. He became only the third Irish forward after Willie John McBride and Fergus Slattery to reach 50 caps, and retired from Internationals after his 51st game in 1984. He would play two more seasons for Lansdowne before calling it a day completely.

In retirement he remained a big figure in every sense in the Irish game, with stories of his exploits on and off the pitch told in bars and after-dinner speeches up and down the country.

As is the way with these things, many prove to be tall tales. One story does the rounds about Moss entering a drinking competition, where the aim is to drink eight pints in five minutes. The story goes that he slips out before the competition starts, and when asked where he's been, replies that he went next door to another pub for a practice run.

Keane certainly enjoyed the social aspect of the game, but he never would have played eleven years without missing a Five Nations if he was as fond of the socialising as some of the stories claim.

His Ireland teammate Ciaran Fitzgerald gave his own views on this reputation:

> There were a lot of myths about Willie [Duggan] and Moss Keane at the time in terms of drinking and lack of training. That's rubbish. I was living beside Moss and training every other night with him. I'm not exaggerating one bit when I say I was going flat-out just to keep up with him.[145]

One story that is just too good not to share is from a club game in Northern Ireland at the height of the Troubles. A bomb scare had cancelled trains and disrupted the Lansdowne team's plan for some beers on the way back down to Dublin, and after a long wait, a bus arrived. Unfortunately, there weren't enough seats for Moss and a few others from the team. Having already drunk his beers, he was in no mood to hang around further. So, according to folklore, he strode onto the bus and said, "Excuse me, this bus is going to crash." At first nobody moved. But then a little old man stood up and said, "Sorry, but where did you say this bus was going to?"[146]

Sadly, Moss Keane passed away in 2010 following a battle with cancer. He was just 62 and died at his home outside

Portarlington, Co. Laois surrounded by his family, including his wife Anne and daughters Sarah and Anne-Marie.

The outpouring of sadness from all corners of the rugby world was remarkable and showed what a not just respected but truly loved figure he was.

The Irish Republic's Sports Minister at the time, Mary Hanafin, said, "Moss will be remembered as one of Kerry and Ireland's greatest-ever sporting heroes. He was one of Ireland's best-loved figures, both on and off the pitch; a gentle giant of Irish rugby."

IRFU president Caleb Powell said the rugby world was all the poorer for Moss's passing. "Quite simply, Irish rugby has lost one of its most genuine characters and legends of the game. His reputation will live long in the memories of not only Irish rugby, but world rugby," he declared.

Keane's legacy can be found not just in the warmest of memories of his performances on the pitch, his sense of fun off it, and his position in Irish sporting history as the first man to make the move from GAA to international rugby. He was truly a big man both on and off the pitch.

Since Rule 27 was lifted, further changes have followed. Rule 21, which banned members of British security forces from membership of GAA and therefore from playing Gaelic sports, was lifted in 2001 after 104 years. The Police Service of Northern Ireland (PSNI) and British Army regiment the Irish Guards both now have GAA teams, something unthinkable just a generation ago. In 2005, Rule 42, which prohibited non-Gaelic games in GAA stadiums was relaxed, with both Irish rugby and soccer teams then playing at Croke Park whilst the Aviva Stadium was being built.

More recently, the summer of 2021 saw Ireland and Lions full back Rob Kearney return to his roots after a spell in Australia and turn out for GAA side Cooley Kickhams in his native Louth – his boyhood club, which he last represented in 2005. A fine handler of the ball, he regularly cited his years playing Gaelic football as helping with his rugby skills. He was welcomed back with open arms, being described by the club secretary as "one of our own".

The link between the great games of rugby union and Gaelic football is stronger than ever and would not have been possible without the freedom that meant Moss Fenton could be Moss Keane.

Gone too soon, I could fill pages with tributes for this rugby maverick, but I think the one that best summed up Keane's unique spirit comes from his fellow Kerryman and friend, journalistic legend Con Houlihan, who described him as "a man of few airs and many graces."[147]

SERGIO PARISSE

"You can't go to Twickenham to play England and say, 'Well boys, we are probably going to lose but...' Fuck that... Sometimes games are strange."

FACTFILE

Full name: Sergio Matteo Parisse

Born: 12 September 1983, La Plata, Buenos Aires Province, Argentina

Positions: No. 8, Flanker

Representative teams: Barbarians, Italy

Clubs: Universitario de La Plata, Benetton Treviso, Stade Français, Toulon

IN THE MODERN game it's easy to be overwhelmed with statistics. From caps and points to defenders beaten, offloads and metres gained even to lean body mass (LBM) and thermoregulation levels, every professional player now has a whole file of numbers against their name. Many International teams place GPS devices in their players' shirts, helping track information about movement on the pitch and distances covered as well as heart rates and levels of fatigue – the coaching staff can access this data in real time and make decisions accordingly. You know when a player is having a great game then gets seemingly inexplicably substituted? That might well be because their GPS data is showing the coach they are in the 'red zone' and about to run out of energy. And when we look at Italy legend Sergio Parisse, his remarkable career is packed full of remarkable numbers – but with one startling, standout statistic. The giant back-row forward played 142 times for Italy but was on the losing side in 106 of those matches, a loss rate of 75%.

No one has lost more International matches than Parisse.

His International career began in 2002 with a 64-10 hammering against the All Blacks in Hamilton and his last cap at time of writing (he has not yet officially retired) came in a 49-3 loss against South Africa in the 2019 World Cup. His debut defeat would be the first of seven against New Zealand, versus Australia it's ten consecutive reverses and he's winless in 15 of 15 games against England. Parisse is the third-most-capped player in rugby history, after Alun Wyn Jones and Richie McCaw, but when it comes to losses, he's way out front: the closest to his total of 106 is long-term Italy teammate Martín Castrogiovanni, who chalked up 88 defeats. The inauspicious list of most International defeats is dominated by Italians, with only Welshman Gethin Jenkins (70 losses in 134 caps) breaking up the list of Azzurri players in the top ten.

One New Zealand newspaper rather meanly referred to Parisse as "rugby's biggest loser" – whilst statistically you could make an argument for this, anyone who has seen him play would be unlikely to ever think it, and with him coming in at 6' 5" and over 19 stone, even less likely to say it to his face. Considered one of the all-time great No. 8s and regularly a shining light in a losing team, he has normally been the sole world-class player in the Azzurri line-up.

Neil Francis, the ex-Ireland forward and often-controversial columnist, isn't always that effusive in his praise for players, but for the big Italian he makes an exception:

> There are no weaknesses in Parisse's game. If there is one, it is that the rest of his game pales into insignificance when you

> watch him indulge in his passing game. Very few people on the planet can pass accurately without looking. Very few people can catch a ball in a lineout one-handed behind their field of vision and guide it down perfectly to a scrum half that you only half know is there. Very few people have the sort of physical presence to take contact from two, maybe even three, tacklers and execute the right pass accurately without taking anything out of the ball.[148]

Twice nominated as IRB World Player of the Year, Parisse's combination of determination, first-class technical ability, flair, charisma and leadership has put him at the heart of most of Italy's greatest-ever moments and has shone even in some of their heaviest defeats. His commitment to the cause has never wavered, and when asked if he ever wondered what it would be like to pack down in a stronger team, he replied:

> I have no regrets at all... it never occurred to me not to play for Italy. My parents are Italian, we were brought up speaking Italian and returned home to L'Aquila every summer. To play for Italy was a dream, to play for my culture and my family. When you pull on a jersey, it is not just a piece of clothing for the day, a convenience. Loyalty, honour and trust – these are the things that mean a lot to me.[149]

So whilst his commitment to Italy is unquestionable, he wasn't actually born there.

The Sergio Parisse story begins in the Argentine city of La Plata, where he was born in 1983 as part of the huge Italian diaspora in the South American nation. Italians began to flock to Argentina in the late nineteenth century to escape war and turmoil and seek better economic opportunities, and the immigration levels remained high into the 1960s. Today over 30 million Argentines – about two thirds of the total population – claim at least some Italian heritage. Other Argentines with recent roots in Italy include another rugby legend, Felipe

Contepomi, footballing superstar Lionel Messi and the current Pope, Francis, who was born Jorge Mario Bergoglio, to name just a few.

Parisse's parents are both Italian. His father – Sergio Senior, a winger – won the Italian club championship in 1967 with L'Aquila, before his work with the airline Alitalia took him to Argentina in 1970.

Parisse the younger started playing the game at just five years old and shone at youth and junior levels before enjoying his first taste of senior rugby at Club Universitario de La Plata in his hometown. And as hard as it is to believe now, Italy could have missed out on him had their two youth coaches – visiting La Plata to play two warm-up games ahead of the U19 World Cup in nearby Chile – not heard, second-hand, of this talented local lad of Italian origin dominating the local league.

The Italian coaches must have blessed their lucky stars when they tracked him down and invited him to train with the squad. He impressed them so much that he was drafted into the squad at the last moment and played in the tournament.

During the tournament, the Argentine coaches spoke to him to try and lure him back towards the Pumas, but the path was set: both Parisse's heritage and future was solidly Italian. Clubs in Italy, alerted to this previously unknown gem, quickly scrambled to sign him up and the following year he joined Benetton Treviso, where he would spend two seasons.

Parisse had not long arrived in Italy when national coach and former All Black John Kirwan called him up for his International debut – in the toughest possible fixture, away to New Zealand. A true baptism of fire, he started in an Italy team facing an All Blacks side which boasted the likes of Christian Cullen, Andrew Mehrtens and Reuben Thorne and had the luxury of keeping Jonah Lomu on the bench. Watching the slightly grainy VHS of the match uploaded to YouTube, the 18-year-old Parisse, wearing a scrum cap with tufts of black hair poking out, refuses to be overwhelmed by the opposition. He wins a great turnover from Mehrtens early on, acrobatically catches a kick on the touchline before starting a counterattack, puts in some big hits and is a danger with the ball in hand. At one point he even chips the Kiwi defence, catching Christian Cullen flatfooted, and regathers the ball before it bounces, to some bemused glances from the All Blacks.

Despite his best efforts, Italy would lose 64-10, and a precedent was set for his International career.

In 2003, the 20-year-old Parisse would play in his first World Cup. Opening with the standard hammering (7-70) by New Zealand before defeating Tonga 36-12 and scoring a try in a hard-fought 19-14 win over Canada, they then faced Wales to decide who would go on to the quarter finals. They came up just short, and Italy went home after the group stage. In Parisse, however, they had a player who was both willing and able to play at the highest level.

With Treviso he won the Coppa Italia plus two Italian league titles before being lured by millionaire owner Max Guazzini to join his French giants Stade Français in 2005. There he would link up with another of our mavericks, Christophe Dominici, and fellow Italian legends Mauro and Mirco Bergamasco, to name just a few of the rugby superstars he'd play alongside during his remarkable 14 seasons in Paris.

In 2004, he'd feature in his first-ever Six Nations victory, a 20-14 home victory over Scotland. Lining up in the Italian XV that day would be Santiago Dellapè, also from Parisse's home city of La Plata, alongside the Argentina-born Martín Castrogiovanni and Gonzalo Canale plus Cristian Stoica, who was born in Romania but moved to Italy as a child, and Aaron Persico, a New Zealander whose grandfather, Liberato, hailed from Sorrento. The diaspora served the Azzurri well that day!

The following year, Parisse would score a try in what must have been a particularly satisfying 30-29 win over Argentina in Córdoba, but the Six Nations woes would continue – an 18-18 draw in Cardiff in 2006 being a rare highlight, and the first time that Italy had not lost away from home since joining the tournament in 2000.

2007 seemed to be a breakthrough year, with consecutive Six Nations wins – away to Scotland then home to Wales – and a solid World Cup that year in France, with wins over Romania and Portugal. It was however, not to be. Despite Parisse being named Italy captain in 2008 and becoming the first Italian to be shortlisted for the IRB's World Player of the Year Award, Italy would manage only one win in that year's Six Nations – over Scotland, 23-20 in Rome – and he would play in 17 straight International defeats through into 2010.

Italy picked up the Wooden Spoon in the 2010 and 2011 Six Nations tournaments and had a disappointing World Cup before recording wins over Scotland in 2012 and France in 2013, when they also claimed their first-ever Six Nations win over Ireland. These would prove just brief highlights, with them losing every game in the 2014 Six Nations then enduring another flat 2015 World Cup.

In 2016, in the 81st minute of the Six Nations fixture against France in Paris, the home team were leading 23-21 with Italy hammering away on the edge of the 22. The pressure on the French was mounting when the ball came to Parisse, he looked up, took a step and sent a kick spiralling towards the post.

It went wide.

He can't quite do it all.

Later that year Parisse's Italy did, however, defeat a South Africa team including the likes of Bryan Habana and Damian de Allende, 20-18 in Florence. From this triumph, though, he'd win only three of his remaining 21 games for the national team: against Fiji, Russia and Namibia. Intending to step down from the International game after the 2019 World Cup – astonishingly, his fifth instalment of the tournament – he decided to postpone retirement after a typhoon meant that Italy's fixture against New Zealand was cancelled, and instead play in the 2020 Six Nations. But then Covid-19 struck and the end of the tournament was postponed and then played in the October in empty stadia, scuppering his chance to say goodbye to the home crowd during a fixture in Rome.

Whilst talk of his returning to the International side bubbled along until 2022, at the time of writing it does look like he has played his last game for the Azzurri – though we should never rule anything out when it comes to Sergio Parisse!

When Italy coach Franco Smith was asked how Parisse could be replaced, his answer was simple:

> You don't. The more you want to replace him, the more difficult it is going to be. He's one of a kind. There are a lot of rugby personalities around the world that have never been replaced. You lose them forever, but there are new personalities that can develop. He's overshadowed Italian rugby, for the right reasons, for a very long time. Now it's time to shine a light on others who can develop with Sergio as their example.[150]

The club game is keeping Parisse busy, though in the summer of 2019, he abruptly quit Stade Français a year before his contract was due to expire. According to *L'Équipe*, Stade were concerned that Parisse's injuries were catching up with him, limiting both his abilities and time on the pitch, and wanted to offer him a player-coach role that would get him off their wage bill. But the Italian declined.[151] It was alleged that their Italy talisman was increasingly dissatisfied with the new management of South African Heyneke Meyer and had shared some strong views with the current owner, Capri-Sun magnate Hans-Peter Wild, on where the club could improve.

In his social media sign-off he thanked the former owner, Max Guazzini, but tellingly not the current leadership:

> Thank you, Max. Thank you to the players, friends, brothers. Thank you to the fans and all those who have contributed to making this incredible love story possible!! Thank you, Paris!!

Stade's announcement was a curt six-line statement. A sad end to 14 years of service.

Whilst some thought this would be the end of his career, another French giant, Toulon, came calling and he has prospered with this new challenge. In November 2020 he set rugby Twitter ablaze with an outrageous cross-field kick straight into the arms of winger Erwan Dridi, enabling him to score a try, in a win over Brive in which Parisse also set up another try with a stunning one-handed offload. In June 2022 the 38-year-old Parisse agreed a one-year contract extension, with Toulon coach Franck Azéma telling journalists:

> He listens to his body and he has a good feeling about it. In your career, depending on your age, it is above all your feelings that matter, and knowing what you are capable of absorbing.[152]

Writing about Parisse's career, it's hard to escape the grind of the International defeats. It's different to any other player in this book, but I think that's what makes him such an interesting figure, maintaining his high standards and world-class standard even alongside players and in team performances far below his level. His mental resilience is something that many young players can strive towards.

But it's not all been hard graft for Parisse. He's played most of his club career for French aristocrats Stade Français, winning two national championships and one European Challenge Cup with the Parisian club. His first marriage was to Alexandra Rosenfeld, a former Miss France and Miss Europe, and he now spends a lot of his year on the Côte d'Azur with his second wife and children. Although he lost his hair somewhere around the age of 24, it has not affected his popularity in the eyes of some sections of rugby fans and he has regularly posed in the annual Stade Français calendar, *Les Dieux du Stade* (the Gods of Stade/the stadium), in which he's typically wearing very few clothes, if any.

And as always seems the way when writing about a high-profile player in France, some unusual off-the-pitch activities complete the CV. For Parisse, they include lending his voice to a character in the French-language version of Disney film *Wreck-It Ralph* and its sequel.

There's no one quite like Sergio Parisse. In some ways he reminds me of Ryan Giggs, the best player by a distance in the otherwise disappointing Wales football sides of the late 1990s and early 2000s. But Giggs wouldn't always be there – as the years went on, he'd increasingly pick and choose the matches he played in. Parisse has only one setting as a player – full velocity, and it's the same today as it was 20 years ago.

For a large portion of his career, he's undoubtedly been Italy's most talented forward, often their strongest ball carrier and at times possibly even their best kicker. At times he'd be guilty of trying to do too much. However supreme his talents, rugby is still the ultimate team game. Still a dominant force on the pitch for Toulon, his continued efforts are a credit to his spirit, his confidence in himself and his own abilities, as well as his professionalism and durability. Playing for Italy, he rarely gets an armchair ride at the back of the scrum – his quiet days at the office are few and far between.

He's always been very honest about the unusual position he has been in, stating in 2020:

> I have always hated defeat but that does not make me feel like a failure. I was not playing for New Zealand, so I knew there would be more defeats than victories, but as captain you have to set an example. My job as captain was not just to make speeches. The day after a game, you might wake up and feel dead because you've given a lot of emotion, but you've failed to win.
>
> You lose by three points and you're overthinking. "Why did we lose? How do we get better? Why didn't our plan work?" But you have to keep going. Again. Again. Again. It is easier to captain a team when you are winning 80 per cent of the time, sure, but you stay positive.

> You can't go to Twickenham to play England and say, "Well boys, we are probably going to lose but..." Fuck that... Sometimes games are strange. When you see how Japan did at the World Cup [a shock win over South Africa in 2015], that is the beauty of sport... the underdogs. Italy will never be the favourites, especially in the Six Nations, but never give up. That's what I want these young guys to carry on.[153]

In the 2022 Six Nations, a youthful and vibrant Italian side ended a run of 36 successive losses spread over seven years with a stunning late win over reigning champions Wales in Cardiff. And with Benetton and Zebre now more competitive than ever in the United Rugby Championship, if Italian rugby does permanently step out of the doldrums, they will be standing on the shoulders of a giant called Sergio Parisse.

KEITH MURDOCH

"I am not the same as you ordinary blokes, you know."

FACTFILE

Full name: Keith Murdoch

Born: 9 September 1943, Dunedin, New Zealand

Died: 27 February 2018, Carnarvon, WA, Australia

Position: Prop

Representative team: New Zealand

Clubs: Zingari-Richmond, Otago, Hawke's Bay, Auckland

It was a sweltering hot Saturday afternoon in early March when they buried Keith Murdoch.

After decades of wandering, his final home was a small patch in Carnavon cemetery in the far west of Australia, a nine-hour drive north of Perth. The ground is covered with red sand, the sky blue and the searing sun unforgiving. The green grass around some of the graves is of the plastic variety you find in greengrocers' shops; no other type would survive. About a dozen people stood under the beating sun: a sister, some friends and a few New Zealanders who lived locally, there to represent their country in saying goodbye to All Black number 686.

His gravestone was adorned with the Silver Fern and his cap number, name, dates and a short text: 'Here lies a man some call a legend, a mystery man, but to his family and friends he was a very much-loved man with a big heart, who loved a beer with his mates and found his peace in the solitude of the Outback. We miss you mate. Rest peacefully Keith.'[154]

One of the mourners, with true Antipodean bluntness, remembers the funeral director needing some extra pairs of hands getting the casket out of the hearse: "Christ, he was heavy. Then we had to shovel the dirt on top of the big bastard. It was a job-and-a-half, let me give you the tip."

At the peak of his rugby career, Murdoch had been 17st 3lbs, and at the time of his death he was bigger.

There's something bleakly poetic about the 74-year-old Murdoch being laid to rest in a place with a Welsh name (albeit the anglicised version – the town was named in honour of a nineteenth-century Secretary of State for the Colonies, the 4th Earl of Carnarvon, father of the 5th Earl, who financially backed the excavation of Tutankhamun's tomb and then apparently fell victim to 'the Mummy's Curse'), given that his rugby career had come to an abrupt halt in Cardiff 46 years earlier.

What happened in those intervening years is a fascinating, sad and mysterious story.

Born in Dunedin in 1943, Murdoch was educated at King Edward Technical College and played his first adult rugby match for Zingari Richmond before breaking into the Otago team in 1964, aged 20. He made an immediate impact, being named one of the season's five most promising players by the *Rugby Almanack of New Zealand*. A hugely powerful player, with natural bulk and strength – there were no gym sessions or protein plans in 1960s New Zealand – his (48") barrel chest was so large that when he was called up to the All Blacks, panels of extra material had to be sewn into his shirts. His bulk plus his black Mexican bandit moustache gave him a look that was part cartoon villain, part South American freedom fighter.

A superb scrummager and surprisingly rapid in the loose, there were perhaps some clues to his later itinerant lifestyle.

He bounced between clubs through the late Sixties and appeared to not play any rugby at all in 1968. But the following year, whilst back with Otago, he impressed Kiwi coach Ivan Vodanovich and was selected for the All Blacks' 1970 tour of South Africa. Although he broke his ankle mid-tour, he managed to recover and made eight appearances against local club sides before his full International debut in the fourth and final Test against the Springboks. He put in a powerful performance in the match, despite being in constant pain from an infected appendix.

He then suffered two years of injury disappointment before winning back his place in the squad and being selected for the 1972–73 tour of the UK, Ireland, France and North America. This was an epic tour, spanning 32 matches including five Tests, which began in October in 1972 in Canada and eventually concluded in southern France in February 1973. There were several memorable occasions on the tour: the loss to fellow maverick Ray Gravell's Llanelli, a draw with a Munster team containing Moss Keane, wins against Wales, Scotland and England, a draw with Ireland and a loss to France, and a first-ever defeat to a star-studded Barbarians side, in a match where Gareth Edwards scored 'that try'.

Murdoch settled into the squad well, but his relationship with the press had been fractious in the past. In 1971, in response to a request from one journalist, Murdoch had invited him into the changing room for a chat, then proceeded to drag him into the showers and hold him there until he was soaking wet.

On the 1972 tour, Kiwi journalist Norman Harris made the mistake of correcting Murdoch, who was clowning around at check-in at a hotel in Peebles in Scotland. Murdoch was pretending to be fellow tourist Graham Whiting, but Harris told an exasperated receptionist his real name.

In a flash, as Harris would later describe, "Murdoch reached out a huge hand, grasped my scalp, and with a swift downward movement deposited me on the floor."[155]

He also allegedly threatened to assault a cartoonist attached to the tour, for reasons lost in the mists of history.

It was the Test against Wales that would prove to be the highlight of Murdoch's International career, then in the hours that followed it, its end.

This was a Wales team at the peak of its powers, with the likes of JPR, Phil Bennett, Gerald Davies and Mervyn Davies all lining up in the hope of a first win over the All Blacks since 1953. Despite being unknown to the northern-hemisphere press prior to his arrival, Murdoch performed well in the first half of the tour. With the *Western Mail* describing him as "the giant Otago prop" and the "biggest-chested player to ever represent the All Blacks", he was selected to start against Wales.

With the game finely poised, All Blacks scrum half Sid Going chips the ball towards the touchline, Wales wing John Bevan manages to catch it but doesn't control it and Going then crashes into the back of him. The ball is loose, five Kiwis rush forward – "like a great black blanket," says commentator Bill McLaren – and it falls to Murdoch, who picks it up, stumbles forward and crashes over the try line before the Welsh cover can stop him. The home team protest to the referee that the ball wasn't grounded, but the try is awarded and Murdoch emerges from a pile of red shirts, ball in hand but no expression of happiness on his face as he trots back to the halfway line. The try made it 10-0 to New Zealand, and Murdoch would distinguish himself with a strong performance in a hard-fought 19-16 win.

Precisely what happened that evening is still unclear and will probably always remain muddied. Reportedly, after many hours of celebrating, Murdoch was among other All Blacks back at their accommodation, the Angel Hotel in Cardiff, a regular host of rugby teams due to its location just across the road from Cardiff Arms Park. There Murdoch was involved in a scrap in the kitchen, which was closed at the time – with sources differing on whether he was there looking for more food, or drink, or both – and security guard Peter Grant, who somehow got in the way, emerged with a serious black eye.

Different reports of the fracas exist. The most repeated is that Murdoch punched Grant after he tried to block his entry to the kitchen. There's another that Grant got thumped by accident as he tried to stop Murdoch hitting New Zealand team officials. And a third, from the daughter of tour manager Ernie Todd, that Murdoch had not assaulted a security guard at all, but chased and threatened a female member of hotel staff.

The following morning, Murdoch awoke to what I'd assume was a stinking hangover, a possible dull ache across his knuckles and a media storm. The incident made front page news in the Welsh papers and quickly filtered out across the world, all the way to New Zealand.

Peter Grant, 29, of Cwmbran, told reporters that he'd gone into the kitchen after hearing complaints that Murdoch was annoying staff:

> He tried to punch one of his tour officials and I stepped in to restrain him. They managed to get him away but then he came round from some pillars and punched me. They held me back to stop me getting at him. Our men restrained him, with one or two of the New Zealand players helping. It was ridiculous. We were there to protect the New Zealanders. This should never have happened.[156]

As the flames of the story were quickly fanned, the chances of the All Blacks' management being able to discipline Murdoch in-house and brush the incident under the carpet lessened. Under intense pressure from the home unions (who sensed the chance to get a Kiwi scalp one way or another) and the press, a series of meetings and long-distance calls back to New Zealand eventually saw manager Ernie Todd, assistant manager Bob Duff, captain Ian Kirkpatrick and vice-captain Sid Going decide that Murdoch should be sent home immediately.

As the players were boarding the bus for training, Murdoch appeared and made his famous comment, "Hooray boys, I'm off." His teammates had a few minutes to say goodbyes and that was that: Murdoch's tour was over.

Ernie Todd hastily called a press conference: "I've called this conference to give you the news that Keith Murdoch is returning home," he began. "I made this decision, really, for the benefit of the player himself and of the team as a whole. It was not an easy decision to make but I think these are the managerial responsibilities I must face up to."

When asked how Murdoch had taken his dismissal, he replied, "Keith Murdoch took the decision like the wonderful man he is."[157]

There's no record of anyone asking why, if he was so wonderful, he was being sent home in disgrace.

Murdoch, dogged by journalists, was escorted to Heathrow, where he boarded a Qantas plane that would take him to Frankfurt, Singapore and on to Sydney, before a connecting flight would take him home to New Zealand.

Except he never got that far.

With reporters waiting at Auckland for his arrival, he switched flights at Singapore and flew to Perth, where he headed into the outback and promptly disappeared. The New Zealand Rugby Union tried to find him, but failed.

In the 46 years between the incident at the Angel Hotel and his death, despite being a regular fixation of the New Zealand press, he was only tracked down four times, slipping away after each discovery.

In 1974 he was working on an oil rig near Perth when one of the greats of New Zealand rugby writing, Terry McLean, tracked him down. Murdoch was explicit in what he would do to McLean if he didn't leave him alone. McLean went home.

Shortly after that, he was back in New Zealand, working on a farm in a job organised by his old All Blacks teammate Graham Whiting.

In 1980, whilst working on a farm owned by friends in Otago on New Zealand's South Island, the friends' son was found unconscious in their swimming pool. He was dragged out of the pool and Murdoch gave him mouth-to-mouth resuscitation, saving the youngster's life. When word of his heroism got out, the press arrived and Murdoch disappeared again, this time back to Australia.

In 1990 a TV producer, Margot McRae, tracked him down to Tully, a remote town in northern Australia. In a 45-minute off-camera interview, he explained that he liked the nomadic life and was happy in himself. When McRae returned to the banana plantation that he was working at the following day with a camera crew, she was hopeful for a scoop.

Murdoch, however, had other ideas, as McRae remembers:

> He was out in the bush, slashing away with a machete. The camera crew were a hundred yards behind me, but they were afraid. Then he heard me. The slashing stopped and there was this moment's silence. Then he just ran away.[158]

He was gone. She would later recall: "He was a deeply shy person, not very articulate. He felt it was better to be quiet than be embarrassed. He was not going to come home and be confronted by reporters."[159]

The last time that Murdoch came back into the public eye was in 2001, during an inquest into the death of an Aboriginal man, Christopher Limerick, who had been found dead at the bottom of an abandoned mine. The last time he'd been seen in the nearest town, Tennant Creek, he'd reportedly been trying to break into a house that Murdoch was staying in, and the former All Black had apparently chased him off before the police arrived.

Shortly after that, Limerick was reported as missing and it later emerged that Murdoch had told a neighbour: "I don't think he'll come back." Limerick's body was found two weeks later, and Murdoch had moved on when a call went out to appear at the inquest – not as a suspect but a "critical witness."

Australian police eventually tracked him down at a remote cattle station hundreds of miles away, and though he was criticised by the coroner for his cavalier attitude towards the enquiry, no charges were brought against Murdoch.

It was concluded that Limerick had died of exposure, having entered the mine looking for water. There was, however, evidence of assault, and it appeared likely that Limerick had been taken to the mine against his will.

And that was the last the wider public heard of Murdoch until he died in 2018, after living out his final years in Carnarvon, Western Australia.

Despite his famed reclusiveness, Murdoch did remain in contact with some family and a number of his former All Blacks teammates. It was his sister who would confirm his death. He would return to New Zealand from time to time, and those he visited helped protect his privacy. Whilst back home, he never did collect the caps he was owed, or turn up at various team reunions, despite an empty chair being left for him in case he chose to make an appearance.

His decades out of the spotlight, embellished by hundreds of Elvis-like alleged sightings, gave the Keith Murdoch story a romantic element. He never publicly spoke about what happened that night in Cardiff, and why he chose to derail his rugby career so suddenly and dramatically. There's no evidence he ever picked up a rugby ball again. Into this void has flowed speculation, half-truths and outright lies.

It has also thrown a shroud of guilt over New Zealand rugby as a whole.

In 2020, tour captain Ian Kirkpatrick told Sky Sports:

> It should have been, "He goes, we go." I'm not quite sure what that would have done with things. I just feel probably looking back I was too young to make a real stand. The manager had the

> right to do what he [did]. If he wanted to send a player home, he could. I really blame myself for that and I don't mind wearing that. It's not done easy but if you deserve it, you take it and get on with it. It was a bit sad that Keith didn't stay with us, but that's all history.[160]

In a 2018 book, *Murdoch: The All Black Who Never Returned*, acclaimed New Zealand sportswriter Ron Palenski contends that the prop was "sacrificed for doing something much less than what many other players, for New Zealand and other countries, have done on tours." He thinks Murdoch was "hung out to dry" by New Zealand Rugby Union officials, who he sees as having capitulated to demands by British rugby chiefs to banish him.

Newspaper editor Karl du Fresne agrees, describing it as a "piffling episode" and arguing:

> Murdoch didn't kill the hotel security man or even leave him permanently maimed. His transgression looks almost laughably inoffensive compared with the predatory sexual exploits, drunken assaults and drug abuse that are now almost commonplace in some sporting codes. In terms of infamy, his behaviour pales into insignificance even alongside some of the on-field behaviour of more recent All Blacks.

Certainly, rugby players have got away with far worse. But this wasn't out of character for Murdoch. He was a man of immense strength – there's a story of how he once needed to move a broken-down car away from the road, so tied a rope around its tow bar and pulled it himself – and as a prop forward, the full pressure of the scrum would fall on his shoulders. In that era, players weren't as big, but he sure was.

Although at times jovial company, he was also shy and sometimes drank far too much. He was what's often described as a loose cannon. Early in the tour, Murdoch told Kiwi journalist T P McLean:

> I am not the same as you ordinary blokes, you know. Nine-tenths of the time I am OK. On the other tenth I have got to blow. I can't take it. I have got to stand up for myself and explode.

We've already noted that there were other moments of off-field violence from Murdoch whilst in All Black squads.

So, as is often the way, the truth about Murdoch is probably somewhere in between. He probably did act badly that night, but from what little evidence we have, it seems unjust that he should have been punished as publicly and brutally as he was. From that moment on, his life would become part Shakespearean tragedy, and part just a bloke trying to move on from a period of his life that he knew he could never return to even if he wanted to.

The only All Black ever sent home from a tour in disgrace, his official profile on the New Zealand Rugby homepage doesn't pull any punches:

> No All Black has been more controversial, more enigmatic and more tragic than the giant prop Keith Murdoch, whose erratic career at both provincial and International levels ended sensationally late in 1972.[161]

Powerful, talented but ultimately unable to maintain his career, he played just three Tests, but the extraordinary aftermath of that night in Cardiff left a legacy and memory which outweighs that of players with far more caps.

But I doubt he would have seen it that way, if he even thought about it at all. Perhaps it's time to leave his memory alone now – as he told Margot McRae: "This isn't a story, this is my life."[162]

JEAN-PIERRE RIVES

"We must always remember we have to play with a smile in our hearts. That is my philosophy of rugby."

FACTFILE

Full name: Jean-Pierre Rives

Born: 31 December 1952, Toulouse, Haute-Garonne, France

Position: Flanker

Representative teams: France XV, Barbarians, French Barbarians, World XV, France

Clubs: Toulouse Olympique Employés Club (TOEC), Stade Beaumontois, Toulouse, Racing Club de France

Nicknames: *Casque d'or* ('Golden helmet'), Asterix

IT MIGHT HAVE been in front of a 49-floor skyscraper on bustling Second Avenue in Manhattan, just a block from the UN, but even the busiest New Yorker would have taken a moment to stop and look at what was placed there in 2010.

The large, oxidized golden-brown welded steel beams, twisting in and out of each other, could not be ignored. At first you might think that if you stared long enough at it, a word would become visible, but no: it's actually almost organic, like willow branches dipping into water or whispering streams running down a hillside. The neat curves and energy-filled straight lines remind me a little of the ramps I used to build as a child to hurl toy cars down. As with all art, there's no prescription for what you can see in a piece, but this sculpture – called *Les Rubans de la Mémoire* ('Ribbons of Memory') – was constructed in memory of the murdered civil rights leader Dr Martin Luther King Jr. and is part of global series of works that commemorate those no longer with us.

Five years later these ribbons would appear again, not in one of the many exhibitions around the world – from Sydney to San Francisco and Dubai to Brussels – where the series featured, but on the 2015 Rugby World Cup French shirt. Look closely and you can see the same curvature seen in New York running up from below the famous cockerel badge to over the shoulder, almost like a tattoo on the famous blue material.

Inside the shirt is a message from the artist, explaining the significance of the ribbons to him and why they are on the shirt. Translated from the original French, it states:

> The ribbons of memory are at the centre of our origins and the start of all hope. Each individual has a unique experience which forms part of our community, and the history of these communities is the memory of a nation.[163]

It's poetic, it's powerful and, to be honest, it's quintessentially Jean-Pierre Rives.

There is no one else who could straddle the worlds of International rugby and art as successfully and confidently as Rives. Capped 59 times, 34 as captain, he led France to two Grand Slam triumphs in 1977 and 1981, and the nation's first-ever win over New Zealand in 1979. Since his retirement in 1984, he has focussed his seemingly boundless energy on art, winning global acclaim a second time and having his work exhibited around the world – including in the famous Jardin du Luxembourg in Paris, the first-time sculptures had been on show there since Auguste Rodin's exhibition more than a century earlier. Alongside his sporting and artistic awards, he has also collected the highest decoration in France, the Order of the *Légion d'Honneur*.

But this only tells a fraction of the story.

His achievements are extraordinary, but it is perhaps his spirit and his relationship with rugby that are the most remarkable.

Rives may have Saint-Simon, a suburb of the rugby-mad city of Toulouse, as his birthplace, but his love of the game was far from assured. His childhood was spent mainly in colonial Africa, where his father served as a pilot in the French Air Force, and home was variously Morocco, Nigeria and Ivory Coast. For the expatriate community, one sport ruled all: tennis. Both his parents were enthusiastic players, and the young Jean-Pierre – classified as a 15-year-old when just 12, on account of his talent – went as far as the junior French Championships at Roland Garros, where he lost in the final of the boys' doubles.

He only began playing rugby when sent back to France for schooling as a teenager, but once committed to the game, it was clear he was a natural. Rives claims that he actually played his best rugby between the ages of 17 and 20: "I played differently in those days. Everywhere, at every moment, I was attacking. That was my role. I never thought about defence."[164]

He was playing for the University of Toulouse team and had already established a reputation for a compelling combination of speed, skill, and fearlessness when the French selectors became interested. They invited him for a trial match.

Rives declined.

Years later he recalled:

> My mind was just not on rugby at that time; in fact, I was playing it only for pleasure... I loved so much the game between 3 and 4.30, but after that the life did not mean much. For me, rugby is not a monopoly of friendship or anything else... I told the selectors, sorry, I was not free to play. I said I am already playing and would prefer it to be with my university.[165]

The snub was met with astonishment, and I doubt any of those selectors would at that moment have imagined he would ever don the shirt of Les Bleus, let alone be arguably their greatest captain of all time.

But this is classic Rives. He was a man who knew what he wanted and wasn't afraid to tell others. People thought this was all part of an act, but no: this is really who he is. In fact, he even needed some persuading to join Toulouse after graduating from university. Eventually he relented, starting his senior career as a 21-year-old in 1973 and playing for his country just two seasons later, resplendent with a mane of golden hair.

Even by the standards of the time, at 5'11" and 13st he was small – a stone lighter and three inches shorter than Jean-Claude Skrela, his great friend and back-row partner for club and country, and positively tiny compared to Dylan Cretin (6' 5" and 16st 5lbs), who fills this role for France today. Some considered Rives too small for the International game. But he was fast and fearless, ferocious in the tackle, and an expert roaming off his flank or in the maul. His handsome face was typically bloodied and bandaged, a by-product both of his bravery and of being the scourge of bigger, meaner opponents.

The call to join the French national team came in 1975, in the fixture against England at Twickenham.

His preparation for this debut was typically unorthodox. Taken under the wing of the more experienced and wonderfully named Claude Spanghero, the day before the game was spent in some of Soho's finest adult-entertainment venues and then, whilst the rest of the team went to bed at 10.30 p.m., he stayed up until 3 a.m. playing poker.

When he took the field, he was instructed to closely follow fellow maverick Andy Ripley, the England No. 8, and tackle him every time he got the ball – as a huge ball carrier, stopping the Rosslyn Park man was deemed essential if the French were to succeed. The only problem was that Rives was the only person in the entire stadium who didn't know who Ripley was.

He had to ask one of his teammates to point him out once the game had started.

But once his target was identified, he didn't let him out of his sights. His tackling and work rate was astonishing in a 27-20 win, and his pal from the Soho sortie, Spanghero, scored a crucial try. Rives had arrived in International rugby.

The Peter Bills book on Jean-Pierre Rives is an excellent and personal view, with its vivid language matching the flow and creativity of the man himself. The English journalist described this moment in his career, following his first season of International rugby:

> Like the launched rocket, his light was ascending. France had discovered, from a fog of mediocrity, a blond beacon to light the future path. And what a path it would become.[166]

In 1977 he was instrumental in helping France to a Grand Slam, and only a defeat to Wales in Cardiff stopped the feat being repeated the following season.

The tussles between Wales and France in this era were legendary, with silky backs and bulldozing forwards, outrageous skills and some of the darker arts of the game all summoning up some monumental clashes. The Welsh great Gareth Edwards, who became a good friend of Rives' (and this is something of a trend when it comes to the Frenchman's interaction with his opponents), saw him and Skrela as the best back-row partnership he ever faced.

Edwards was fascinated when he first came up against Rives, recalling years later:

> ...this good looking, blond-haired player who looked more like a pop star than a rugby player. A lot of people thought, early on, it was more of a gimmick, because he wasn't really good enough. But they soon changed that view. He was always first to the ball, and always brave.[167]

Ireland also proved a combative fixture in this era, with Rives' French forwards packing down against another of our mavericks, Moss Keane, the lively Fergus Slattery and the legendary Willie John McBride, among other fierce opponents. And with the Irish, Rives found a deeper connection, as he proudly told *The Irish Times*:

> I would have been happy to represent Ireland. I like the tragic, their empathy, their taste for all things larger than life... I have a real weakness for them. Their dramatic fighting spirit. More than fondness, I feel a certain kind of admiration. If I hadn't been born French, I would have been very happy to be Irish.[168]

By the time the French tour of New Zealand tour of 1979 came around, Rives had been national captain for a year. This was a tour of almost Lionsesque proportions: 10 matches, beginning in Fiji and finishing in Tahiti, with a run of fixtures against a hardcore group of Kiwi club sides warming up (or should that be 'breaking down'?) the French ahead of a two-Test series against the All Blacks, a team the French hadn't beaten on home shores in eight attempts.

The going was predictably tough. Relentless games against skilful and doughty opposition in the cold, wet New Zealand winter makes this probably the toughest tour in world rugby. The French lost the first Test 23-9 in Christchurch, and followed this up with a 12-11 defeat to modest club side Southland. Few would have given Les Bleus much of a chance ahead of the second Test, but what could have been a disappointing end to a damp squib of a tour would prove to be one of the greatest-ever French performances.

An unexpected piece of encouragement came to Rives from his opposite number – New Zealand captain, the thoughtful but intense Graham Mourie – who assured him after that first Test defeat: "You never know what may happen in rugby. Don't dismiss your chances, your hopes, for this second Test match, Jean-Pierre. Nothing is certain in this great game."[169]

A forensic look at the video of the first Test, hard training, the curtailing of any kind of freewheeling tour antics added to Mourie's words, and the French arrived at Auckland's Eden Park in good condition. And they struck a first psychological blow by conducting a 45-minute, no-holds-barred, full-contact warm-up session on the pitch just before kick-off in front of a presumably puzzled home crowd.

Prior to kick-off, fans were also treated to a bizarre pageant featuring an oversized papier-mâché figure that I think, given the blonde hair and headband, was meant to be Rives. Carrying a French flag and riding around atop a cardboard cockerel, he is chased by what is possibly an English player, who proceeds to pull a rugby ball out of the backside of the animal. Once the ball has been 'laid', two similarly grotesque figures that I think are meant to be New Zealand enter the field of play dragging a wooden guillotine and all the characters run off the pitch. I urge you to check the YouTube link as I don't think I am able to explain what I have just watched![170]

Perhaps Mourie, in his assessment of French chances, and the pre-match 'entertainers' were both noting the significance of the date of the fixture: 14 July – Bastille Day. A national holiday when France remembers the storming of a symbol of oppressive power through an act of bravery and unity. Rives wouldn't be one for hyperbole, but it's likely that some parallels between the situations were noted before the match.

Early moments in the match proved crucial. The French pack, bullied in the first Test, won the first scrum contests, with the All Black forwards feeling the rare sensation of going backwards. With the Kiwis under pressure at the set piece, the French backs had space to create, with rejuvenated fly half Alain Caussade, who had laboured badly in the first Test, and recalled scrum half Jérôme Gallion both producing electrifying performances, as well as a try each.

But at the core of the French team that day was Rives. Never was his ability to pop up in positions completely unexpected of him more apparent than versus the All Blacks. His blond hair seemed to stand out even more than usual when swimming against a tide of black shirts. Always identifiable and ever in the thick of the action, he fought for every ball and made tackle after tackle. Lightning quick to the breakdown, and ruthless in the contact against his bigger New Zealand opponents, his hard work helped ensure that France were leading 24-19 with just moments to go.

The final moments of the game illustrated perfectly how the match was won.

A scrum gives New Zealand possession on the halfway line. The ball moves quickly across the back line before a Frenchman slips, opening up a gap, which All Black winger Stu Wilson greedily slices through. He is in space approaching the 22 and has time to assess his options before issuing a beautiful chip over the remaining flatfooted defenders. If he can gather the kick, he'll be under the posts and will win the game.

Suddenly a bolt of blue appears from the left of the screen. It is winger Frédéric Costes, who has been causing New Zealand problems all afternoon but must now plug a gap in his own defence. He hurtles across from his own flank, eyes fixed all the time on the ball spinning in the sky and, quicker than anyone else in pursuit, catches it, takes a few steps, looks up to see precisely where he is and – just before he can get flattened by a Kiwi attacker – boots the ball off the pitch.

That's it. The referee blows the final whistle. The Bastille has been stormed. And France have secured their first win on New Zealand soil.

In an outstanding team performance, Rives was its beating heart. Jérôme Gallion recalled his importance:

> Jean-Pierre was the basis of our success in Auckland, because he took hold of the team. We were near the end of tour, we had lost the previous match before the Second Test, and I would say the morale of the troops was at its lowest... But Jean-Pierre allowed

> the revolt or rebellion... he asked each player to think... he allowed the team to rebel and that is why we were successful.[171]

For the players afterwards, there was no loud singing or bellowing of celebration in the changing room. It was quiet. Almost silent. Instead, the exhausted players luxuriated in the feeling of deep satisfaction over a job very well done. Among them sat Rives, bloodied but unbowed, this unorthodox, unexpected but thrilling and historic victory being the perfect symbol of his many talents as a player and a captain.

The pioneering triumph over the All Blacks following standout Grand Slam performances made a Rives a global star. His distinctive, handsome appearance, his all-action style of play, his natural charm and his ability to speak English saw his appeal cut across national boundaries and he became famous outside the game in a way that few others have.

A story from this era has Rives doing some filming with a British TV crew ahead of a match in the early 1980s. They invite him out to dinner but he declines, stating that he has other plans, but agrees to meet them at a club later that night. He arrives later than arranged, explaining that he had been summoned to dine with François Mitterrand, the President of France. When asked who else was there, he replies, somewhat sheepishly, that it was just the two of them.

His life during the peak years of his rugby career was a whirl of training and playing, his professional role in public relations for Pernod, plus extensive society engagements, travel and attendance at other sporting and creative events. A chapter in *Jean-Pierre Rives: A Modern Corinthian* follows him for a week and paints a picture of a truly unique lifestyle. There are moments when he seems almost like a James Bond or Don Draper from *Mad Men* kind of character – sipping champagne at the Roland Garros tennis tournament, playing golf with Formula One driver Alain Proust, and chatting to a steady stream of beautiful women. At other times, he cuts an eccentric figure, picking at food when he can, drinking cups of coffee that are hours old, fussing over his small garden and receiving phone calls at all hours from rugby connections seeking help and advice.

In 1981 he left Toulouse for Racing Club de France in Paris. The same year he won a second Grand Slam, secured with a 16-12 win over England at Twickenham.

That summer he would travel to Australia, and although there would be no famous victory, even in defeat his legend would grow. In an early game against Queensland, Rives was trapped at the bottom of a ruck and a rogue boot smashed against his shoulder. As he was helped off the pitch, it was clear that the bone had been twisted horribly out of position and was almost bursting through the skin. He had suffered regular injuries through his career, but this was particularly serious. He missed the first Test, a narrow 17-14 defeat, and the odds of him playing in the second Test looked very slim.

The crowd in Sydney were therefore shocked when, his shoulder wrapped in padding, he ran out gingerly with the team to take his place in the French XV. The Australian full back that day, Paul McLean, recalled:

> He took the field looking like Quasimodo. One shoulder was about six inches lower than the other, and the strapping and padding holding it together gave his body a weird, contorted shape.[172]

McLean's teammate, No. 8 Mark Loane, was similarly shocked to see the French captain:

> I was staggered he tried to take on the game, let alone finish it. It was bravery to the point of insanity... Rives always led from the front. Perhaps all rugby is folly in the end. But I certainly would have found it impossible to play with that. He could not tackle but he tried to take the ball off players several times. It made me think of Napoleon's troops bravely retreating from

> Moscow. Battered and beaten but still attempting to make a contest of it.[173]

France went down 24-14 that day despite their captain's best efforts. Effectively playing with only one arm, he could only lean on the side of scrums, and attempt to disrupt rather than stop attacks. But the courage that pushed him through the full 80 minutes won the respect and admiration of the rugby world. Rives would later admit that perhaps he shouldn't have played but, quite simply, his team wanted and needed him – he did it for the boys.

He would continue to play with distinction for club and country before the injuries finally caught up with him, retiring from International rugby in 1984 and from the game entirely two years later.

But that is not the end of the story for Rives. There'd be no drift into media work, after-dinner speeches and golf for him. Throughout his playing career, he'd had a keen interest in art, in particular the work of his good friend, the sculptor Albert Féraud, and from this initial curiosity has sprung a successful second career as an artist himself.

The two men found a common aesthetic, and many of Rives' earliest sculptures were created in Féraud's workshop, where both artists worked side by side. The connection between art and rugby is a natural one for Rives: "In sports you make movement, and you are maybe sculpting or painting in the space with your body," he told *The Sydney Morning Herald*. "In art you use instruments. Art is just energy; you have to do it; it has to come out."

Today Rives works out of a disused railway shed in the north of Paris, where his sculpture focuses on the forms and twists of found steel, which he cuts strategically to ally the hardness of the material with the softness of its curves. French newspaper *La Dépêche du Midi* has described his sculptures as being "a marvellous mixture of suffering, grace and beauty."[174]

He paints as well, and his work is found in numerous public, private and corporate collections around the world. Many of his pieces are in places where his rugby exploits will be little known and his first career is normally a mere footnote, if present at all, in the descriptions and biographies that appear next to his work.

Rives still has a keen interest in rugby – and every Six Nations the world sees one of his works, as he designed the Giuseppe Garibaldi trophy, which is awarded to the winner of the match between France and Italy. It's no silver cup or plate, this: no, it features elegant black curls of metal, almost like a ball's trajectory, and is one of the most eye-catching trophies in the game. He is also closely involved with the French Barbarians, which he co-founded in 1979.

As befitting his role as a true Renaissance man, he has also helped run a restaurant and has, like so many French rugby greats, acted in a few feature films. Rives played the role of Teuton Chief in *Druids* (2001), an action film about a Gaulish rebellion against Roman rule starring Christopher *Highlander* Lambert, and Morholt in *Connemara*, another historical film, of which I can find little aside from the DVD cover, on which Rives looks resplendent in a black tunic, holding a huge broadsword.

Now married with two children, he divides his time between his Paris studio and houses in the South of France and Ibiza.

Rives is a remarkable character whose approach to playing the game, both in not taking it too seriously but also in committing fiercely to it each time he crossed the white line onto the field of play, created part of his immense appeal. His fame transcended the sport at a time when this was rare – no social media, few televised games, and still in the amateur period, with all the rules and restrictions that brought. To achieve this you had to be something special.

He played the game in glorious technicolour. I am not sure how much he would have enjoyed today's game of video analysis, gym sessions, dour defences, rolling mauls and kick tennis, though I have no doubt he would still be a world-class operator. Even if he probably would be the smallest man on the pitch.

I'll let the great man himself offer his thoughts on how to play the game:

> We must always remember we have to play with a smile in our hearts. That is my philosophy of rugby. The game is for the spirit: to improve yourself, to express yourself. To take pleasure from the game; playing the game you love with those you love... We need communication, and for me, rugby communicates. It is about sharing emotion.

Amen to that!

JAMES SMALL

"Jeez, even the President knows I'm supposed to be the bad boy."

FACTFILE

Full name: James Terence Small
Born: 10 February 1969, Cape Town, South Africa
Died: 10 July 2019, Johannesburg, South Africa
Position: Winger
Representative teams: Barbarians, South Africa
Clubs: Transvaal, Natal Sharks, Western Province, Golden Lions, Stormers, Cats
Nicknames: No Rules, The Englishman

NELSON MANDELA APPEARED to be the most relaxed man in the stadium when introduced to the teams before the 1995 Rugby World Cup Final. Although now a little stooped and dwarfed by most of the players he was meeting, the President of South Africa was smiling, joking and as twinkly eyed as ever on this most special day in rugby history. Wearing a Springboks jersey, for so long a symbol of apartheid, the eyes of the world were on him and Johannesburg for the meeting of the Springboks and the All Blacks. Sport loves to pretend it changes lives. Normally it doesn't. But sometimes it does, and today – 24 June 1995 – it would change a country forever.

As Mandela stopped in front of New Zealand winger Jonah Lomu, he looked up, gave him his big megawatt smile and, placing his hand on his arm, said, "You. You are the one." The 6' 5", 18st All Black, largely unknown prior to the tournament, had become its undoubted star – running largely unchecked against the three Celtic nations, then pulverising England with four remarkable tries in a semi-final rampage. The first is still striking all these years on. Just four minutes into the game, Lomu picks up a bouncing loose pass 30 metres out, rounds England speedster Tony Underwood, steps out of Will Carling's diving tackle and then runs straight through Mike Catt – think more American football than rugby union – and over the try line. The try was converted and although the score at this point was still only 7-0, the match as a contest was already over.

A few minutes after speaking to Lomu, Mandela was meeting the Springboks. He stopped in front of James Small, the South Africa wing, who was positioned directly in front of Lomu. The spry 76 year old fixed the 26 year old with a smile and said, "You've got a big job to do today, Mr Small."

He certainly had. All week in the lead-up to the Final, the media had been in a frenzy about Lomu and particularly about how, or indeed *whether*, he could be stopped. In this contest, Small lived up to his name, coming in at 'only' 6' 1" and 14st, and the way the two men were discussed was more like boxers ahead of a title fight than players in a team game.

But whatever the subject, Mandela's confidence was usually rooted in something more than just hope. And his relationship with Small turned out to be a moving and surprising one that extended beyond just the turf of Ellis Park on that bright June day in 1995.

The son of Vernon Small, a South Africa soccer International turned electrician and plumber, James Terence Small was born in Cape Town in 1969. His parents divorced when he was young, and he was a sporty, high-spirited but often ill-disciplined pupil. The young Small was a keen participant in athletics, running for Transvaal in 100 m and 400 m, and was offered a place at San Diego State University in the USA as a result, but his working-class family couldn't afford to take advantage of the opportunity. His other great love was soccer, which he played until 17 – when, in a fit of rage, he headbutted a referee and was banned from the sport, thereafter turning his focus fully to rugby.

He didn't attend one of the classic South African rugby schools, and was of British rather than Afrikaans descent in an era when rugby was almost entirely dominated by those of Dutch heritage, so getting spotted for representative teams proved more challenging than it would be for others. But he shone whilst representing Transvaal Schoolboys at Craven Week – the giant annual interprovincial tournament organised for schoolboys – was selected for South African Schoolboys and his career took off. He joined the Wits rugby club and was representing Transvaal (now the Golden Lions) at just 18.

Known as much for his aggressive style of play as for his speed, his combative approach made him a firm favourite with fans. First Transvaal then Natal and soon the national team came calling.

Small would make his International debut in a 1992 fixture against New Zealand at Ellis Park later known as the Return Test, as it was South Africa's first Test match since 1984, when their apartheid system finally saw them banned from playing Test rugby by the International Rugby Board.

It wasn't just a first cap for Small – it marked the re-emergence of a sporting nation, coming blinking into the light from the dark decades of such a cruel regime. Nelson Mandela's political party, the African National Congress (the ANC), agreed to support the match under three conditions: the South African national flag would not be flown officially (this flag, synonymous with apartheid, would be replaced with the country's current flag soon after); the national anthem, '*Die Stem van Suid-Afrika*', would not be played (like the flag, this too would soon change); and there would be a minute's silence to remember the victims of township violence.

The traditional flags were still to be seen in the crowd, a section of which sang *'Die Stem van Suid-Afrika'*, and the minute's silence was disrupted by some chanting in Afrikaans, *"Fok die ANC!"* ('Fuck the ANC!').

New Zealand held off a late South African rally to win 27-24 but Small acquitted himself well in managing the giant Kiwi winger Inga Tuigamala. Unfortunately, far from the match being a celebration of unity, the actions of some in attendance sparked a political row. South African paper *The Star* described the atmosphere like this:

> For that moment inside the concrete bowl, it seemed like a besieged tribe had gathered to take strength in their numbers and to send, from the protected citadel, a message of defiance to their perceived persecutors.[175]

The ANC threatened to withdraw support for South Africa's next Test match against Australia, but in the end agreed to give the supporters a second chance. This time, before the match – in the more liberal Cape Town – two national anthems were played (*'Die Stem van Suid-Afrika'* and *'Nkosi Sikelel' iAfrika'*, a pan-African liberation song linked to countries gaining their independence), and both were sung by players and fans.

For those closely observing the Springboks singing the anthems that day, they will have noticed it was Small who would appear to be the most emotional whilst singing *'Nkosi Sikelel' iAfrika'*. With a growing reputation for hijinks and loving the nightlife as well as for his off-field interests (he'd just started doing some modelling work), some would have been surprised that it was this emerging bad boy of the game who was moved to tears while singing a song that had previously belonged to his nation's black community.

Small was also overcome by emotion when the Springboks toured the brutal prison on Robben Island where Nelson Mandela had been captive for 27 years. It was then still a prison, with all the prisoners being black or 'Coloured'. He recalled the visit from the nearly entirely white team, and when the prisoners started singing and cheering for their visitors:

> I just burst into tears. This was when the sense really took hold of me that I belonged to the new South Africa, and when I really got a sense of the responsibility of my position as a Springbok. There I was, hearing the applause for me, and at the same time thinking about Mandela's cell and how he spent twenty-seven years in prison and came out with love and friendship. All that washed over me, that huge realization, and the tears just rolled down my face.[176]

He was aware that had he not channelled his energies into rugby, his life could have taken a very different turn, as he would freely admit:

> I'm so fortunate. I was a hard guy, I could have ended up in prison. I'd go to those rough Johannesburg clubs late at night. I could easily have taken a bullet.[177]

I spoke to Small's Springboks teammate Joel Stransky about the passion that Small brought to the team:

> He was a really special guy and crossed the generations through his Springboks career. When he started, Naas Botha was still playing, and so when the new guard came in, we all looked up to Small a great deal. He was massively talented but very complex, different to most of us. He felt very strongly about things, and at times was misguided and wrong, but he had a massive heart and huge ability.

Further fuel for Small's fire was that South African rugby wasn't just divided into black and white, but also between those of Dutch and those of British origin, giving Small a particular insight into discrimination:

> I know what it's like to be on the receiving end too. I was an Englishman playing a Dutchman's game. When I began in the game at provincial level, I got fucked around badly by Afrikaner players. I was made not welcome by my own team and by the rival. Players in my own team tried to get their Afrikaner mates ahead of me in the team. They ostracized me, and I was badly beaten too. At my Springbok initiation, they fucked me up so badly my dad wanted to report them to the police.
>
> But I used all that to spur me. And I got my way in the end. I became a Springbok. Yet the whole experience taught me an appreciation for the outsider, a sympathy for those in my country who did not have the opportunities I'd been so lucky to have.[178]

Small would later recall overhearing four fans in a bar the day before his debut Test, dismissing his selection.

> They went through the whole side, player by player. And I was the only guy they didn't want. I went over to the loudest guy and said to him: "Give me your business card and I'll call you after the game." Shakily it was handed over, and after a good performance, the call was made. I phoned the guy who had dissed me and I said, "There, Fuck You!" – and I put the phone down. That's how I feel my whole life has been – proving people wrong.[179]

The mixture of talent and fire which made Small such a maverick figure was rarely more on show than in the twelve-match, three-Test series in Australia in 1993, the Springboks' first tour there since 1971. In the first Test he scored two tries in a 19-12 win. In the second, he made history for the wrong reasons when he became the first Springbok to receive a red card in a Test. Small's marching orders were for dissent, when he backchatted English referee Ed Morrison after his team had been marched back several times due to complaints from his teammate Robert du Preez at a penalty given wrongly (as watching the game on YouTube confirms) for offside. Small finally blew his top:

> I couldn't resist any more so I shouted, "Why don't you just give them a fucking penalty try?!" Those were the exact words I used. "Off!" he shouted. "Off you go, son."[180]

Red cards were such a rarity in those days that Morrison didn't actually have one on him to brandish. Instead he just somewhat theatrically pointed off the pitch, and Small began his lone trudge. The decision did appear harsh and was criticised by many, but the referee backed up his decision in the post-match press conference:

> I stand by what I've done. James abused me verbally on two occasions and as far as I am concerned there is no place for it in the game. James and I spoke [afterwards] and shook hands and what's happened is water under the bridge.[181]

Small was handed a token one-match suspension, enabling him to return for the third and final Test of the series a week later in Sydney – a 19-12 defeat, but one in which he again scored a try.

The following year he was dropped from a South Africa tour to the UK and Ireland after a bizarre fracas at the appropriately named Barney's Tavern in Port Elizabeth. It began with Small having his bum pinched by the girlfriend of Ian Macleod, a champion wave skier, and ended with the two men fighting on the beach outside the club, and the winger being booted out of the national squad.

Whilst his teammates made short work of most of their northern hemisphere opponents, Small went to New York on his own, and would later admit a bitterness that his career with the Boks ended on 47 caps, when he would have achieved his half-century if he'd made this tour.

He may have been out of the tour, but wouldn't be in exile for long. He was back in the squad for the following year's World Cup on home turf. A truly landmark tournament, it was the last of the amateur era, the first to include South Africa and the first major sporting event to take place in the country since the end of apartheid.

An opening-day win over Australia set the tone for the Springboks' surge out of their group. They walloped Western Samoa in the quarter finals before edging past France in a nervy semi-final and into the showdown against New Zealand and Jonah Lomu.

The All Blacks had demolished everyone in their path, but their momentum came to a shuddering halt in the final. The gauntlet was laid down by the Springboks during the pre-match haka. Around halfway through, Lomu broke its ranks – a small but significant break with protocol. He advanced towards Small, eyes fixed firmly on his opposite number. Then came an important moment: the giant lock Kobus Wiese, standing next to Small, took a few steps forward and out in front of Small.

"Kobus broke the line, as if to say to Lomu, 'To get to him, you have to get through me first,'" remembered Springboks skipper François Pienaar.[182]

On the final, Stransky told me:

> I remember he [Small] felt the focus on him, and yes, he was apprehensive, but he thrived under pressure – it was inspiring to him. The final was emotional for him, but when it came to facing the opposition, he said, "I'll do it, I'll set an example to the team." And that's exactly what he did.

Once the whistle blew, the South Africans rammed home this early psychological edge. They embodied the proudest of African animals, lions, and adopted the tactics of a pride in tackling in groups, with what they labelled "the gang tackle".

Small would later recall:

> Before we went out, Chester Williams [the other South African winger], said to me, "You just hold him, James, and the rest of us will pull him down." Then Kobus [Wiese] said, "Just cling on

> to him and I'll fuck him up." Chester hit him. Kobus hit him. Japie [Mulder] hit him, Joost [van der Westhuizen] hit him. I hit him...

When asked how it felt to tackle Lomu:

> When you hit him hard, it's like hitting a wall. But I got his attention. Jonah's very aware of me on the park. He knows what I bring to the party. I'm the psycho-kid who's not going to stop at anything. He knows I'm capable of going a little ballistic.[183]

The Boks kept the Kiwi attack under lock and key, but failed to score any tries themselves and in a tense, hard-fought match, neither side could gain any significant lead. South Africa led 9–6 at half time, and New Zealand levelled the scores at 9–9 with a drop goal in the second half, which is how it stayed for the rest of the regulation time. Both teams scored penalty goals in the first half of extra time, before Joel Stransky scored a late drop goal for South Africa to secure a 15-12 win and send the Rainbow Nation into raptures.

James Small was a world champion. And he would quickly become one of the poster boys for both the new South Africa and the brave new world of professional rugby, with commercial endorsements including his own underwear range, magazine front covers and the press following him as closely off the pitch as they did on it.

In the wake of the World Cup win, the team attended a function at which the President stopped for another chat, as Small would remember:

> Mandela comes up and says, "James Small, my son has posters of two white men all over his wall. One of them is François Pienaar, which I can understand. But for some unknown reason, the second man is you!" He laughed, but it made me think, "Jeez, even the President knows I'm supposed to be the bad boy."[184]

I found a copy of the August 1996 edition of the South African magazine *Cosmo Man*, which featured a topless Small carrying a toddler on the front cover. The feature about him is entitled 'Gentle Giants: the soft core of rugby's hard men' (other stories in this issue include 'Wilt or Wild – we test novelty condoms' and 'A Month in a Monastery').

The women's magazine *Femina* also had an article on him in January 1997, in which he is described thus: "like a local Johnny Depp, James is the rebel with a cause and loads of talent... utterly aware of the effect he has on women but not always sure of how to deal with it."

There were so few figures like Small in rugby (aside from some featured in this book) that the press looked to football for comparisons, with Paul Gascoigne – for his electric, if sometimes unfocussed, talent – and in particular Eric Cantona – for his combustible mix of sublime skill and mercurial temperament – being the most commonly cited.

"When I was compared to Eric Cantona," he enthused, "I took that as my biggest-ever compliment. If I had just one ounce of the skill Eric Cantona has in his left foot, I'd be a happy man. But Cantona also has the immense intelligence."[185]

I asked Joel Stransky to share some more memories of Small's approach to life:

> He certainly had his own unique lifestyle. When I roomed with him, I'd be going to bed at 10 p.m. and he'd be going out. When I woke up, he was coming back in! But his sort of lifestyle doesn't happen overnight, you descend into it. Yes, elements of his life he could have changed, but as a player, he always delivered. He never would have achieved what he did without his talent and commitment. He was also one of the hardest trainers there was – he worked his socks off, but a lot of people probably didn't realise. James also loved coaching kids: it was when he was happiest. Sure, he had problems with adults but I remember saying once to him that he'd rather spend time with kids than anyone else. He laughed but said, "Yes, I would!"

Small would continue to play, make headlines and score tries, winning his last cap for South Africa in 1997 with a brace of tries against Scotland to break his country's try-scoring record, before injury forced his full retirement in 1999.

Rugby had focussed Small's considerable energies, but without it he drifted. Still a sporting icon, he worked as a model and had plenty of opportunities coming his way, but would later admit that a lack of professional support, and his own indiscipline, stopped him taking full advantage of them – he admitted once spending all the money he had on six Armani suits. He became involved in real estate, house renovation, the restaurant business, e-sports and some commentating and coaching. Small was in a high-profile relationship with South African model Christina Storm, whom he met on a photoshoot. Twice engaged but never married, their relationship ended badly, with Small admitting he'd been violent to Storm, and an ugly custody battle over their daughter, Ruby.

This break-up sent him into a spiral, and in 2009 he woke up in a padded cell in a psychiatric hospital after a drink and drug binge ended with him cutting his wrists. He was committed for three months before being released into his mother's care.

In the depths of his despair, the phone rang. His mother picked up. The voice on the line said they were calling from the office of the President and that Mr Mandela wanted to speak to Small. On hearing this, he thought it was a cruel prank, and ordered his mum to hang up.

The phone rang again. This time Small answered, and recognised the familiar voice, a little frailer than in 1995, but still clear.

"Hi James, how are you?"

It was Nelson Mandela.

He asked what was happening, and Small opened up to him. He said that being away from the game and the spotlight meant he'd lost his sense of identity. And things had gone south from there.

The President listened, and said he knew, from his time in prison, what it was like to feel that people have forgotten about you. But that Small was still important.

Mr Mandela said, "James, you still have a big role to play, and even a responsibility. You are from the class of '95, and even if you think people have forgotten about you, they have not. You still have much to give and you are still a hero to many. That is your identity."

Small would say this call changed his life. The fact that the President had asked someone to track him down, then put in the time to call and offer him both perspective and reassurance, made him stand back up again. Mandela had taken a shine to this bad boy of the 1995 World Cup team and didn't forget about him in his moment of need.

From this moment, Small started on the road to recovery, attributing his new-found strength to the call from Mandela, his friendships across rugby and his young daughter, who would later be joined by a son.

Whilst his last years were more settled, the James Small story would be cut short in 2019, when he suffered a fatal heart attack at a strip club in Johannesburg. Aged just 50, there were no suspicious circumstances – instead the autopsy found he had been suffering from undiagnosed coronary heart disease. He was survived by his daughter Ruby, son Caleb, his sister and mother.

Small was the third of the 1995 team to die, after Ruben Kruger and Joost van der Westhuizen. A fourth, fellow wing Chester Williams, would die a few months later, also of a heart attack. Their coach, Kitch Christie, had died in 1998 after a long battle with cancer.

Their greatest opponent, Jonah Lomu, had died in 2015, from a heart attack linked to his long-term kidney disease, aged just 40.

Because of what happened that day in 1995, the lives of Lomu and Small will always be intertwined. Shortly before

Lomu passed away, a film was being made about the final and the two wingers were reunited. As they chatted, Small turned to Lomu and quietly said, "I think the only reason people remember me is because of you."

Yes, his defence on that date helped define his legacy, but he was so much more than that. A hard-running, hard-tackling winger, and a proper predator when the try line was in his sights, his 20 tries in 47 Tests was then a South African record. He was the kind of player that gets you off your seat. Not being from the conservative Afrikaner rugby tradition, he created his own philosophy – or, as he put it, "I played the game with no tradition in mind, I just wanted to get the ball and run with it."[186]

Then there's the bad boy reputation: the drink and drugs, the tattoos, the Harley Davidson, disciplinary issues and bust-ups in changing rooms and bars across South Africa. But again, this doesn't tell the full story. It's easy to pigeonhole James Small, but you'd be wrong.

In a land of diamonds, South African rugby had lost a particularly rough one, but the tributes that flowed in following his death showed just what he meant to people, even if he hadn't always been so sure himself.

The ANC, in a glowing tribute, said:

> He was a member of the legendary South African Rugby squad that won the World Cup in 1995, a year after the ushering in of a democratic government in South Africa. The class of 1995 contributed enormously towards uniting the nation and displaying to the world South Africa's sporting prowess. James Small was a patriot who fought like a soldier in the field of play and was prepared to die with his boots on. He played with extraordinary passion and commitment, for he knew that every time he walked onto the field, he carried the hopes of the nation on his shoulders.[187]

Among the tributes from players, I particularly like this one from former Springboks lock Victor Matfield:

> James was probably the first rebel in South African rugby, but everyone loved him for that because he was himself; sometimes difficult, sometimes awesome to be around — but he made a difference.[188]

So, to finish up, perhaps we should give Small the final word:

> The thing is, I'm not just that one-dimensional guy they write about. I don't want to be known as the nut who got kicked out because of a fight in a night club. I want to be known as someone who did some interesting things off the field. But, maybe most of all, I want to be known as a great competitor, as a guy who is good to play with, and hard to play against.[189]

DAVID POCOCK

"I would be doing this regardless of what career I had. It is part of being a human being and taking on the challenges we face as a society."

FACTFILE

Full name: David Pocock

Born: 23 April 1988, Gweru, Midlands Province, Zimbabwe

Positions: Flanker, No. 8

Representative teams: Australia A, Australia

Clubs: Western Force, The Brumbies, Panasonic Wild Knights

Nickname: Bam Bam

FOR THOSE (WISELY!) uninitiated in the ways of Twitter, when a name, place or phrase is listed as 'trending', it means that it's one of the main topics being discussed at that moment on the platform. It is often less than edifying: a gaff, a faux pas or something similarly negative. But when in mid December 2021, having already begun research on this chapter, I saw *David Pocock* trending, I knew it would be something both positive and interesting.

And I wasn't disappointed.

The recently retired 33-year-old former Wallabies skipper had announced he would be seeking election as an independent candidate for a Senate seat representing Australian Capital

Territory (ACT), the federal territory containing Canberra, in the 2022 elections.

Rugby players becoming politicians was not unknown in the amateur era. Wing Derek Wyatt was capped for England in the 1970s and later represented Sittingbourne and Sheppey as a Labour MP under Tony Blair and Gordon Brown. Full back Dick Spring played for Ireland (also in the 1970s) and was Tánaiste (the deputy head of government) three times in the 1980s and 1990s, as well as leading the nation's Labour Party. Bernard Laporte, who won the French championship with Bordeaux-Bègles and managed France, had a spell as Secretary of State for Sport under President Sarkozy. Whilst in New Zealand, Grahame Thorne enjoyed a remarkable career, first as a well-known International, then a City Councillor and a Member of Parliament, before losing his seat and making the switch to being a TV chef.

But with Pocock, it's slightly different. He's from the professional era.

He's young.

And he's angry.

His motivation to switch to politics is born of a frustration with the current crop of Australian politicians. He said of his decision to stand:

> Like everyone, I've been watching politics over the last three years and getting increasingly frustrated at the way politicians aren't addressing the big issues we're facing and aren't actually representing communities.
>
> We know we need bold climate action to have a great future as a country. We are living with the effects of climate change already and we need politicians who are looking further ahead than the next three years. We've got to reframe climate action as the economic opportunity it is – it's no longer a cost: the cost is not acting.[190]

Those of us who had read his comments at the COP26 climate change conference in Glasgow in November 2021 perhaps shouldn't have been surprised at this move into politics. He told assembled climate activists, international delegates and the press:

> Australia is at the sharp end of climate change. We are a huge and hot nation that see the direct and early effects of carbonisation, yet we as a society here are failing on a governmental and social level to deal with the change. You asked me earlier if this was about a marginal gain philosophy – us all doing 100 things 1% better – but I say no, it's much bigger than that and we need to change the big things.[191]

To go from hitting rucks to hitting environmental targets – for Pocock, at least – is not as big a step as you might expect. An outstanding captain and openside flanker, he is one of the most talented, engaging and interesting players of the modern game, and has consistently championed social and environmental causes. Since his retirement, he has committed full-time to making a bigger difference to the world.

Pocock was born just outside of Gweru in central Zimbabwe on a family farm that produced flowers for export and cash crops like tomatoes. He began playing rugby at school at the age of 8, but family life was shattered by the chaotic and aggressive land reforms ordered by Robert Mugabe.

In 2002 David, aged 14, his parents and two brothers fled to Brisbane after a neighbouring farmer was shot and killed and their own farm was confiscated in the Mugabe land grab.

When the Pococks relocated, they left behind a lifetime's work and their extended family, and arrived in Australia with few possessions and little money. Dad Andy worked as a gardener and factory worker before finding a new career as a counsellor and therapist.

Rugby became a way of dealing with what had happened in Zimbabwe. Pocock told *The Sydney Morning Herald* in 2016:

> I remember being pretty scared, mostly just at night. As a kid, all the different scenarios are going through your mind... I knew I had some trauma stuff in there that I needed to actually tell people about and talk through, but in my mind there were people way worse off. I've got this opportunity, I've got sport.[192]

The young Pocock played alongside another free spirit, Quade Cooper, in an all-conquering Anglican Church Grammar School team. Initially playing at inside centre, he switched to the forwards aged 16. At 18 he made his Super Rugby debut for Western Force and by 20 he became a full International, coming off the bench versus New Zealand. His selection for the Wallabies came exactly six years to the day after the Pocock family had first landed in Australia.

He quickly became one of the first names on the team sheet, and in 2010 Pocock won the first of two John Eales Medals – an award given to the best Australian player each year, as voted for by the Wallabies themselves.

At the 2011 World Cup, he shone in the doughty 11-9 quarter final win over South Africa. With Australia having only 24% territory, Pocock's defensive power and discipline were probably never better nor more in demand.

In 2012, Pocock became the Wallabies captain at just 24, and in the same year left the Western Force to join the Brumbies in Canberra. Pocock was part of the exciting Australian squad that reached the 2015 World Cup Final, scoring a try in the defeat to New Zealand and being named in the team of the tournament. *Talking Rugby Union* wrote: "There are just not enough superlatives to do Pocock's performances at this tournament justice. He was by far the RWC's best individual performer."

Although Pocock is universally regarded as the one of the very best defensive openside flankers of all time, the brutality of the modern game and how he played it began to take its toll. He suffered a series of knee injuries, including two reconstructions, but made it clear that these weren't the deciding factor in his retiring at just 32. Instead, we can turn to the remarkable array of projects and protests that have run in parallel to his rugby career to give a clue as to why he felt that sport was only a part of his journey.

In 2008 – the year he made his Australia debut, at just 20 years old – he co-founded EightyTwenty Vision, a charitable foundation working in partnership with a rural Zimbabwean community-development organisation. Their goal was to improve maternal health, education, food and water security for the underprivileged.

Two years later he announced that he would not legally marry his long-term partner Emma Palandri until all couples in the country were able to marry. Speaking about their decision to hold a commitment ceremony instead, Pocock told *The New Zealand Herald*:

> Being brought up in a Christian home and still identifying as Christian, I get pretty annoyed with the Christian lobbies around the world who say gay marriage destroys the family and all that kind of rubbish. They claim to follow someone who always stood up for the oppressed and marginalized.
>
> I guess it is a fear of the unknown – if you talk to someone who doesn't like gay people, you can almost guarantee that they don't know too many. These are the prejudices that you have to challenge and break down. Emma and I decided not to get legally married until our gay friends could do the same.[193]

In 2013, the ACT Legislative Assembly passed a bill to allow Australia's first same-sex marriages. Pocock clarified that their commitment was to wait until everyone in the country was able to legally wed, and not just in this state.

True to his word, in December of 2018, shortly after the federal Marriage Act had been amended to offer marriage equality to all in Australia, David Pocock and Emma Palandri tied the knot. The ceremony was a minimalist's dream: no dress, no suit, no flowers – just the couple and a celebrant outside in the countryside. It was announced on Pocock's Twitter account, with a few photos and the ultra-relaxed description – "Married my best mate yesterday" alongside a smiley face emoji.

Whilst there is a small but growing number of openly gay professional rugby players and officials, the game has a long way to go in terms of openness and inclusion.

In 2015, NSW Waratahs' South African forward Jacques Potgieter apologised for a homophobic slur reported on the pitch to the referee by Pocock and his teammate Stephen Moore and was fined $20,000 by the Australian Rugby Union. As part of his apology, Potgieter visited the Sydney Convicts, Australia's first gay rugby team, at training to say sorry in person. Pocock would later tweet a picture of a very cheery Potgieter with the Convicts, with the message, "Huge respect to @JacquePotgieter! If we were all so willing to engage, we'd stamp out homophobia in no time."

Then there's David Pocock's Australia teammate, Israel Folau. One of the most exciting talents in the modern game, his career has, however, been littered with homophobic and transphobic comments. An evangelical Christian, he was ultimately sacked by the Australian national team for posting a message on Instagram stating that "hell awaits" for homosexuals and atheists unless they "repent their sins".

Pocock remained phlegmatic when asked about Folau:

> It's been a really tough situation for rugby and at the end of the day we have so much more in common than the few things we might divide us. As a sport we want to be inclusive and create a safe space for people so when they turn up to play rugby, they feel like they can be whoever they are.
>
> I've always said sport is at its best when it's inclusive and it's actually challenging society to be more inclusive. Rugby has done a great job over the years of doing that. It's been dealt with now by Rugby Australia. I'm really sad to see him go but I really hope we can continue with the great work that has been done in creating that safe space.[194]

It's not just marriage equality and the LGBTQ+ community, however, that Pocock has publicly and powerfully supported.

In 2014 Pocock was arrested after chaining himself to a digger in protest at a coal mine being opened in a forest in northern New South Wales. Opponents to the mine claimed that by opening it up, Australia's carbon emissions would go up by nearly 10%, and more than 4,000 hectares of forest would be cleared.

Whilst out of the game injured, he joined several local farmers and campaigners in a blockade of the site. The protest was live-Tweeted, with one particularly eye-catching photo showing that Pocock was physically locked into the digger with his arm rammed into a close-fitting metal pipe attached to the metal giant. Dressed in shorts, T-shirt and a wide brimmed hat, Pocock looks the picture of happiness in the photo.

After ten hours occupying the super digger, Pocock and a local farmer were taken into custody by local police. But not before he conducted an interview, still chained to the digger, with the Australian Associated Press. He told them that he hoped his protest would send a message to his adopted country about a need for action:

> I believe it's time for direct action on climate change, standing together as ordinary Australians to take control of our shared future.
>
> This mine is about so much more than climate change. This is something that's beginning to impact the community and will have far greater impacts in the future in terms of the water table, the health implications of living next to a coal mine. I would be doing this regardless of what career I had. It is part of being a human being and taking on the challenges we face as a society. It is about giving back and getting the conversation going.[195]

Within a day of his arrest, he'd received a formal written warning from the Australian Rugby Union, who made the following statement:

> While we appreciate David has personal views on a range of matters, we've made it clear that we expect his priority to be ensuring he can fulfil his role as a high-performance athlete. The matter is now subject to legal proceedings, and we will now let the legal process take its course.

At his trial in February 2015, Pocock was initially charged with three offences, including entering enclosed land without lawful excuse and hindering the working of mining equipment. But after he pleaded guilty to the charge of hindering a workman in use of property, the other offences were withdrawn. As a result, the charge was proved but no conviction was recorded, with the magistrate – clearly favourable to Pocock's cause (or at least his ability on the pitch) – stating that a conviction would be "disastrous". Pocock was a free man and returned to the Brumbies and Wallabies with no further censure.

Pocock & co. stopped work for a day, but didn't stop the mine. It became fully operational in 2015 and has since been repeatedly fined for environmental breaches.

In 2017, at 29 years old and with 66 Wallaby caps, he took a sabbatical. No reality TV, giving cricket a try or trekking across the Andes for Pocock. Instead, he returned to the land of his birth, Zimbabwe – then still suffering under Robert Mugabe – to pursue his interest in animal conservation and agriculture.

Before acknowledging it could have easily backfired, Pocock told journalists:

> It was something I wanted to do, in rugby terms it was a risk. Yeah, yeah, but it was something I really wanted to do, six months away from rugby.
>
> We based ourselves in Zimbabwe. I guess we hadn't been back there before that for more than a few weeks. It was challenging: it was sort of before the President resigned, so it was pretty tough going economically. The country was struggling. We were trying to farm, trying to sell tomatoes; no one had money, the markets were not doing that well.

> It was a bit of an eye opener, but it has got a special place in my heart. I love it, I love the land, love the people, and I guess at the end of the day, if you are a Zimbabwean, everyone is a victim in some ways.[196]

After seven months living and working on a farm in rural Zimbabwe with his wife, he went to Harvard Business School to complete their Authentic Leader Development Course.

This time away from the game – which was agreed as part of a three-year deal to keep him in Australia through until the 2019 Rugby World Cup – wasn't without controversy, with some angry that he was still being paid by the Union whilst he was overseas.

But he came back to rugby, with the first of two stints in Japan with the Panasonic Wild Knights, then a final two seasons with the Brumbies and Wallabies. He took part in his third World Cup, receiving the last of his 83 caps in a 40-16 quarter-final defeat against England. In October 2020, after a second spell with the Wild Knights, Pocock called it a day aged 32. He did so not because of injury – although he had suffered many in his 15-year career at the top – but because it was "time".

On the announcement of his retirement, Pocock told a journalist:

> There's this author in the States, Rob Bell… I've really enjoyed his stuff over the years, and I've heard him say, "You can leave when it feels like a graduation, or you can hang in there and you have to leave when it feels like a divorce." I'm hoping that it's going to feel like a graduation.[197]

Unsurprisingly for a man with such clear convictions, hanging up his boots as one of Australia's all-time greats was followed not by a drift into punditry, golf and a touch of self-pity, but by a renewed focus and new projects. Starting every day at 6.15 a.m. with yoga before focussing on his Master's degree in sustainable agriculture, there was little time to dwell on his memories in the weeks after his first career came to an end.

Within months, David and his wife Emma co-founded FrontRunners, an organisation that works with athletes and sporting organisations to develop solutions to tackle climate and environmental challenges. As part of his work with FrontRunners, David headed up The Cool Down, a 2021 campaign that saw over 470 Australian athletes from 40+ sports call on their country to do more to stop climate change. David and his youngest brother, Steve, have also co-founded Rangelands Regeneration in Zimbabwe, working to restore ecosystems, develop greener forms of agriculture and help struggling communities.

Pocock is also a supporter of indigenous Australian culture. In December 2020 when the national anthem was sung in both English and Eora for the first time before a Test match, he spoke positively of it but called for more, telling a radio station:

> In some ways, it's a great gesture. In other ways, I think the anthem is problematic in itself, singing about being young and free when we live on land that's the oldest living culture in the world — it's probably important that these are part of the conversation.[198]

And then at the end of 2021 came the announcement that he was running for the Senate.

It will come as no surprise to you, having read this chapter, that in the election in May 2022 he was successful. He is now Senator Pocock, having run on a platform of liberal values including taking more effective action on the climate crisis, assuring equal rights for the LGBTQ+ community and bringing in Voluntary Assisted Dying laws to the ACT, defeating an incumbent who opposed these positions. He appealed to Canberrans from across the political spectrum and his campaign had more than 2,000 volunteers, many getting involved in politics for the first time.

David Pocock is a highly unusual figure in modern rugby. He is widely regarded as the world's best openside flanker of his generation, and a dominant force at the breakdown at Super Rugby and Test level since he first burst onto the scene as an 18-year-old – but that only tells a fraction of his story. He was not so much a maverick spirit on the pitch, but a powerful, passionate voice off it, for causes that aren't normally taken up by professional athletes.

Not that his stands have been without criticism. Following the mine protest, there were those who labelled him an extremist. After the Jacques Potgieter incident, there was disquiet from some about him breaking the code of 'what happens on the pitch stays on the pitch'. And as noted, his sabbatical drew criticism too, seen by some as self-indulgent and unnecessary. A look at social media shows there are people who actively dislike him, labelling him "woke" and a "virtue signaller", with the particularly childish "David Woke-Cock" being one of the slurs. Others call him a hypocrite, pointing at his wearing of an Australian jersey sponsored by Qantas for many years, and the carbon impact of regularly flying between his home, Asia and Africa.

But despite these criticisms, his beliefs shine through, and he is confident that he is on the right side of history when it comes to his work on equality, culture and the environment. There's a good chance that his barnstorming rugby career could end up being a mere footnote to far greater achievements.

David Pocock is only really getting started.

ACKNOWLEDGEMENTS

THIS BOOK WOULD not have been possible without the work of a host of rugby authors and journalists spanning the last 90 years. Without their hard work, I would not have been as easily able to delve into post-apartheid South Africa, rural Ireland in the 1960s, the impact of Pacific Islanders on the growth of sevens, the lifestyle of an exiled Russian aristocrat, modern-day Australian politics or how to seamlessly switch between tobogganing and rugby, to hint at just some of the stories in this book. A huge thank you to every single name in my bibliography.

Similarly, I would not have been able to write this book without the generous time of the former rugby players who replied with a 'yes' to a speculative email, Tweet or LinkedIn message asking them for a quick chat. I'll always be grateful to everyone that I called, and I particularly hope that the warmth from those who spoke about teammates no longer with us comes through in these pages. A very special thank you to David Campese, who took time from his busy schedule to share his open and honest thoughts for the Foreword as well as some memories for his chapter. And to Paul Cunningham, for the insights into the life of his late Uncle Marnie and for supplying the fantastic image of him for the photo section of the book. Thank you also to Donal McAnallen for his invaluable GAA expertise.

A huge thank you the team at Y Lolfa for trusting me with a third book since 2018, after *Absolutely Huge* and *Hard Men of Rugby*: it's a pleasure to work with you all. I'd particularly like to thank Lefi Gruffudd for his continued confidence and support. And to Carolyn Hodges, my very talented editor, for her positivity, hard work and indulgence of the occasional nonsensical rugby term – her expert skills improved the text greatly. *Diolch i'r ddau!*

I'd like to give a shout out to Matt Cutler, my partner in a silly idea over a decade ago that set the ball rolling on these books. And to the 23rd Old Gorians, a constant source of entertainment and friendship – and yes, occasionally the odd piece of maverick behaviour too.

My love of rugby and reading comes direct from my parents, John and Anne Upton in Swansea, and for that I will be always very grateful. And thank you also to my family in South Wales and London – Jamie, Lucy, Pablo, Marion, Elliot, Oscar, Daphne and Josephine – for your continued positive vibes!

A huge thank you too to my Irish family – my father-in-law Pat, Chris, Aoife, Caroline, Catherine, Paul, Henry, Éala and Méabh. And for those of you reading in Monahan's Bar in Athlone, I'm happy to debate who I did (and didn't) include next time I am in!

I owe an enormous thank you to my wife, Eimear, who has once again massively supported me doing 'book stuff' in the middle of a very busy house. Our daughter Iseult was born during the writing of *Absolutely Huge,* our son Séamus arrived during the production of *Hard Men of Rugby* and for this book, we were blessed with a baby girl, Úna, who made her appearance around the 80-page mark. Several chapter introductions were conceived, and textual problems solved, whilst pushing the buggy or when attempting to shush her back to sleep in the early hours. I also work full time, so I could not do any of this without Eimear's patience, support and love.

I'd like to thank all the players featured in this book. It's been a privilege learning more about them all and diving into their varied worlds. If some think I've been unduly critical of anyone – or perhaps too lenient, in some cases – I apologise, but I've tried to be honest about what makes them mavericks. None of them are angels, but then none of us are. What they are is true to themselves, and for that they are included.

And finally, I'd like to thank you for reading. I hope you've enjoyed it as much as I have enjoyed writing it.

Thank you.

Luke Upton
London, September 2022
@MrLukeUpton
LukeUpton84@gmail.com
www.lukeupton.co.uk

BIBLIOGRAPHY

Books

BILLS, Peter: *Jean-Pierre Rives: A Modern Corinthian* (Allen & Unwin, 1986)

BISHOP, Nick and CARTER, Alun: *The Good, The Bad and The Ugly: The Rise and Fall of Pontypool RFC* (Mainstream Publishing, 2013)

BROWN, Geoff and HOGSBJERG, Christian: *Apartheid Is Not a Game: Remembering the Stop the Seventy Tour Campaign* (Bookmarks Publications, 2020)

CAMPESE, David with BILLS, Peter: *On a Wing & a Prayer: The Autobiography of David Campese* (Queen Anne Press, 1991)

CARLIN, John: *Playing the Enemy: Nelson Mandela and the Game That Made a Nation* (Atlantic Books, 2009)

COUGHLAN, Barry: *Rags to Riches: The Story of Munster Rugby* (The Collins Press, 2009)

ELLA, Mark: *Running Rugby* (ABC, 1995)

ENGLISH, Tom: *No Borders: Playing Rugby for Ireland* (Arena Sport, 2016)

FITZSIMONS, Peter: *Nick Farr-Jones: The Authorised Biography* (Hutchinson, 1993)

GRAVELL, Ray (BEVAN, Alun Wyn, ed.): *Grav: In His Own Words* (Gwasg Gomer, 2009)

JENKINS, Peter: *Wallaby Gold: The History of Australian Test Rugby* (Random House Australia, 2003)

KEANE, Moss with KEANE, Billy: *Rucks, Mauls and Gaelic Football* (Merlin Publishing, 2005)

MCGEECHAN, Ian: *Lion Man: The Autobiography* (Simon & Schuster, 2009)

MCLAREN, Bill: *Rugby's Great Heroes and Entertainers* (Hodder & Stoughton Ltd, 2003)

MCLAREN, Bill: *Talking of Rugby* (Hutchinson, 1991)

MCRAE, Donald: *Winter Colours: Changing Seasons in World Rugby* (Mainstream Publishing, 1999)

MEIRION, Rhys (ed.): *Grav: The Legend of Ray Gravell* (Y Lolfa, 2021)

MOURIE, Graham with PALENSKI, Ron: *Graham Mourie: Captain* (Moa Publications Ltd., 1982)

MOYSE, Heather: *Redefining 'Realistic'* (Red Roots Publishing, 2017)

PALENSKI, Ron: *Rugby: A New Zealand History* (Auckland University Press, 2015)

REYBURN, Wallace: *Wallace Reyburn's World of Rugby* (Elek Books Ltd., 1967)

RICH, Gavin: *Our Blood is Green: The Springboks in Their Own Words* (Polaris Publishing, 2020)

RIPLEY, Andy: *Ripley's Rugby Rubbish: The Essential Ego and Massage Book* (Allen & Unwin, 1985)

RIPLEY, Andy: *Ripley's World: The Enthralling Story of the British Lion's Most Crucial Victory* (Mainstream Publishing, 2008)

SCALLY, John: *Giants of Irish Rugby* (Mainstream Publishing, 1996)

SCALLY, John: *Odd-Shaped Balls: Mischief-Makers, Miscreants and Mad-Hatters of Rugby* (Mainstream Publishing, 2004)

SHELFORD, Buck and GRAY, Wynne: *Buck: The Wayne Shelford Story* (Moa Publications, 1990)

STAFFORD, James: *An Illustrated History of Welsh Rugby* (Polaris Publishing, 2021)

THOMAS, Clem: *The History of the British Lions* (Mainstream Publishing, 1997)

TOSSELL, David: *Nobody Beats Us: The Inside Story of the 1970s Wales Rugby Team* (Mainstream Publishing, 2009)

VAN ESBECK, Edmund: *Irish Rugby, 1874–1999: A History* (Gill & Macmillan Ltd., 1999)

VEYSEY, Alex: *Colin Meads: All Black* (Collins NZ, 1974)

WILLIAMS, Sonny Bill: *You Can't Stop the Sun from Shining* (Hodder & Stoughton, 2021)

Periodicals and magazines

Belfast Telegraph

The Cork Examiner

Daily Express (UK)

Daily Mail (UK)

The Echo (Cork)

L'Équipe

The Evening Standard (London)

The Guardian (UK)

The Independent (UK)

Irish Examiner

Irish Independent

The Irish Times

Judiciary UK

Rugby Dump

The Rugby Journal

The Rugby Paper

Rugby Pass

Rugby World

South China Morning Post

South Wales Evening Post

The Telegraph (UK)

The Times (UK)

Western Mail (Wales)

Websites

www.abc.net.au

www.archyde.com

www.bbc.co.uk

www.chicagotribune.com

www.dib.ie

www.edition.cnn.com

www.espn.co.uk
www.foxsports.com
www.gaa.ie
www.ladepeche.fr
www.lequipe.fr
www.lionsrugby.com
www.mirror.co.uk
www.news24.com
www.nzherald.co.nz
https://rmcsport.bfmtv.com/
www.rnz.co.nz
www.rugby.com.au
www.rugbyshirtwatch.com
www.skysports.com
www.smh.com.au
www.stats.allblacks.com
www.stuff.co.nz
www.sustainabilityreport.com
www.theoffsideline.com
www.theroar.com.au
www.thescotsman.com
www.thestar.com
www.The42.ie
www.women.rugby
www.world.rugby
www.youtube.com

NOTES

NB All website URLS were correct at time of publication.

1 https://www.rugbypass.com/news/the-inside-story-on-what-happened-the-day-cipriani-was-punched-out-in-england-camp-bust-up/

2 https://www.rugbydump.com/news/danny-cipriani-and-josh-lewsey-box-and-makeup/

3 https://www.thetimes.co.uk/article/interview-danny-cipriani-s9ng56ljf8d

4 https://www.standard.co.uk/sport/my-mum-s-singleminded-dedication-helped-me-get-to-the-top-in-rugby-says-england-hero-cipriani-6637258.html

5 https://www.judiciary.uk/wp-content/uploads/2016/09/cps-v-cipriani-judgment.pdf

6 https://www.youtube.com/watch?v=gMlnqlWXlbE

7 https://www.theguardian.com/sport/2019/dec/13/danny-cipriani-england-rugby-union-interview-eddie-jones

8 https://www.dailymail.co.uk/sport/rugbyunion/article-10162389/DANNY-CIPRIANI-Eddie-Jones-negative-Im-sure-Marcus-Smith-deliver-England.html

9 https://www.instagram.com/tv/B804EcRHKus/?hl=en

10 https://www.thetimes.co.uk/article/wales-mourns-viking-who-wore-heart-on-sleeve-in-career-that-defined-an-era-vxg85l66lnr

11 Gravell, *Grav: In His Own Words*, p.36

12 Tossell, *Nobody Beats Us*, p.192

13 *Nobody Beats Us*, p.192

14 Max Boyce, *Live at Treorchy* (EMI Records, 1974)

15 *Grav: In His Own Words*, p.85

16 *Grav: In His Own Words*, p.134

17 Meirion (ed.), *Grav: The Legend of Ray Gravell*, p.42

18 *Grav: In His Own Words*, p.190

19 *Grav: The Legend of Ray Gravell*, p.43

20 *Grav: In His Own Words*, p.155

21 https://www.the42.ie/andy-lee-sonny-bill-williams-5669231-Jan2022/

22 https://www.rnz.co.nz/national/programmes/ninetonoon/audio/2018816031/sonny-bill-williams-the-man-on-and-off-the-field#:~:text=But%20controversy%20has%20also%20tracked,and%20accusations%20of%20chasing%20money

23 https://www.skysports.com/rugby-league/news/12196/12433433/sonny-bill-williams-cross-code-new-zealand-rugby-star-opens-up-on-therapeutic-autobiography

24 https://www.foxsports.com.au/nrl/nrl-premiership/nrl-2021-sonny-bill-williams-book-bulldogs-exit-release-2008-season-airport-french-rugby-union-toulon/news-story/2baf27bbf6449d2a5b4b5bf42a472f37

25 https://www.the42.ie/andy-lee-sonny-bill-williams-5669231-Jan2022/

26 https://www.irishtimes.com/sport/rugby/international/rwc-moments-sonny-bill-williams-gives-medal-to-stunned-fan-1.4002442

27 https://www.bbc.co.uk/sport/rugby-league/50406738

28 https://www.the42.ie/andy-lee-sonny-bill-williams-5669231-Jan2022/

29 Williams, *You Can't Stop the Sun From Shining* (digital edition)

30 https://www.chicagotribune.com/news/ct-xpm-1991-03-01-9101190716-story.html

31 https://www.youtube.com/watch?v=HfrWvWw2ckg

32 Ripley, *Ripley's World*, p.157

33 *Ripley's World*, p.55

34 English, *No Borders*, p.61

35 *Ripley's World*, p.61

36 *No Borders*, p.63

37 https://www.lionsrugby.com/2010/06/18/merv-leads-ripley-tributes/

38 Thomas, *The History of the British Lions*, p.164

39 *Ripley's World*, p.94

40 Ripley, *Ripley's Rugby Rubbish*, p.16

41 *Ripley's Rugby Rubbish*, Foreword

42 *Ripley's World*, p.98

43 https://www.theguardian.com/sport/2010/jun/18/andy-ripley-obituary

44 Moyse, *Redefining 'Realistic'*, p.36

45 *Redefining 'Realistic'*, p.134

46 https://www.women.rugby/news/569560/between-the-lines-heather-moyse

47 *Redefining 'Realistic'*, p.173

48 *Redefining 'Realistic'*, p.126

49 https://www.youtube.com/watch?v=jI4asH41CnQ

50 https://www.thestar.com/sports/amateur/2016/11/14/canadian-heather-moyse-to-enter-world-rugby-hall-of-fame.html#:~:text=Longtime%20national%20team%20standout%20Gareth,Cup%20Sevens%20tournament%20in%20Moscow

51 https://www.heathermoyse.com/a-very-daunting-idea-heather-moyse-attempting-bobsleigh-comeback-for-2018-pyeongchang-olympics/

52 https://www.theguardian.com/sport/blog/2021/aug/07/finn-russells-invention-helps-lions-lose-with-a-roar-rather-than-a-whimper

53 https://www.scotsman.com/sport/rugby-union/lions-tour-2021-warren-gatland-offers-qualified-praise-for-finn-russell-as-he-rues-high-penalty-count-3338117

54 https://www.espn.co.uk/rugby/story/_/id/15340213/finn-russell-stonemason-scotland

55 https://www.stuff.co.nz/sport/rugby/international/101777043/how-canterbury-rugby-helped-shape-scotlands-six-nations-giantkilling-team

56 https://www.rugbypass.com/news/zebo-explains-the-origins-of-finn-russells-racing-92-nickname/

57 https://www.thetimes.co.uk/article/finn-russell-the-true-story-about-gregor-townsend-and-me-pvq86vgv0

58 https://www.theoffsideline.com/keith-russell-not-good-guys/

59 McLaren, *Talking of Rugby*, p.166

60 http://edition.cnn.com/2014/05/08/sport/waisale-serevi-rugby-sevens-hong-kong/index.html

61 https://www.youtube.com/watch?v=9tFHiT_CqbY

62 https://www.scmp.com/sport/rugby/hk-sevens/article/2140261/he-may-be-king-sevens-waisale-serevi-slept-floor-hong-kong

63 https://www.scmp.com/article/493623/serevi-eyes-fiji-romp-through

64 https://www.scmp.com/sport/rugby/hk-sevens/article/2140261/he-may-be-king-sevens-waisale-serevi-slept-floor-hong-kong

65 https://www.the42.ie/karl-keane-usa-u20s-5104905-May2020/

66 https://www.theguardian.com/sport/2014/oct/01/serevi-rugby-sevens-new-york-contact

67 'Few Limerick Citizens Join in Anti-Springboks Protest March', Irish Times Reporter, *The Irish Times*, 15 January 1970

68 *No Borders*, p.24

69 *The Echo*, December 2020

70 *The Echo*, December 2020

71 https://www.irishtimes.com/life-and-style/people/the-only-catholic-priest-to-play-for-ireland-in-international-rugby-1.650724

72 Brown and Hogsbjerg, *Apartheid Is Not a Game*, p.41

73 https://www.mirror.co.uk/sport/rugby-union/john-taylor-british-lion-whose-23036957

74 *Apartheid Is Not a Game*, p.50

75 https://www.mirror.co.uk/sport/peter-hains-apartheid-battle-bid-23037099

76 https://www.dib.ie/biography/foster-alexander-roulston-alec-a9798

77 *No Borders*, p.49

78 'Few Limerick Citizens Join in Anti-Springboks Protest March', Irish Times Reporter, *The Irish Times*, 15 January 1970

79 Coughlan, *Rags to Riches: The Story of Munster Rugby*, p.57

80 Letters to the Editor, *Irish Times*, 19 January 1981

81 Letters to the Editor, *Irish Times*, 19 January 1981

82 Campese with Bills, *On a Wing and a Prayer*, p.104

83 McGeechan, *Lion Man*, p.170

84 *The History of the British Lions*, p.210

85 *On a Wing and a Prayer*, p.44

86 *On a Wing and a Prayer*, p.75

87 *On a Wing and a Prayer*, p.142

88 Ella, *Running Rugby*, p.42

89 Jenkins, *Wallaby Gold*, p.316

90 FitzSimons, *Nick Farr-Jones: The Authorised Biography*, p.236

91 McLaren, *Rugby's Great Heroes and Entertainers*, p.187

92 *Rugby's Great Heroes and Entertainers*, p.185

93 https://www.therugbyjournal.com/rugby-blog/non-evans

94 https://www.youtube.com/watch?v=a6ea2hLS1Qw

95 https://www.world.rugby/news/700639/six-nations-memories-non-evans-wales-womens-rugby-interview

96 https://www.therugbyjournal.com/rugby-blog/non-evans

97 https://www.walesonline.co.uk/sport/rugby/rugby-news/wales-women-rugby-players-offered-22056020

98 https://www.therugbyjournal.com/rugby-blog/non-evans

99 https://www.youtube.com/watch?v=m0fez2Ch0rU

100 https://www.theguardian.com/rugbycup/Story/0,,202643,00.html

101 https://www.theroar.com.au/2021/10/22/zinzan-zinny-brooke-definitely-not-a-murray/

102 *Rugby's Great Heroes and Entertainers*, p.228

103 https://www.theguardian.com/sport/2003/oct/05/rugbyworldcup2003.rugbyunion1

104 https://www.nzherald.co.nz/sport/zinzan-brooke-tough-no-8-always-had-the-special-wow-factor/QTWXTDEM5GHEOF3HF27KMKC7G4/

105 Shelford and Gray, *Buck: The Wayne Shelford Story*, p.213

106 Veysey, *Colin Meads: All Black*, p.218

107 https://www.stuff.co.nz/sport/rugby/124461833/all-black-legend-zinzan-brooke-urged-to-engage-with-scientists-over-covid-stance

108 *Rugby's Great Heroes and Entertainers*, p.228

109 http://en.espn.co.uk/2011-rugby-world-cup/rugby/story/83333.html

110 https://www.irishtimes.com/sport/detonator-primed-to-ignite-1.391332

111 https://www.therugbypaper.co.uk/features/featured-post/39128/jackson-column-christophe-dominici-so-strong-on-the-pitch-so-fragile-off-it/

112 https://www.theguardian.com/sport/2003/nov/12/rugbyworldcup2003.rugbyunion2

113 https://www.therugbypaper.co.uk/features/featured-post/39128/jackson-column-christophe-dominici-so-strong-on-the-pitch-so-fragile-off-it/

114 http://news.bbc.co.uk/sport1/hi/rugby_union/international/3509445.stm

115 https://www.thetimes.co.uk/article/christophe-dominici-obituary-0dwzj58bh

116 https://www.archyde.com/death-of-christophe-dominici-his-last-injury-the-abortive-recovery-of-the-beziers-club/

117 https://www.archyde.com/death-of-christophe-dominici-his-last-injury-the-abortive-recovery-of-the-beziers-club/

118 https://www.youtube.com/watch?v=vHoY_FT6fqs

119 https://www.walesonline.co.uk/sport/rugby/rugby-news/david-bishop-60-bitter-welsh-19277844

120 https://www.therugbypaper.co.uk/all/columnists/brendan-gallagher/19292/brendan-gallagher-bish-is-an-angel-with-a-dirty-face/

121 Bishop and Carter, *The Good, the Bad and the Ugly*, p.142

122 https://www.therugbypaper.co.uk/all/columnists/brendan-gallagher/19292/brendan-gallagher-bish-is-an-angel-with-a-dirty-face/

123 https://www.therugbypaper.co.uk/all/columnists/brendan-gallagher/19292/brendan-gallagher-bish-is-an-angel-with-a-dirty-face/

124 *The Good, the Bad and the Ugly*, p.148

125 https://www.audible.co.uk/pd/David-Bishop-The-Exclusive-Interview-Podcast/B09ZVFHJ4S

126 https://www.walesonline.co.uk/sport/rugby/rugby-news/rugby-hero-david-bishop-begged-23928347

127 *The Good, the Bad and the Ugly*, p.147

128 Reyburn, *Wallace Reyburn's World of Rugby*, p.82

129 Palenski, *Rugby: A New Zealand History* (digital edition)

130 *Rugby: A New Zealand History* (digital edition)

131 https://www.youtube.com/watch?v=Wjb8eO0bJ3U

132 https://www.ipswichwarmemorial.co.uk/h-h-prince-alexander-sergeevich-obolensky/

133 https://www.ipswichwarmemorial.co.uk/h-h-prince-alexander-sergeevich-obolensky/

134 https://www.irishtimes.com/sport/gaelic-games/the-ban-vigilance-committees-and-the-policing-of-irishness-1.4526195

135 https://www.irishexaminer.com/opinion/columnists/arid-40207337.html

136 Keane with Keane, *Rucks, Mauls and Gaelic Football*, p.47

137 *Rucks, Mauls and Gaelic Football,* p.49

138 *Rucks, Mauls and Gaelic Football,* p.58

139 Van Esbeck, *Irish Rugby, 1874–1999: A History*

140 *Rucks, Mauls and Gaelic Football,* p.107

141 *Rucks, Mauls and Gaelic Football,* p.118

142 https://www.irishexaminer.com/sport/rugby/arid-30882183.html

143 *Rucks, Mauls and Gaelic Football,* p.126

144 https://www.independent.ie/sport/rugby/munster-rugby/they-were-knocked-to-the-ground-like-skittles-how-we-reported-munsters-famous-victory-over-the-all-blacks-40-years-ago-today-37477793.html

145 Scally, *Giants of Irish Rugby* (digital edition)

146 Scally, *Odd-Shaped Balls,* p.127

147 https://www.belfasttelegraph.co.uk/sport/rugby/my-great-pal-moss-keane-had-few-airs-but-so-many-graces-28562907.html

148 https://www.independent.ie/sport/rugby/world-cup/neil-francis-sergio-parisse-is-sublime-but-im-embarrassed-for-those-who-underestimate-jamie-heaslip-31580035.html

149 https://www.telegraph.co.uk/rugby-union/2020/07/12/sergio-parisse-would-still-love-have-last-game-italy-rome/

150 https://www.dailymail.co.uk/sport/rugbyunion/article-7949323/Sergio-Parisse-hands-Italys-young-brigade-No-8-heads-international-retirement.html

151 https://www.lequipe.fr/Rugby/Article/Stade-francais-sergio-parisse-les-raisons-d-un-depart/1034855

152 https://rmcsport.bfmtv.com/rugby/toulon-sergio-parisse-vers-la-prolongation_AV-202204190254.html

153 https://www.dailymail.co.uk/sport/rugbyunion/article-7949323/Sergio-Parisse-hands-Italys-young-brigade-No-8-heads-international-retirement.html

154 https://images.findagrave.com/photos/2018/308/194503127_4c91b681-7178-4136-9b2f-4bf5afa2e945.jpeg

155 https://www.stuff.co.nz/sport/rugby/super-rugby/102737159/the-murdoch-myth-all-blacks-legends-life-of-a-recluse-after-infamous-punch?rm=m

156 https://www.stuff.co.nz/sport/opinion/106900494/mark-reason-keith-murdoch-is-now-more-myth-than-man#:~:text=Grant%20said%2C%20%22He%20tried%20to,It%20was%20ridiculous

157 https://www.stuff.co.nz/sport/rugby/all-blacks/106060590/hooray-boys-im-off-what-really-happened-when-keith-murdoch-was-sent-home?rm=a

158 https://www.stuff.co.nz/sport/rugby/opinion/102743494/phil-gifford-keith-murdoch-was-a-boy-in-a-big-mans-body?cid=facebook.102743494&fbclid=IwAR2GmwlHo725U85qfCRNvcACNDFPcwZ56vPcYTXP09RHXRckBlIoWWT0EgE

159 https://www.rugbypass.com/news/remembering-keith-murdoch-one-sports-strangest-stories/

160 https://www.stuff.co.nz/sport/rugby/all-blacks/300031711/all-blacks-legend-ian-kirkpatrick-i-still-blame-myself-for-keith-murdoch-banishment

161 http://stats.allblacks.com/asp/profile.asp?ABID=641

162 https://www.rugbypass.com/news/remembering-keith-murdoch-one-sports-strangest-stories/

163 https://rugbyshirtwatch.com/2015/08/20/france-rugby-adidas-rugby-world-cup-2015-home-shirt/

164 Bills, *Jean-Pierre Rives: A Modern Corinthian*, p.27

165 *Jean-Pierre Rives: A Modern Corinthian*, p.27

166 *Jean-Pierre Rives: A Modern Corinthian*, p.50

167 *Jean-Pierre Rives: A Modern Corinthian*, p.54

168 https://www.irishtimes.com/sport/rugby/international/if-the-spirit-that-made-playing-france-so-terrifying-has-gone-what-is-left-1.3378009

169 Mourie, *Graham Mourie: Captain* (digital edition)

170 https://www.youtube.com/watch?v=0Ou-dmXdGg4

171 *Jean-Pierre Rives: A Modern Corinthian*, p.19

172 https://www.rugby.com.au/news/wallabies-v-france-the-day-jeanpierre-did-the-impossible-2021711

173 *Jean-Pierre Rives, A Modern Corinthian*, p.9

174 https://www.ladepeche.fr/article/2010/07/20/876003-jean-pierre-rives.html

175 https://journals.sagepub.com/doi/abs/10.1177/101269029603100104?journalCode=irsb

176 Carlin, *Playing the Enemy*, p.190

177 *Playing the Enemy*, p.177

178 *Playing the Enemy*, p.178

179 McRae, *Winter Colours*, p.178

180 James Small quoted in *Our Blood is Green: The Springboks in Their Own Words* (digital edition)

181 http://en.espn.co.uk/blogs/sport/story/365587.html

182 *Playing the Enemy*, p.179

183 *Winter Colours*, p.80

184 https://www.thetimes.co.uk/article/james-small-obituary-wntllzk8v

185 *Winter Colours*, p.83

186 https://www.youtube.com/watch?v=94i0pp7erVU

187 https://www.news24.com/sport/Rugby/Springboks/anc-pay-tribute-to-patriot-james-small-20190710

188 https://www.thetimes.co.uk/article/james-small-obituary-wntllzk8v

189 *Winter Colours*, p.84

190 https://www.abc.net.au/news/2021-12-17/former-wallaby-david-pocock-to-run-for-act-senate/100705718

191 https://sustainabilityreport.com/2021/10/28/cop26-a-decisive-moment-for-athlete-climate-activism/

192 https://www.smh.com.au/sport/rugby-union/david-pocock-fear-in-zimbabwe-a-rugby-obsession-and-an-injury-nightmare-20160216-gmvag8.html

193 https://www.nzherald.co.nz/sport/the-man-apart-in-the-australian-rugby-world-cup-pack/C2JVWSJ22KAA4LE72B26XKLWYQ/?c_id=4&objectid=10757439

194 https://www.espn.co.uk/nrl/story/_/id/33210279/nrl-does-opening-month-nrl-season-really-matter

195 https://www.abc.net.au/news/2014-11-30/former-wallabies-captain-pocock-arrested-at-coal-mine-protest/5929024

196 https://www.irishexaminer.com/sport/rugby/arid-20471852.html#:~:text=The%20gamble%20paid%20off.,regime%20of%20President%20Robert%20Mugabe

197 https://www.rugby.com.au/news/2020/10/23/wallabies-great-david-pocock-announces-retirement-and-reveals-his-next-move

198 https://www.abc.net.au/news/2020-12-12/david-pocock-calls-for-climate-action-national-anthem/12978202

Also by the author:

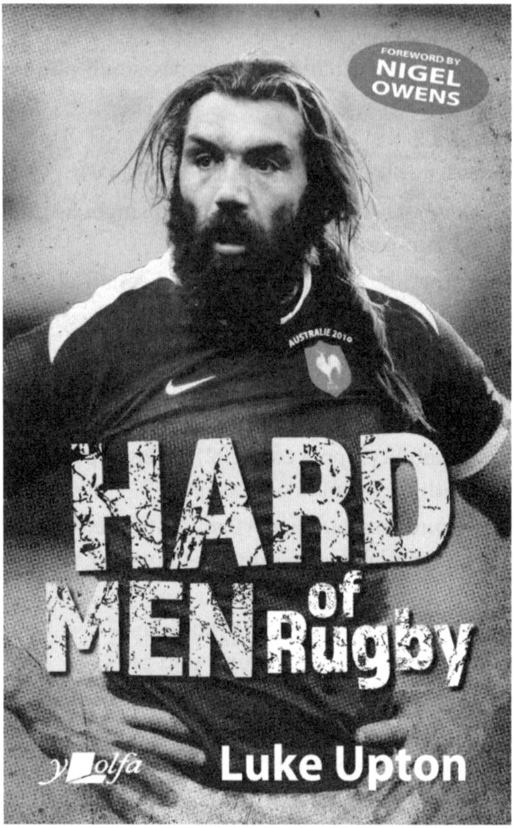

£9.99

The true stories behind the toughest characters to ever play the game, from pre-WWI firebrands to modern-day YouTube sensations.

£9.99

Hilarious spoof biography exploring the highs and lows of Gethin 'Huge' Hughes' often controversial career. An affectionate satire of Welsh rugby and the media hype that surrounds it.

£7.95

The stories of the toughest Welsh players who fought valiantly for pride and honour in the days prior to the game turning professional in 1995. With profiles of legends such as John Bevan, Graham Price, JPR, Scott Gibbs and many more.

£14.99

A history of Wales and New Zealand matches, from their first in Cardiff in 1905. The book focuses on the curiosities of off-field activities, obligations and functions. From forgotten facts unearthed in dusty old newspapers to first-hand anecdotes and recollections from Wales and All Blacks greats.